AF235268

IRRFAN

Shubhra Gupta is a film critic and columnist with the *Indian Express* and the curator of the enormously popular Indian Express Film Club, a unique platform for cinema appreciation. One of India's most well-regarded and influential film critics, she has travelled extensively around the world to film festivals both as reporter and jury member, and served as a member of the Central Board of Film Certification (CBFC) between 2012 and 2015. She received the prestigious Ramnath Goenka Award for Best Writing on Film in 2012. Her first book, *50 Films that Changed Bollywood*, 1995–2015, was published in 2016. This is her second book.

Praise for *Irrfan*

'[Gupta] brings to this book not only her in-depth knowledge of her subject's career and Hindi films, but also her deep access to the industry ... She has been able to interview for the book the who's who of Bollywood ... What emerges from these interviews are some remarkable stories'
Uttaran Das Gupta, *Business Standard*

'Film critic Shubhra Gupta's tribute to Irrfan brings alive the man who is not in our midst, but well-entrenched in our hearts. [She] presents ... Irrfan as no one else has'
Vijay Lokapally, *Hindu BusinessLine*

'A must-read for movie junkies [and] those who are interested in life and its falsafa in general'
Raya Ghosh, *India Today*

IRRFAN

A Life in Movies

SHUBHRA GUPTA

PAN

First published in India 2023 by Macmillan
First published in paperback 2024 by Pan
an imprint of Pan Macmillan Publishing India Private Limited
707 Kailash Building
26 K. G. Marg, New Delhi 110001
www.panmacmillan.co.in

Pan Macmillan, The Smithson, 6 Briset Street, Farringdon, London EC1M 5NR
Associated companies throughout the world
www.panmacmillan.com

ISBN 978-81-19300-85-3

Copyright © Shubhra Gupta 2023

Image Credits:
'Irrfan and Sutapa, over the years': courtesy Sutapa Sikdar
The Namesake photographs © Sooni Taraporevala 2005
Qissa photographs: courtesy Anup Singh
D-Day photographs: courtesy Emmay Entertainment
Qarib Qarib Singlle photographs: courtesy Ritam Banerjee/Zee Studios
Angrezi Medium photographs: courtesy Homi Adajania

The views expressed in this book are the author's and interviewees' own and the
facts reported by them have been verified by the publisher to the extent possible.
The publisher hereby disclaims any liability to any party for loss,
damages or disruptions caused by the same.

All rights reserved. No part of this publication may be reproduced, stored in or
introduced into a retrieval system, or transmitted, in any form, or by any means
(electronic, mechanical, photocopying, recording or otherwise) without the prior
written permission of the publisher. Any person who does any unauthorized act in
relation to this publication may be liable to criminal prosecution and civil
claims for damages.

1 3 5 7 9 8 6 4 2

This book is sold subject to the condition that it shall not, by way of trade or
otherwise, be lent, re-sold, hired out, or otherwise circulated without the publisher's
prior consent in any form of binding or cover other than that in which it is
published and without a similar condition including this condition being imposed
on the subsequent purchaser.

Typeset in Minion Pro by R. Ajith Kumar, New Delhi
Printed in India by Gopsons Papers Pvt. Ltd., Noida

For Madhusudan

CONTENTS

Contents

Contents

Contents

INTRODUCTION

An Actor Nonpareil

Nahi karoonga kahaani poori. Aadhi chhod jaaoonga beech mein.
I will not complete the story. I will leave it halfway.

— *Madaari*, 2016

Some lines are prescient. On 29 April 2020, Irrfan Khan left his story halfway. In his passing, the world lost an actor nonpareil.

This was not the way it was meant to be. His journey was one of a kind – from television in the late eighties and nineties to his first steps in cinema in the new millennium; his gradual climb from bit parts to lead roles written solely for him; from films that were on the fringes of Hindi cinema to moving front and centre, all the while challenging, slowly but surely, the definition of the mainstream, and of stardom.

Irrfan gave us unalloyed joy, the kind only a true performer can. In his best roles, you could not see Irrfan. What you got instead was the character, full-bodied, believable, built with the exquisite awareness of the self and the other. These were parts which had provenance, a rare quality in Hindi cinema. When we meet characters essayed by Irrfan, we implicitly become aware of their histories – and some of those characters walk out with us when the film ends.

There is no doubt that he was an actor who filled us with pleasure. But was Irrfan a star? He made us grapple with this question much more seriously than anyone who came before him. This was not, and is still not, a rhetorical question. Mainstream Hindi cinema thrives on the star–actor binary. Most stars rely upon their charisma to get the job done. Unlike such stars, great actors are not automatically offered great movies which have the potential to go big; that space is still a work-in-progress, but Irrfan gave it an unparalleled boost.

Whether they are from Hollywood or Bollywood, stars tend to choose films that ride on their stardom and burnish it. Stars do starry stuff; their 'market' mandates it. Experimenting with their 'image' isn't something risk-averse mainstream film industries veer towards. What if die-hard fans turn their back on the film and it turns into a resounding flop? True actors like Irrfan, on the other hand, gravitate towards films which give them a chance to hone their craft, spread their wings, explore yet another facet of life through story and performance.

With each film, Irrfan was pushing boundaries. He was creating a space for himself, filling it with the enticements that got people to buy a ticket for an 'Irrfan film', and there came a time when Irrfan blurred the lines between actor and star – another of those rarities in Hindi cinema.

Once you get there, you change something. You are no longer confined to films made on a small canvas. Big producers are willing to take a punt on you because you bring the crowds in. You become a boon for smart screenplay writers, who are always looking for opportunities to create something original. It's a win-win.

The last actor who managed to do this was Amitabh Bachchan. And before that, to some extent, Dilip Kumar. Consummate actors, towering stars, their films had huge cultural footprints. They changed the script, the groundswell of opinion and, as a consequence, the industry. The three Khans – Aamir, Salman, Shah Rukh – who grabbed our attention during the end of the eighties and the early nineties (when Irrfan, stuck in his TV rut, was struggling to break into the movies) became superstars before they could start shifting a few registers here and there.

But Irfan Khan, who added an 'r' to his first name and dropped his surname, worked to ensure that he was no prisoner of any image. Singlehandedly he lifted the status of 'character actors'; he became that actor who made us fall in love with his characters. He managed to do the near-impossible – create a magnetic hold over his audience despite being a chameleon. He could become anybody, and he could keep us watching.

When he was diagnosed with an incurable endocrine cancer in 2018, it must have been a cruel blow, as he was, at that time, right on top of his game. He had breached the box-office barrier, finally, with his 2017 dramedy *Hindi Medium*, breaking into the so-called '100-crore club'. With that, he was finally the actor who could 'open' a Friday. That was all it took for big-studio Bollywood – which keeps a sharp eye on the films that make money – to fully wake up to him. If he could do this with a film which had a distinctly indie spirit, what would he have achieved if given a bigger budget, bigger play, and the promise of a big opening?

If he was still around, Irrfan would have changed the rules of the game.

There was no one quite like him. As we mourn his loss, and feel his absence keenly, it's becoming quite apparent that there may never be. Sure, there are superlative actors in the Indian firmament, but someone like him, who held within his self a multitude of selves, and presented them with great empathy and assuredness, may be hard to find.

Recounting Memories

Remember that you and I made this journey together to a place where there was nowhere left to go.

The Namesake, 2006

The idea of the book came from my friend, the literary agent Mimi Choudhury, who called me in May 2020, a month after Irrfan's passing. The world was reeling under the pandemic. The first of the stringent lockdowns had begun. We were in our homes, unable to let off steam or process the devastation caused by the Covid-19 virus; people were dying and vaccines were still some ways off. It was a time out of time.

Despite knowing about the gravity of Irrfan's illness, we had hoped that he would overcome it, and feel well enough to be back on set again, doing what he did best. But it was not to be. His death unleashed unprecedented waves of grief; it was as if someone close to us had gone.

After several rounds of conversations, Mimi and I hit upon some clarity. The book would be from the perspective of a long-time film critic, someone who had seen him in the movies since the beginning of his career, and would be able to put into context his extraordinary journey, and what it meant for the Hindi film industry.

It was then that I thought of a book of conversations, with his family, friends, co-stars, and collaborators in the film industry.

These would be people who had known him closely, as well as those who would be able to give us an insider's view of how the industry functioned, and how it responded (or not) to an actor like Irrfan.

My knowing of Irrfan was limited to his films. I met him just once, very briefly, on a set; there was time only to exchange pleasantries. And so, I was very interested in understanding what these others made of him, and use their insights to build a composite picture of the actor and his terrain, through what I hoped would be leisurely, informal, anecdotal conversations.

To my delight, almost everyone I reached out to said yes, without any reservations. The pandemic meant that most people were home and not out shooting. They were unfailingly generous with their time: the conversations took place over Zoom, and most stretched out to an hour or more. The result was an outpouring of love, respect, and grief – subdued in some cases, more apparent in others. As I listened, a detailed picture of Irrfan's many facets began to emerge – actor, star, entertainer. Husband, father, friend. Artist, thinker, nature lover.

———

TV Beginnings

Kismat ki ek khaas baat hoti hai, ki woh palat-ti hai.
There's one thing to be said for fate and fortune: it changes.

– *Gunday*, 2014

For a hard-to-please critic whose viewing life is significantly more full of soul-sapping duds than satisfying sagas, Irrfan was a joy. Even in his indifferent or plain bad films – he did several where you catch him repeating a look or a gesture – you could see he was striving to surprise. People who knew him well speak of his tendency to get bored (as some of his directors and co-stars attest in this book) all too quickly. Perhaps this is what pushed him to dig deep into the part, to find a distinctive *sur* (note) while exploring that key question that plagues the best performers – what makes this character tick – because clocking that crucial aspect is the way to distinguish one part from another.

When you do a series of cops or crooks – as he did in several of his mainstream Bollywood forays – as well as other more distinctively written roles, the challenge lies in building in those differentiators that would make the audience take notice. Coming upon such singularities became key to savouring an Irrfan performance.

That he was going to be someone special was quite evident from his early days. You may have caught only a glimpse of him in Mira Nair's *Salaam Bombay!* (1988), after his part as a slum boy was scrapped from the film 'because he looked so much older than the others', as Nair recalled during our conversation. It was as blink-and-miss as a role can be, but you remember him. He appeared in just a few episodes in Shyam Benegal's landmark epic *Bharat Ek Khoj* (1989) on state-run Doordarshan – at the time India's only TV channel – and managed to hold his own in a crowded frame.

In *Banegi Apni Baat* (1993–97), an extremely popular Zee TV series about modern families navigating the confusing strands of a newly liberalized India, he plays a husband and father, a man older than himself. The series was written by Sutapa Sikdar, Irrfan's wife, and it became a hallmark of new-age TV fiction, a much required antidote to the stodgy programming on Doordarshan.

But the series that turned out to be a godsend for Irrfan was *Bestsellers* (1999–2000) on Star TV, another new channel which started amassing eyeballs with its trendy programming. An anthology of stories based on literary works, *Bestsellers* was the brainchild of Shailja Kejriwal, who had recently joined Star. Now a veteran media maven, Kejriwal remembers those 'fabulous, crazy times', so full of ferment and excitement, where they became 'a tribe' going full tilt at creating something original. Not only Irrfan, but a host of names which would soon become well known were on the *Bestsellers* roster: Tigmanshu Dhulia, Imtiaz Ali, Sriram Raghavan, Anurag Kashyap, Hansal Mehta, Anup Singh, among others.

Despite its massive popularity, the series came to an abrupt end, as it failed to become a money-spinner. Television's loss was cinema's gain. The noughties were different not only because Bollywood was being forced towards novelty, but also because these fresh entrants did not hail from film families with their built-in safety nets; they came armed only with the confidence of those who have nothing to lose, bent upon changing the world. And they did. These new filmmakers began fashioning a new idiom, and Irrfan was right there, hungry, waiting.

――――

Arriving in Bollywood

Yeh shehar humein jitna deta hai, badle mein kahin zyada humse le leta hai.
What this city gives us, it takes away in spades.

– *Life in a… Metro*, 2007

For perspective, *Salaam Bombay!* released the same year Aamir Khan broke out in *Qayamat Se Qayamat Tak*, a star-crossed romance. One year later, in 1989, Salman Khan professed undying love for a pretty young thing in Sooraj Barjatya's *Maine Pyar Kiya* and won her hand. And Shah Rukh Khan played a brash young lover in *Deewana* (1993) and also got his lady. All three films were smash hits, making their heroes and the genre of youthful musical romances Hindi cinema's flavour of multiple seasons thereafter. In 1995, Shah Rukh did *Dilwale Dulhaniya Le Jayenge* – a blockbuster love story that is still running in a Mumbai theatre – and that was that. The three young Khans who made hearts throb back then – and are astonishingly still going strong, powering their brand, over thirty years later – sealed the fate of other kinds of cinema.

What could Irrfan, who had graduated from the National School of Drama in 1987, working through student productions of classical dramas, have done in the Bollywood of the nineties? Short answer: nothing. The Aamir–Salman–Shah Rukh trio had decisively taken over the decade. Legacy studios fell over themselves to make movies coasting on romance, parental opposition, societal differences, stuffed with songs-and-dances and bright costumes. This was happy, shiny Bollywood, raking in the good stuff, in no mood to do anything different.

Both Aamir and Salman belonged to established film families, and Shah Rukh had arrived in Bombay riding high on his massive popularity as the lead of *Fauji*, a 1989 series that aired on Doordarshan. The audience was bewitched by the three Khans. They were a bonanza for the film industry, which was hurting from the previous decade's home entertainment hegemony, facilitated by easy access to colour TVs and DVD players. With viewers returning to theatres in droves, why would filmmakers do anything to rock the boat?

It made sense then, in retrospect, that this was the decade Irrfan spent in television, biding his time. Apart from *Banegi Apni*

Baat, he appeared in several shows, a handful of which became hugely popular. Many of them are available on YouTube and, if you are a completist, you may want to catch up with the episodes which feature him in such series as *Chandrakanta* and *Chanakya*. But it would only be of academic interest. For the most part, you see a clearly disinterested actor buried under loud costumes and dialogues. My only good memories are from *Banegi Apni Baat*, which he outgrew long before it came to an end and, of course, *Star Bestsellers*, which, as Kejriwal says laughingly in her interview, came to be known as 'Irrfan's Bestsellers'.

After a surfeit of banal TV fiction in which he had come to despise his rote, exaggerated parts, and walk-on roles in films that went nowhere, Irrfan was on the verge of quitting acting. It was then that his NSD mate Tigmanshu Dhulia, who was casting director on Asif Kapadia's *The Warrior* (2001), got him the breakthrough for which he was desperate. An initially reluctant Irrfan was talked into meeting Kapadia. Sikdar recalls in the opening interview how she persuaded Irrfan to wear his 'lucky black kurta' for the meeting. Whether it was the kurta or the instant connection between actor and director, or both, there was no doubt that *The Warrior*, which made great use of Irrfan's striking face, and those magnificently hooded eyes, gave him the strength to stay the course. The film, which picked up a BAFTA* award, made the right people notice Irrfan, and it became his calling card in the West.

But after *The Warrior*, things slowed down again. The film hadn't made it to India, and once again Irrfan was beginning to feel disheartened. The roles he was getting, with a few exceptions, were strictly forgettable: the one I do remember him vividly in

---

* British Academy of Film and Television Arts

is *Kali Salwaar* (2002), an NFDC* production of a Saadat Hasan Manto story, directed by Fareeda Mehta, and starring Sadiya Siddiqui. But it was limited to the arthouse.

What an outsider like Irrfan needed were more outsiders, as intent as him to break into the charmed circle of Bollywood. To challenge the gatekeepers who would only back a certain kind of cinema was extremely tough, and it took all the way to the early 2000s for these new entrants to get a foot in.

Again, for perspective, it must be noted that at the start of the new millennium, in the name of new-age Bollywood, debutant Hrithik Roshan had starred in a youthful romance called *Kaho Naa… Pyaar Hai* (2000). There was nothing new-agey about the film, but it was helmed by a fresh face which belonged to another old Bollywood family: Hrithik is the son of Rakesh Roshan, and the grandson of J. Om Prakash. It helped, of course, that Hrithik was tall, fair and handsome – mandatory Bollywood hero traits – and that he danced like a dream. Gifted with a pair of lightning feet, which rivalled and, in some instances, outdid older singing-dancing stars like Mithun Chakraborty and Govinda, Hrithik was one of the last 'star sons' to rapidly ascend to stardom. The film was a blockbuster.

Hindi cinema went on to roll out highly successful films in 2001–2003. Farhan Akhtar's 2001 *Dil Chahta Hai* was a gamechanger in the way it portrayed the rich urban Indian. *Gadar*, a Partition drama starring the brawny Sunny Deol, and *Lagaan*, a Raj-era entertainer with Aamir Khan in the lead, released on the same day in June 2001, and established new box-office records.

Around that time, there were many other bright newcomers trying to break into Bollywood. The very talented Manoj

---

* National Film Development Corporation of India

Bajpayee, an outsider just like Irrfan, was also struggling to find his place during this period. Bajpayee, who had made an impact with *Bandit Queen* (1996), Shekhar Kapur's stark, chilling biopic about the dacoit Phoolan Devi, and had broken out in Ram Gopal Varma's stylish gangster flick *Satya* (1997), co-starred with Irrfan in a soggy crime thriller called *Ghaath* (2000). It did neither of them any good.

When Bajpayee's new avatar in Shyam Benegal's period piece *Zubeidaa* (2003) didn't find too many takers, he went into a slump. It was clear that actors with 'unconventional' looks, who took their craft seriously, would find it hard to secure good work in mainstream Bollywood. At the time, Bajpayee and Irrfan, as well as Kay Kay Menon, another talented 'outsider', were around and available, and yet the Hindi film industry kept dishing out more of the same.

One of the biggest hits of 2003 was the romantic comedy-cum-family drama *Kal Ho Naa Ho*, produced by Karan Johar, directed by Nikkhil Advani, starring Shah Rukh Khan, Saif Ali Khan, Preity Zinta and Rani Mukerji. Big stars, flashy foreign locations, song-and-dance, sentiment, sacrifice, it had all the elements that make for a hit. Could any other kind of film breach this seemingly invincible combination? Were lovers of formulaic masala movies ready for a change? As it turned out, they were.

The change which had started with *Bandit Queen* and *Satya*, films clearly at odds with star-studded, formula-heavy Bollywood, had begun making itself felt. In the same year, there arrived a clutch of movies – Prakash Jha's gritty cop-versus-hinterland-crook drama *Gangaajal*, the Pritish Nandy-produced perky musical *Jhankaar Beats*, the Pooja Bhatt-produced erotic thriller *Jism*, Anant Balani's slice-of-life drama *Joggers' Park*, Rajat Kapoor's quirky dark comedy *Raghu Romeo* – spanning various genres, none featuring stars.

It wasn't a 180-degree pivot, but Bollywood's small chink was large enough for the newbies to step in. That was the year Irrfan found his Bollywood launchpad, in Tigmanshu Dhulia's *Haasil*, revolving around student politics in an Uttar Pradesh town. His riotous 'negative' character garnered a huge positive response. A few months later came Vishal Bhardwaj's terrific gangster film, the *Macbeth* adaptation *Maqbool*, in which Irrfan played the titular role with such brio that he blew us all away. The film was marked by a bunch of excellent performances, from Pankaj Kapur, Naseeruddin Shah, Om Puri and, of course, the stunning Tabu, but it is Irrfan, with his coiled intensity and his passionate but doomed embrace of Tabu's Lady Macbeth, that you remember most.

With *Haasil* and *Maqbool*, he was off and away. At last.

Producer-director Honey Trehan, who began his Bollywood life as casting director-cum-assistant director with Vishal Bhardwaj, shared with me a first-hand story about how Irrfan secured *Maqbool*. There were many actors being considered for the film, but at a trial show of *Haasil*, which they watched together, 'Vishal-ji suddenly said, "*Yeh hai Maqbool!*"' A phone call was made, Irrfan came to their 'small office', and the script was handed over. Within a few hours, Irrfan, who had devoured the script in a single gulp, turned up and said, '*Main kar raha hoon* – I'm doing it.' And that was it.

'That time, Tishu bhai and Vishal-ji were also finding their calling. They were beginning their innings in Bollywood, as was Irrfan,' said Trehan, who worked closely with Irrfan on several films subsequently. His directorial debut *Raat Akeli Hai* (2021) was meant for Irrfan but finally went to Nawazuddin Siddiqui; it released a year after Irrfan's passing. '*Irrfan ko khona bilkul ek neelam ko khone jaisa hai* [losing Irrfan is like losing a gem]; it is not just a loss, but an *abhaav* [absence] we will always have to live with.'

———

The roles that stay with us

Bheed mein kho jaaun, aisa toh main koni.
I am not the kind that will get lost in a crowd.

– *The Song of Scorpions*, 2012

Which is your favourite Irrfan film?

This question brings up such a swirl of characters that it's hard to choose, but some of these faces fill me up with a leaping happiness, the kind that comes with indelible movie moments, mixed with an aching regret that we will never see him do something new on screen.

Rannvijay Singh, in Dhulia's crackling debut feature *Haasil*, was a riot as a 'student leader' and all-round lout, who desperately wants to be more than he can ever be, rampaging through the corridors of a once-great university now fallen upon bad days. This was his triumphant arrival in Bollywood. He was finally where he wanted to be.

Maqbool in Bhardwaj's marvellous eponymous film, conflicted between loyalty to the gravelly-voiced ganglord and an insatiable passion for the latter's wife Nimmi (Tabu). In a Bollywood never comfortable with adult, grown-up desires, the illicit trysts between Maqbool and Nimmi burn up the screen. The scene where the two stand face to face, as Nimmi exhorts Maqbool, '*Bolo "Meri jaan, jaan meri"*' [Say 'My love, my life'], is wild, pulsating poetry.

It stings, it burns. Oh, my beating heart.

Paan Singh Tomar, with his large appetite and larger heart, discovering his talent for speeding up at the right time on the race track, jumping, flexing, winning. His anguish at being let down by the very system that he serves with his entire being. The army jawan and award-winning athlete being forced to turn into a dacoit is one of Hindi cinema's greatest roles, in a great movie of the same name, directed by Dhulia. And who can forget the line: '*Beehad mein baaghi hote hain, dacait milte hain parliament mein.*' [Rebels are found in moors, dacoits in parliament.] It cracks me up every single time.

The shy, self-effacing Ashoke Ganguli in Mira Nair's *The Namesake*, setting up house in the US with his new bride Ashima (Tabu), becoming a father, teaching his son lessons that are not to be found in books. Ashoke with little Gogol on a day out at sea, Ashoke standing in line, waiting to board the plane, tilting his head in a tiny farewell nod. It is a role that is made of these little shimmering, magical moments, and I can't ever watch the film without a catch in the throat.

Monty in Anurag Basu's *Life in a... Metro*, your average inexperienced jerk, chasing away a woman he is instantly attracted to, and then circling back to her in a series of beautifully crafted moments. Irrfan's track with Konkona Sen Sharma is an abiding delight, a guaranteed bringer of wide smiles.

Umber Singh in *Qissa: The Tale of a Lonely Ghost*, Anup Singh's beguiling period gender-bender about identity, corrosive love and loss, leaves you stunned. Its audacious premise turns conventional gender constructs on their head and blurs the lines between them. Trying to be the man he wants to be and being left with unfulfilled inchoate desires that he himself cannot understand, Umber is an endlessly fascinating portrait of a man in search of himself.

Saajan Fernandes, middle-aged widower, grey of mien and testy of temperament after years of working in the same office, coming to life again after a wrong-but-right *dabba* lands on his desk. The aroma wafting from the lunchbox in Ritesh Batra's *The Lunchbox* makes Saajan want to taste life again in this unexpectedly tender, flavourful romance.

Rana in Shoojit Sircar's *Piku* is just a guy looking bemusedly at a girl, and her obsessed-with-his-digestive-track dad, ducking to stay out of their crotchety crossfire. Romcom, family drama, road movie, will-they-won't-they-get-together, the film has all of these elements, with Irrfan in his element. There's Amitabh Bachchan, clearly wanting to chew up the scenery, and Deepika Padukone whose long-limbed litheness can swallow the screen. Yet it is Irrfan who is the stickiest glue in the film.

Yogi in Tanuja Chandra's opposites-attract romance *Qarib Qarib Singlle* is the kind of irritating fellow you aren't meant to fall for instantly. But his insistence on getting in your face and demanding your attention, just like he does with the neatly squared-away Jaya, played by Parvathy, makes you look at him again. This time for good.

There are so many other Irrfan characters who grabbed me and wouldn't let me go: a couple of his characters in *Bestsellers* ('*Ek Shaam Ki Mulakaat*', '*Fursat Mein*'), the wife-beating poet in Vishal Bhardwaj's *7 Khoon Maaf*, the mysterious Roohdaar emerging from the falling snow in *Haider* (also directed by Bhardwaj), the bright-shirts-clad mobster in Aditya Bhattacharya's sadly unreleased *Dubai Return*, the ten-headed Raavan whooping it up with Arshad Warsi in Rohit Shetty's loud laughathon *Sunday*, the investigating officer working on his toughest case in Meghna Gulzar's *Talvar*.

It's ironical that the actor who couldn't wait to get out of Indian

TV, landed a couple of great roles in international television. In the third season of HBO's *In Treatment* (2010), he plays Sunil Sanyal, an elderly Bengali widower trying to make a place for himself with his son and the latter's American wife. It feels like an extension of his Ashoke Ganguli character, greyer, older, but not wiser. His resentment that bubbles barely under the surface comes through in therapy, and those episodes with Irrfan on the couch, so to speak, are exceptional. In the NHK* miniseries *Tokyo Trial* (2016), based on a group of Allied judges asked to decide the fate of Japanese World War II criminals, he plays Radhabinod Pal, the only one in the group who is a conscientious objector, holding on steadfastly to his views.

I can go on, but I will stop here, even if I'm missing many, many more Irrfans, in all the good, bad, indifferent films that he did: if there was one actor who got me dangerously close to gushing, something I do very seldom, it was him.

―――

Crossing over

Life is very busy these days. There are too many people, and everyone wants what the other has.

– *The Lunchbox*, 2013

After *Haasil* and *Maqbool*, two of Irrfan's most important films were *Life in a... Metro* and *Paan Singh Tomar*, both emerging from the leading production house UTV Motion Pictures, which had launched Spotboy, a division meant to focus on more offbeat

---

* Japan Broadcasting Corporation

but realistic subjects. Both films took him up the mainstream Bollywood ladder, and were instrumental in cementing his position as a spellbinding actor.

'Around the time both films were in development, Irrfan had become extremely busy with his international assignments. But [Anurag] Basu [the director of *Metro*] refused to shoot without Irrfan,' recalled Rucha Pathak, then Senior Creative Director at UTV, currently producer with Excel Entertainment, who had worked closely on the two films. 'He shot the rest of the film, and then waited for Irrfan. Oh my god, what it was on paper ... and what Irrfan actually did to that character was to die for.

'The same thing happened with *Paan Singh Tomar*, which suffered delays before its release. By that time, he was already a certain age [the film required a great deal of gruelling physical effort], but Tishu was adamant that this film would only be made with him. Irrfan was already a name overseas, but we in India didn't know just how big he had become. And he really stuck by the film. The industry was going through a crazy recession at the time, and he agreed, like everyone else working on that film, to a pay cut.

'Thanks to *Metro* and *Paan Singh*, people in India started seeing him as that amazing actor who could also work in the mainstream,' she said, recalling how Irrfan was always enquiring about interesting projects, and then, when she would pitch them – she was 'constantly pitching because he was top-of-mind for all the directors he worked with' – he would say, '*Yeh toh kiya hai maine* – I've done this before. I want something new.'

Irrfan had, by now, already crossed over to the West. Or rather, he had got to the enviable point where he was able to cross back and forth between India and the West, and he had managed it so organically that we don't give him enough credit for being India's first genuine crossover star. No one before him had straddled both worlds quite so successfully.

It was during this period that Irrfan appeared in his major international projects. In *The Darjeeling Limited* (2007), about three brothers on a spiritual journey in India, he had a barely there part, but he did that film because he wanted to work with the director Wes Anderson. After that, the parts got bigger and, in a few fortuitous instances, more germane to the plot – as the Pakistani investigating officer in *A Mighty Heart* (2007), the Bengali bhadralok in *The Namesake* (2006), the belligerent cop in *Slumdog Millionaire* (2008), the grown-up Pi in *Life of Pi* (2012), the innovative scientist in *The Amazing Spider-Man* (2012), the big businessman in *Jurassic World* (2015), the fixer in *Inferno* (2016). The optics were great – Irrfan with Angelina Jolie, Irrfan with Tom Hanks, Irrfan in an Ang Lee film – even if his roles did not drive the narrative.

During a chat with Michael Winterbottom at a film event in Doha in March 2023, I asked him about Irrfan's role in *A Mighty Heart*. The director, quite an experienced India hand, having shot a few films in the country, said that he remembered it being one of Irrfan's earliest roles in an English film. 'Initially he was quite reluctant to do the role of Captain, the investigating police officer, because he would have to act in English', he said. 'But fortunately, we were able to persuade him, and he was fantastic in that part.'

Why was he doing these roles? Was he not getting his due in Bollywood? Is that why he was gravitating towards Hollywood? It was clear that Hollywood, which had kept an eye on him since *The Warrior*, was making space for him in massive tent poles. But it was equally clear that Irrfan's heart was always more at home. He had gone on record several times to say that he was never tempted to move base to Los Angeles. The intention was always to travel there to make the movies, after which he would return to where he belonged.

I enjoyed most of his turns in his big Hollywood movies. By the time he came to *Puzzle**, he had clearly got to the point where he was not going to be boxed anymore into the standard brown-guy roles, the token desis Hollywood dreams up in the name of inclusion. In the film, which wasn't particularly good, he was the male lead (not an Indian or South Asian) opposite the white female lead, who even, whoa, gets to kiss her as an equal.

But they were not *his* films. Even in Ang Lee's *Life of Pi*, where he looks back at an adventure which changed his life I found Irrfan underutilized, not quite at home. Even though Lee won an Academy Award for Best Director, Irrfan's character seemed to me much more effective in the other international film which also won multiple Oscars, Danny Boyle's *Slumdog Millionaire*. As a cop, he tortures the poor protagonist with gusto, all the while darkly muttering imprecations against 'murderers, rapists and bum-bandits'. If you haven't heard Irrfan say 'bum-bandits', I tell you, you haven't lived.

But none of his 'foreign' acts gave me as much pleasure as did his roles in Hindi cinema, even those to which he appeared to have said yes strictly for the pay cheque – the fate of all working actors. He did several of those, but I will leave you with one of my top so-bad-it's-beyond-ghastly films, *Hisss*, in which the sinuous Mallika Sherawat plays an *ichhadhari naagin*, and Irrfan brings up the rear. Oh, my eyes.

The extent of Irrfan's fame outside India became apparent slowly, but once it did, the tabloids kept faithful track of what he was

---

* A 2018 Marc Turtletaub film, where he plays a character who is an expert at assembling complicated puzzles.

doing and, more importantly, what he was letting go. He refused two huge projects – Ridley Scott's *The Martian* and Christopher Nolan's *Interstellar* – for Bollywood films that he was either already committed to, or which he felt would be more expedient.

What would have happened to Irrfan's trajectory in the West had he appeared in those films is a matter of conjecture, but it's clear that in choosing *Piku* over *Interstellar*, he made the right choice. 'By that time, he had become a casting favourite across Hollywood; he didn't have to audition or screen-test,' Manpreet Bacchhar, his manager who worked with him 2014 onwards, told me. But Irrfan knew that *Piku* could change his life.

It did. *Piku* made it possible for him to be ranged alongside an enviable A-list companion cast. That same year, in 2015, he also appeared in *Jazbaa*, *Talvar* and *Jurassic World*: in the first, an action thriller, he plays a mouthy, dialogue-spouting cop; in the second, a police procedural, he leads an investigative team; and in the third, he is the billionaire owner of a theme park which houses dinosaurs.

Not one of the biggest names in Bollywood could boast that mix. The three Khans and two other major stars, Akshay Kumar and Ajay Devgn, were on top of the heap at home. But outside the country, it was Irrfan who made it to the wishlist of some of the biggest helmers in Hollywood: a global Spielberg franchise is as big as they come. Shah Rukh, with his flowery romances, has always enjoyed an unmatched reach, further expanded by his 1000-crore-and-counting mega success *Pathaan*. Of the three Khans, Shah Rukh is the one with the maximum global appeal.

But Irrfan was the Khan international directors reached out to.

———

Brand Irrfan

Pack a pillow and a blanket and see as much of the world as you can. You will not regret it. One day it will be too late.

– *The Namesake*, 2006

After the startling success of *Hindi Medium*, Irrfan could well have turned into Brand Irrfan. It wasn't as if that hadn't been in progress. You cannot be a successful actor without parlaying that success into making other brands successful, especially those that align with your persona. He had been getting the endorsements, making the red-carpet appearances, enjoying the financial trappings that come with that kind of glory. And his brand value would have only grown stronger. 'The beauty of Irrfan sir was that he didn't need an agency; you didn't need to pitch him,' said Bacchhar. 'Those who wanted him … wanted him.'

But while Irrfan wanted everything that goes with being a star, and why should he not, he did not want to be distilled into a 'brand'. Because that would have been reductive, making him one-dimensional.

For someone who believed that his work should do the talking, the publicity and marketing that has become such an important aspect of the business, was anathema. Parull Gossain, one of the most experienced publicists in Bollywood, recounted a hilarious encounter with Irrfan, which was precisely about this tricky issue. She had bumped into him outside a Mumbai theatre. Irrfan was standing there smoking. '*Mere liye kuchh karo* – please do something for me,' he said. '*Iske liye kya karein* – what can be done for him? He is so much in his own space, like a babaji, you know,' Gossain told me. 'If you want publicity to help you,

you need to be driven yourself. But he was chill like that. He would do interviews, but hated selfies,' she laughs. 'My feeling is that he knew he was bigger than this whole circus of media, PR, marketing. Because *kaam bolna chahiye, yaar*. He wanted his work to do the work.'

'He was never going to be the kind of star who would drive college kids into a frenzy. But after *Piku*, the younger viewers began appreciating him', she said. 'See, no one's a star for everyone. Salman and Shah Rukh are stars for many more people, but Irrfan was no less a star for others. He epitomized the changing arc of Hindi cinema.'

The marketing–branding–publicity machine didn't quite know what to do with this man, just like the big studios. A chameleon is hard to capture, because that's the nature of the beast: if you are ever-shifting, how would a marketer come up with a pithy one-liner? 'He was like a bird,' said Rucha Pathak, 'always on the move. Even physically he kept moving from Madh to Malad to Lokhandwala [localities in Mumbai]. He would pick up my calls, but you would never know where he was.'

Maybe that's why it's so hard to classify Irrfan. He was an actor, he was a star. But he was much more. He was a keenly aware, deeply political person who did not wear his politics on his sleeve (even though on a couple of TV panels he did comment on the polarized times we are living in), a believer who was not a practising Muslim. I asked several people during my conversations whether he was left out of big movies, not given significant parts, or impacted in any other way because of his religion, but almost everyone said that his phenomenal talent superseded everything else.

In the end, as he struggled with his cancer, he revealed something even more significant about himself – that he was human, with all the attendant strengths and frailties.

———

The story of a life

Ek baar toh yoon hoga, dil mein sukoon hoga. Na dil mein kasak hogi, na sar mein junoon hoga.
One day my heart shall find contentment. Neither will sorrows afflict the heart, nor will passion stir the mind.

– 7 Khoon Maaf, 2011

I began working on the book in earnest around March 2021. The first person I had reached out to was Sutapa. I wasn't going to proceed without her on board, so I was immensely grateful when she agreed to speak to me at length, whilst still struggling to come to terms with the loss of her partner, and the father of their two boys, Babil and Ayaan.

On Sutapa's request, the Zoom calls – spread over a couple of days – included the couple's great friend, confidante and collaborator Shailja Kejriwal. Despite the occasional grief that would overcome Sutapa, the conversation, peppered with charming anecdotes, flowed easily. They were disarming in their candour, reminiscing about Irrfan's early days in NSD, his television and film journey.

It took me over a year to speak to everyone on my list. Most came through quickly. It took much longer with others. I will always regret not managing to include in the book two people on my wishlist: Asif Kapadia, whom I could not reach despite several attempts, and Tabu who, I was told, was still so overwrought that she didn't want to speak to anyone. But almost everyone else that I wanted is all in here.

You will find within these pages Irrfan's people, who were part of his most arresting films: Tigmanshu Dhulia, his old friend from drama school, who gave Irrfan some of his best films; Vishal Bhardwaj, also very close to Irrfan, who created a clutch of remarkable roles for him; Anup Singh, director of *Qissa* (2013) and another close friend; his *Qissa* co-actors Tillotama Shome and Rasika Dugal, who spoke at length to me about their experience on set. Rajat Kapoor, in whose debut feature Irrfan played a police inspector, was more measured in his observations of Irrfan; Naseeruddin Shah, who co-starred with Irrfan in the same film, was as incisive as only he can be.

Most conversations would begin with talk of Covid, of the dispiritedness engulfing us, of what we would find on the other side, if we ever came that far. Once those preliminaries were over, all talk would revolve around Irrfan, and I came to know him anew through the minds and hearts of Shyam Benegal, Anurag Basu, Pooja Bhatt, Sudhir Mishra, Mira Nair, Sooni Taraporevala, Priyadarshan, Nikkhil Advani, Sanjay Gupta, Shoojit Sircar, Ritesh Batra, Tanuja Chandra, Meghna Gulzar, Pankaj Tripathi, Saket Chaudhary and Homi Adajania.

A few others I spoke to had not worked on films with Irrfan – Anurag Kashyap, Dibakar Banerjee, Karan Johar. But being part of the industry, and by association, they offered valuable insights. Johar said he never did have a script worthy of Irrfan's 'monumental talent' but was proud to have presented *The Lunchbox*. I also spoke to Sunil Doshi, veteran industry watcher and independent producer, and Santosh Desai, among the most acute Indian cultural commentators. Both provided sharp observations on the phenomenon that was Irrfan. Cameron Bailey, CEO of the Toronto International Film Festival, is the only international figure in the book, whose comments crucially underline Irrfan's impressive impact in the West.

Across these conversations, I have repeated some questions: memories of first meetings, for example, or how he will be remembered. The conversations have been shortened and edited for clarity, but I have tried to retain their raw essence and the voice of each interlocutor, maintaining their particular cadences and rhythms. Some use both present and past tense when referring to Irrfan. Most conversations were bilingual; Pankaj Tripathi and Vishal Bhardwaj spoke extensively in Hindi. Their answers, for the most part, appear in English translation.

So here's the inspiring journey of Sahabzade Irfan Ali Khan turned Irrfan – an artist who thought long and deep about his craft, and who was concerned not just about his own performance but also of his co-stars. With each opinion, perspective, memory, the picture gets denser, richer and more complex. You start to see the minutiae of the stuff that makes up a life.

What I came away with was a portrait of a man who worked at being completely at home in the world, while retaining a great sense of himself. I hope you find your Irrfan in this kaleidoscopic volume.

———

Being Irrfan

I suppose, in the end, the whole of life becomes an act of letting go …

– Life of Pi, 2012

'When he first arrived at NSD, he looked very unmade, completely disjointed,' theatre veteran Prasanna Heggodu, one of Irrfan's most beloved teachers, told me. Heggodu was instrumental in taking Irrfan well beyond the mundane style of acting that used to be so prevalent when the latter joined the drama school. He showed Irrfan how to communicate with his whole being. 'During one of the plays, we tried out a method of communication that became a signature with Irrfan: communication through sense, touch, feel, flash of the eye, tension of the hand – which he became so good at. They confuse it with method acting, but it is much more than that.'

'In the beginning, he was among the three or four students who were very good, but by the end of the course, he was far, far superior,' said Prasanna, whom Irrfan and Sutapa kept in touch with over the years. 'From an unmade man, he became so made.'

At his peak, Irrfan had everything going for him. He had conquered the classy-sexy space, and had managed to loosen up enough to get into a pool with a swarm of scantily clad ladies, and do a jig. He could carry off pink and pastel, nailing the natty-man-around-town look, and he could get into a *pagri* and wear his rumpled grey locks with pride. Versatility is for lesser actors; Irrfan literally could do anything he wanted.

It took Irrfan more than thirty years to get where he did. All through, riding the ups and downs, waiting for the right films, and arriving at that point where an Irrfan film would become a much-awaited event; from that one-scene-only letter writer who crumples little Chaipau's letter and throws it away in *Salaam Bombay!* to the loving father who will do anything for his beloved daughter in his last film *Angrezi Medium* (2020), Irrfan always managed to preserve himself. He did not fritter himself away; he held on to that essential Irrfan-ness, kept nurturing it with support from Sikdar, and opened himself up to the roles that needed all of him.

And he really had to wait for those roles.

I've posed this question to many in the book: why did it take big-budget Bollywood studios so long to find Irrfan, and give him a tailor-made role, and not just expect him to buoy the cop-hood parts they handed out to him routinely? He did make it to the coveted Yashraj* roster, playing a cool cop whipping off snappy lines in the Ranveer Singh–Arjun Kapoor starrer *Gunday* (2014) – but the heroes were the legacy stars. The answers all boil down to this one fact: the mainstream Hindi film industry doesn't make movies for actors. It makes them for stars, and those stars, in turn, make money for the industry. It's a tight circle which has no place for disruptors, and Irrfan, indubitably, was one.

It wasn't as if he didn't try his luck in the movies which would have led to him being co-opted by the industry, had they done well. Remember Ishaan Trivedi's *7½ Phere*, which came out in 2005? Don't kill yourself if you don't. It's an eminently forgettable family drama-cum-romcom which allowed Irrfan a meet-cute with Juhi Chawla, who trips and falls over him and asks him archly, 'Are you flirting with me?' Irrfan, flat on the ground, not quite knowing whether he should be pleased or mortified, makes nothing of the moment. And nothing came of the film either. Imagine if the film had succeeded, and Irrfan had got stuck in a series of tacky meet-cutes in bad melodramas

---

* Yashraj Films, a leading Bollywood production house

– would he have got better at those scenes? Short answer again: highly unlikely.

As much as he needed to know what he could do and, more importantly, what he couldn't, the movies needed to shift gears to be ready for him. It happened when it did, and we got the films which Irrfan was looking for, the ones which top-lined the story and the actor, minus the contrivances and clichés that were so much a part of Bollywood's formulaic offerings.

You could see how he had worked on himself over the years, but if there was one thing that he didn't do well, despite having acquired a staggering degree of polish, it was cheese. He was much too self-aware to either be satisfactorily cheesy, or letting himself go on the dance floor. In the rare films where you can catch him trying to groove, he is more awkward than anything else.

The insistence on being as life-like as possible, learning how to make friends with the camera, catching the eye while being still – these are all part of Irrfan's legacy. The declamatory, throw-everything-at-the-kitchen-sink acting style is yet to become a thing of the past, and may never be, but Irrfan's understated yet effective use of actorly tools gradually percolated to newer actors like Ayushmann Khurrana, Rajkummar Rao, Vicky Kaushal, Pankaj Tripathi, Vijay Varma and Jaideep Ahlawat ... These actors now helm some of Hindi cinema's most impactful, entertaining films and web shows. And they are stars in their own right.

Irrfan's most direct legatee, his older son Babil, has already made his acting debut with a dark drama (*Qala*, 2022), and followed that up with a lightweight teen comedy (*Friday Night Plan*, 2023) and an intense web series (*The Railway Men*, 2023). Of course he reminds us of his illustrious father, but he is rapidly proving that he is his own person, and a talented performer in his own right.

And yet – and yet – it will be impossible not to miss Irrfan, so uniquely himself, and so universally us.

PART I
1997–2005

'Generous in every which way'

SUTAPA SIKDAR AND
SHAILJA KEJRIWAL

Sutapa Sikdar, Irrfan's wife, was his constant companion and collaborator, as also his greatest critic, in his remarkable journey as an actor. She was with him when he took his first steps at the National School of Drama, where they were batchmates. She saw him grow and carve out a path through the Hindi film industry, which had no idea what to do with an actor of his calibre. Acknowledging her great script sense, Irrfan ran all his scripts by her. 'He was getting the best scripts when he fell sick,' says Sikdar, who has worked as a scriptwriter, producer and costume designer. Currently she is the script head for two shows, one each on SonyLIV and StarPlus.

Shailja Kejriwal, a pioneer in the entertainment industry, was responsible for getting Irrfan out of the endless loops of soaps and series as he waited for a break in the movies. An accidental visionary, she helped kickstart *Star Bestsellers*, the groundbreaking show on StarPlus [1999–2000] which gave many of Indian cinema's most well-known actors and directors their first airing. Irrfan was one of the biggest beneficiaries of *Bestsellers*; he worked in many of the episodes and found the will to go on at a time he was getting despondent about not finding good work.

Kejriwal also co-produced, with Sikdar, Irrfan starrers *Madaari** and *Qarib Qarib Singlle*†. Currently she is Chief Creative Officer at Zindagi TV.

The conversation with Sutapa and Shailja was conducted together on the former's request. And it turned out to be a perfect *jugalbandi*, as they trained a personal and professional lens on Irrfan, sharing perspectives no one else could have. The free-flowing and easy chat is the result of their years of friendship and affection, mutual support and respect.

—————

I

SHUBHRA GUPTA: You met Irrfan for the first time at the National School of Drama. Why did you join NSD?

SUTAPA SIKDAR: It's a very tricky question, Shubhra. I joined the National School of Drama because I didn't want to do a nine-to-five job. It's not about passion. It's very unlike Irrfan, who did so many things to get into NSD. I was studying in Delhi [Kamala Nehru College], doing English Honours, and there was a teacher from NSD who came to do a *Waiting for Godot* workshop with us – Anuradha Kapur. Anu and I became very good friends. At that time, I thought I wanted to be a tour guide. In the workshop I thought, 'This is not bad, this is interesting – another profession [where] I don't have to sit at a desk.' And that's when I said, 'Okay, let me explore.' Anu was after me. She said, 'You must try, you are so good.' She meant acting, you know? I never wanted to become an actor. I just thought it's interesting and cool. So that's how I joined.

—————

* A 2016 Nishikant Kamat film
† A 2017 Tanuja Chandra film

But the admissions had just [got] over at NSD. So I started my post-graduation from Delhi University and, in [between], I did all this acting-shacting, and did ten plays. We had to do ten plays [as a requirement for admission into NSD]. And I did not lie; unlike Irrfan, I did those ten plays!

SG: You mean he lied? He hadn't done ten plays?
SS: Yes, he lied! He had done three to four and he said ten, because he was so desperate to get in, you know? I think what he learnt at the end of the journey is that you always get what you want when you let go.

My whole thing was to let go. *Hoga, hoga. Nahi hoga, nahi hoga.* [It'll happen if it has to happen. If it doesn't, it doesn't.] And I was very cool with my teachers. I used to call them by their first names. It was a culture shock for Irrfan. He used to say 'ma'am' and 'miss' and all that. So we were very different – chalk and cheese – from the very beginning.

SG: So was it love at first sight? For the both of you?
SS: Not at all! I was quite intimidating; he thought I was his senior. I ragged him, actually. I was friends with some third years before I joined NSD. On our interview day, we ragged him. And he thought I was in [the] third year. Then he got this shock when he saw I was in his class. I slowly noticed that he was most sincere, very honest. Which kind of pulled me towards him. I hate dishonesty, I always have. I think that was one thing which kind of attracted [me towards him] … but no, it was not love at first sight at all. Shailja will vouch for that.

all laugh

SG: Shailja, you got to know Sutapa before Irrfan. How did that happen?

SHAILJA KEJRIWAL: It's a very fun story. I saw her from afar at FTII [Film & Television Institute of India], with Irrfan. It was 1991 or '92 – I'm not sure. And I had gone there to do my FA [Film Appreciation] course. And there was this whispering happening: '*Arre, arre*, Irrfan has come …' because one of Irrfan's films had released … I'm forgetting the name. Which one, Sutapa? The one with Dimple [Kapadia].

SS: *Drishti** … with the hot scenes.
SK: Yeah, *hot* scenes, exactly!

all laugh

So a friend of ours, who was from FTII, came to my house in Calcutta – I still hadn't moved to Bombay – and he said, '*Dekhechhish?*' [Have you seen?] I said, 'What?' He said, 'There's this new boy … *dekhechhish?*' So I said, 'Why are you drooling over a boy?' And then I watched *Drishti* and I was like, 'Wow, man! This guy is really cool.' Cut to: I go to FTII to do my FA course and by then, at least the intellectual FTII types were already familiar with Irrfan.

They said, '*Pata hai? Irrfan aaya hai. Woh jo naya ladka tha na* Drishti *mein? Woh yahaan hai.* [You know, Irrfan is here. That new guy who was in *Drishti*? He is here.] It was like, 'My god, the hottie is here!' So we decided to go and see, and these two were walking towards the pool area, which was dry all the time, and I saw them from behind. I saw one lanky fellow and I see

---

* A 1990 Govind Nihalani film

one hottie. Wearing shorts and some tank top kind of thing, with sneakers, and I'm like, '*Usko chhod; ye kaun hai* – who is she?' [referring to Sutapa] First of all, the heart broke *ki* he's already married. Second, the heart broke *ki* he's married to *this* one. '*Koi chance hi nahi hai,* you know?' So we just ogled them from behind and then, of course, they went on their own private little tour or whatever.

SG: Which year was this?

SK: I think this was '92 … '91 or '92 – I'm not sure. Then I went back to Calcutta because I was finishing my master's at the time. I completed my master's, and I was doing my research for my PhD. Then, finally, I joined Star [TV].

Life happened. I got married, I got divorced. All my friends in Calcutta were from FTII and I was from Jadavpur [University]. So there was this synergy happening at the time. I was the person who would write and they were the ones who would direct. I had met most of them during my stint at FTII because they were the diploma students and I was the FA student. They had all taken me under their wing. Basically, '*Arre! Chal edit kar, ye kar, woh kar*, etc., etc.' This fascinated me. And while I was doing my PhD, I felt *ki* I don't want to be stuck in a seminar room, you know? Which is what you end up doing, and you end up talking to each other. You talk to the initiated – and I didn't want to do that, really. By the way, when I was in Calcutta, I completely skipped that TV era, of Sutapa writing *Banegi Apni Baat* and all of that, because in Jadavpur it was really looked down upon. We were more into watching Tarkovsky, Fellini and Antonioni.

In Calcutta, I was writing documentaries and stuff, so when I came to Bombay I met all these other friends of mine from

FTII, and they said, '*Yaar, tu idhar hi reh ja* – you stay behind.' I asked what will I do? Unlike Sutapa, I don't have the patience to go knocking at producers *ke* doors *ki*, '*Mujhe writing karna hai, ye karna hai.*' I had written some documentaries and some short fiction for Rathikant Basu, who used to be Doordarshan's director-general, right? He had left Doordarshan and become the head of Star. So I thought, '*Chalo*, let me try my luck, who knows?' I was really surprised that he remembered me, because it [had been] a good four–five years since I had met him the last time. I said, 'I've come for a writing job.' He said, '*Nahi*, we don't commission writing jobs. What is it that you want to do – do you know how to cut promos?' I said, 'I don't know what promos are!' He said, 'Okay, what do you like doing?' I said, 'I know only one thing in life. I love telling stories and listening to stories. *Iske ilawa* I know nothing!' So he said, 'Oh, that's cool then. We are going to start a commissioning department and you would be an ideal fit.' I asked what had to be done. He said, '*Kuchh nahi, kahaaniyan kehni hoti hain aur sunni hoti hain. Yeh hi hai, bas!*' [Nothing much – you have to tell stories and listen to stories. That is it!] I said, '*Wah! Aur paise bhi milenge iske liye?*' [Wow! And I will be paid for it too?]

SG: *laughs*

SK: I would've done the job even without getting paid, quite honestly. So that's when I joined the commissioning department, and I started. I entered Star in January 1998 and they shoved me into that room with 500 tapes and said, 'Go!' I had to see all those tapes in the next two to three months. They put a VCR and a TV in my house and told me to watch and decide which out of these tapes are good. I said, '*Ye toh mindblowing cheez hai!*' I would spend days looking at all that content. Then the regime at Star changed and all of us were asked to make a plan overnight. My overnight plan was [Star] Bestsellers. [As I was] from a literature background, I couldn't think of anything else, other than short TV fiction based on classics. And it just got accepted! So it was just chance ... and then I started meeting people and that's how I ended up meeting Sutapa.

Sutapa, you remember how we first ...

SS: Yeah, yeah. I remember how we first met. Also, by then, Irrfan had done some inane films like Kasoor*. He was not interested anymore in working in serials. So that's when we thought ki maybe he'll direct, maybe we'll produce and stuff like that. And then Star Bestsellers happened, and we took our story and went to Shailja. She was very excited to see Irrfan ... during the first meeting (when he had gone to the loo!) she told me the FTII story. This hottie thing!

all laugh

At that time Banegi Apni Baat was a hit. Irrfan was really admired and everybody loved him. But Irrfan was like this Jadavpur [University] faculty, Shubhra; he would make me feel so bad about it ki, 'What shit are you writing?' I still remember Shailja telling me, 'I'm glad of one thing: you will no more feel that you're writing shit. You always felt you were not good enough because Irrfan thought TV's not good enough. And that's why he said, "Let's do different kind of TV."' That's why we were very keen on doing Star Bestsellers. And it was fun!

---

* A 2001 Vikram Bhatt film

SK: *Star Bestsellers* started getting known as a series for Irrfan Khan. So, internally, it was this thing that Shailja casts Irrfan in everything. Because Tigmanshu [Dhulia] was making *Star Bestsellers*, he cast Irrfan Khan. Indranil Goswami was making *Star Bestsellers* – he cast Irrfan Khan.

SS: Even Anup Singh ...

SK: Even Anup ... Everybody, *everybody* would cast Irrfan Khan! Even if no one was casting him, I would say, 'How about Irrfan?' I thought we'd won the lottery because he was willing.

I think Tishu [Tigmanshu] made some five or six *Bestsellers* with Irrfan. Out of the total number we made, I think one-third was with Irrfan. So that's how the relationship grew. Then Sutapa wrote one very nice *Bestseller*, which was hilarious and we used to keep laughing, and that's how Sutapa and I started keeping in touch on a regular basis. She wrote *Hum Saath Saath Hain Kya?* I remember *Hum Saath Saath Hain** had released around then.

SS: But I must thank Ekta Kapoor for one thing. We were doing one show for Star, which was a proper TV show. We were the producers – we wrote it and went to Delhi as new producers who will be doing this revolutionary, pathbreaking show. We shot four episodes and then *Kyunki Saas Bhi Kabhi Bahu Thi*[†] came.

all laugh

---

* A 1999 Sooraj Barjatya film
† A 2000–2008 StarPlus show

The programming changed, *completely*, for television, forever! Thank god for that, otherwise we would have become 'producers' and Irrfan wouldn't have done [*The*] *Warrior* [the film that was his launchpad into the movies]. For me it was bad, but for him it was good that Ekta Kapoor came into the scene.

SG: Sutapa, I'd like to take you back a little bit to the National School of Drama. How did he actually get into his groove?

SS: I think he was always in the groove. Like, he would not be able to laugh like I would. I would be very serious in class. I was the good student [who] always did very well at NSD. And I would come out and say, '*Kya chutiyapa tha!*' [What ridiculousness that was!] And he would look at me *ki* how can somebody be so dishonest?

So that was him … he was always in the groove. I remember, at NSD we did a play which was directed by Ram Gopal Bajaj – called *Lower Depths*. That's when we were quite serious about each other. I think it was in our second year.

SG: The Maxim Gorky play?

SS: Yes, yes. He really was so into it that he literally got depressed. We [the characters] were very poor in the play. We used to live in this one small chawl – that's why it's called *Lower Depths*.

One time I went to my room in the girls' hostel and saw that he was sitting under my table. And I got scared because he did not look normal to me. I called some friends, then, slowly, we [helped] him out from under the table and took him for an auto ride to get him out of that zone. The thing about him is he went wherever [something took] him. Which is very scary! Which, as a partner, as a wife, worried me many, many times. He was less serious about performances in his last years. He was very serious about it initially. He was that serious man, you know? I lived in Chittaranjan Park [a primarily Bengali neighbourhood in south Delhi], but hostel was compulsory, so my mother would call everybody home. We would have fun. See, his family is very different, so he was not exposed to such things. And [with] Bengalis, you know, *na*, everybody is a communist.

all laugh

He was like, 'I have to read everything!' So he got exposed much more than any normal person because of his tremendous curiosity and drive to learn. That's why I think he always was in the groove.

But yes, at NSD you have different kinds of teachers. Finally, it was Prasanna [Heggodu] sir, who is in Bangalore now – he has left theatre and become a social activist. I think his [Irrfan's] life only changed when he could manoeuvre the craft. I think Prasanna sir was helpful in manoeuvring his craft towards what he wanted to achieve.

But my best experience at NSD was my diploma play, *Equus*. I don't remember Irrfan saying 'I love you' to me. I just remember that he, for my diploma production, stood like a pillar. From painting the scrolls to painting my set with his own hands and doing all kinds of stuff, costumes and everything! Just to make it happen well. As a woman or as a girl, that's where you feel that you can trust someone. That's where you get this thing *ki* I can live with this man.

When Shailja saw me at FTII, we were not married; we were living together. We actually got married very late, in '98. I took that long to decide. Because I found that he was also not the type who'd be a typical husband. I was also not the type who'd become a typical wife. So it kept getting delayed, and then maybe he got insecure that I'll marry someone else.

all laugh

SG: Was there a threat?
SK: Always, always. Ask me!
SS: I wouldn't have gone anywhere, Shubhra, but that's what he felt!

SG: So... after NSD?
SS: The first thing he did immediately after NSD was *Salaam Bombay!*. I was in Delhi at that time. He was shooting here [in Bombay] and he wanted me to come to Bombay, and I didn't want to. I am a Delhi girl, you know? After that, Shyam Benegal's *Bharat Ek Khoj* happened.

I came to Bombay regally, with a job. I said, 'I'm not going to struggle.' So I came with a job with Govind Nihalani from NSD itself and I started working. We [Irrfan and I] worked together. He was acting in *Drishti* and I was in the direction department. After that, we went to FTII. Afterwards he was doing some television ... one television show [on Doordarshan] called *Shrikant*. You know the one in which he wears that white kurta-pajama and looks like a *Bangali jamai babu* – I thought he looked very stupid!

all laugh

SG: I thought he just changed the complexion of things on TV. Like he did with cinema. What do you remember most from his TV period?

SS: He was very popular in *Chandrakanta**. But I was terrified of him going to the shoot because he would give me horrible times at home. He hated the way they would tell him to show more anger, more happiness, everything more, more, more. His main problem with television, Indian television, was this. He loved doing *In Treatment*†. So, with Shailja, he really hoped *ki* TV would change, but it did not. He was mentally very tortured. He just couldn't do what he wanted to because he was constantly told, '*Ye toh kuchh karta hi nahi hai, yaar, ye toh aise hi khada rehta hai.*' [He doesn't do anything; just stands there like that.] But he insisted *ki*, '*Waise hi khada rahoonga; main nahi karoonga villain jaise villain kiya jaata hai.*' [I will stand exactly like that; I will not act the way a villain is supposed to act.] He wrote to some television producer *ki*, '*Mujhe maar do, yaar; main nahi kar sakta yeh.*' [Just kill my character; I just can't do this.] And they did! They did kill that character, but then, by popular demand, he had to be called back as his brother or something.

laughs

It's very funny. So slowly people just started accepting that this is working for people. Honestly, at that time, he was so embarrassed *ki* he wouldn't give me any TV scripts to read, otherwise all through our lives he made me read through every script of his – *every*!

---

* A 1994–1996 Doordarshan show
† A 2010 HBO show

all chuckle

You know that is honestly one portion of our life, of two to three years, where I worked differently and he worked differently. After that ...

SG: The rest was always together?
SS: Always together. Like even with [The] Warrior, when the first draft came, he made me read it. So that's one phase where he was not actually proud of what he was doing. I shouldn't say the word 'proud'; he wasn't happy, he wasn't comfortable doing what he was doing. So that's what the television phase was ... except, of course, those Bestsellers. That he always loved doing.

II

SG: And after that, he was done and dusted with TV.
SS: Yes, yes. When we were doing Bestsellers, he also tried directing because that was almost the end of his television career, where we actually thought he didn't want to act anymore. Because of the format and many other reasons – the way television was in India.

So he directed one of the films. It was called Alvida, a BBC film on leprosy. BBC was the main sponsor. Rafey Mahmood was our cameraperson and Nawazuddin [Siddiqui] did a small role in that. What was interesting is that though it was his first directorial thing, it helped because Rafey is a very cinematic cinematographer, not the usual television cinematographer.

SK: Sutapa, wasn't that for *Bestsellers*?

SS: It was! But it was by BBC in a way ... And he introduced Nawaz! I was trying to tell him, 'Why don't you do it?' He said, 'No, no, he is a new guy. He's very good, you'll see.'

We had a lot of scripting back and forth with BBC. They were saying leprosy has to be underlined. But he made it into a spiritual love story [even as] it talked about leprosy. It was the journey of a person [after] he discovers he has leprosy. That's what I saw [in] him in his disease. When he actually had his disease that ... you know ... you need not be depressed. Because we have used those lines also in that *Bestseller*: '*Mayoosi gunaah hai!*' [Sadness is a sin!]

See, this man lost all hope because he had leprosy in the film, and we were shooting in colour and, for that particular portion, Irrfan wanted everything to go black-and-white. So we have this one portion where it's all black-and-white. Because the world for him became black-and-white and, slowly, when again he kind of comes out of leprosy as a stigma, the film again becomes coloured.

gets emotional and voice cracks a bit

What I'm trying to say is that I saw it in his way of battling his own disease. He had [it] in his mind that *mayoosi gunaah hai*. And I used to get angry, Shubhra. I used to say, 'You have to consider your disease an enemy. You *have* to tell him to go away! You can't make him a friend.' But he made his disease a friend. He said, '*Nahi, but woh aaya hai na? Usko rehne do ab ... hum baatein karenge.*' [Now that he is here, let him stay. We will have conversations.] I was feeling very superstitious as well; it was a very difficult period for me. So I just felt we need to tell him [the disease], 'Get away! Get lost!' Many people tell you many things –

manifestation, this, that. And here there was this man talking to his disease: '*Rehne do usko. Usne kya bigaada hai?* He's doing his job.' [Let him stay. What is his fault?]

I was very mindfucked. But somewhere I saw that glimpse which he had shown as a philosophy, in that *Bestseller*. Ages back. How to combat – there was no death involved in that *Bestseller* – but how to combat something when your life has taken a 180-degree turn. I saw a man who is only supposed to be a good actor as a director. I don't know whether he would have become a director finally because he was doing so well in the end as an actor. But he had this keen sense of music. And editing.

I still have those four TV episodes we shot. When the camera was travelling slowly, we used to say, '*Yaar, yeh nahi hold karega.*' But when we saw it with the music and with everything else, it did hold, you know? It was telling a story, it was talking of a language which is not words and it's not in the face of the actors who were speaking. So what is interesting is even so many years ago he had this vision of seeing everything in totality. Even when he was acting, he always saw the whole thing. Shailja and I realized it in *Qarib Qarib Singlle*, how he saw everything in totality. As in, he's not happy with only his scenes *ki*, '*Dekho, achhe se scenes likh ke tum ko de diye hain. Ab tum karo, yaar, apna kaam, humein apna kaam karne do.*' [I have written good scenes for you; now you do your job and let me do mine.]

I learnt a lot while producing with him. Because here I saw an actor who would not say, '*Bhai, mere upar camera rehna chahiye; baaki gaye bhaad mein.*' [The camera should focus on me; to hell with everyone else.]

SG: I was told that he was a generous actor. He was good in almost everything, but in some films he was great. I thought

Maqbool was one of those. He's aware of everything that is happening on screen. Aware of where he is and where everyone else is. It's a mark of great actors, that generosity.

SS: Yeah! Generosity and also, it's about how you chisel your skill. I have not seen many actors closely. Because Irrfan lived with me, I saw him closely. But I failed to understand how he could be so deep in that scene, and yet he knew *ki light idhar se hit ho rahi hai toh mujhe zara sa chehra hilana hai.* [Since the light is hitting me from here, I need to move my face a little.] That is what I found very, very fascinating.

The point is that he has this ... he had this command over the skill, and he could've used it. Unfortunately, it just [*gets emotional, voice cracks*] kind of finished too early because this is the time he actually was at ease with himself. It looks very easy on screen but it took a long, long time for him to be easy with lines, with his body language, with everything ... also to catch the light [*voice returns to normal*] – it takes a lot of time, you know?

For instance, in *Karwaan**, he was offered Dulquer's [Salmaan] role, because that's the main role. And he refused it. They were shocked *ki* why is he doing the secondary role. Manpreet [Bacchhar], his manager, said, '*Sir, kyun kar rahe hain aap aisa?*' He said, '*Mere paas uss mein kuchh add karne ko hi nahi hai.* What will I do with a hero's role if I can't add anything?' I asked him, 'Then why are you doing it – you should've just refused it?' *Bole,* 'No, but Shaukat's character is very interesting. I need to do Shaukat's character.' See, he had different reasons to do different films. Which is very important for an actor, that he should know why he is doing a particular film.

---

* A 2018 Akarsh Khurana film

Initially *toh* of course he had his needs. Later, for the last six–seven years, he made a choice; he knew exactly why he was doing which film, for what. And he gave 'entertainment' a whole lot of importance. Which is so unlike his 'serious' image. He always thought *ki*, 'If I'm not entertaining, or the film is not entertaining, then it's pointless. Because I've not come here to preach. Why should I preach that this is good acting; *main dus–gyarah ghante ka pause loonga aur* I'll be considered an arty actor. My audience should be entertained, and I have to tell the story' – that was very important for him.

He followed Om Puri and Naseer [Naseeruddin Shah] bhai, right? What is interesting is this new breed of actors – which I wasn't aware of, till he actually passed and people sent me messages – had so much faith in themselves because he had faith in himself. Which I think is a huge contribution. He created a camp without creating a camp.

Today I know that an actor can say, 'I will not do this.' They've got this confidence, you know. The way he suffered because he didn't have anybody saying, '*Hum toh dheere dheere hi dialogue bolenge, yaar, aur matlab nikaal ke hi rahenge.*' [I will deliver my dialogue slowly but ensure it makes sense.] *Woh koi uske paas example nahi tha*, you know? So he had to suffer a lot of things in that sense. But there are a lot of actors today who can stand up and say *ki* '*Irrfan sir bhi toh aise hi acting karte thay aur sabko mazza aata tha; humko kyun nahi karne diya jaa raha hai?*' [This is exactly how Irrfan sir used to act and everyone would be entertained by it; why am I not being allowed to do it?] It's not a great thing to say, not a humble thing to say, but I think he is an institution in that sense.

SG: You were work partners, home partners ... partners in everything. Did he insist on getting your approval before he actually said yes to anything?

SS: Yes! I read all the scripts. Of course he would do what he would do, but he made me read all the scripts, ask what I thought. I was very strict. I would say, '*Tum kitna bakwaas gaate ho.*' [You sing so badly.] I didn't appreciate Irrfan properly in the beginning. If I didn't like his performance, I would not say, '*Arre wah, kya kamaal kar diya toone!*' [What a remarkable performance you've given!] Till I actually felt it, you know? Like in *Paan Singh Tomar**, I felt that he lived that character, and I cried. And *he* cried because he said this is the first time I was acknowledging his performance.

It was three in the morning and I just said, 'My god!' And then we sat down with Tishu for a long time. When we came back home, it was very late. I told him ki '*Yaar, main toh kuchh kami nikaal hi nahi sakti, Irrfan, iss mein.*' [I can't find any shortcoming in this.] I'll give you another example. I had a lot of problems with his [*The*] *Namesake* performance. And he always told me *ki*, '*Yaar, tere ko kyun problem hoti hai*; you know people were crying.' But I think his language was not right. Bengalis were all saying, '*Kitna achha Bangali bola.*' I don't think he spoke Bengali well.

This was one point. The other is that – his mother tongue is Hindi, he thought in Hindi. So I personally felt it took him a while to be comfortable in the English language. Very strictly my point of view. I used to always tell him, '*Hollywood ki picture agar Hindi mein bolti na, ab tak tujhe Oscar mil gaya hota!*'

---

* A 2012 Tigmanshu Dhulia film

[If Hollywood movies were made in Hindi, you would have got an Oscar by now!]

all laugh

Because I feel that language *was* a barrier. But he worked so, so hard to make it sound effortless by the end of it. [During] *Inferno**, we were sitting in a cafe, at a personal dinner with Hans [Zimmer, the film score composer] and everybody – their family and our family – it was a very small dinner. He was conversing and I was getting nervous: *abhi ye kuchh na galat bolega hi bolega!* [He will definitely say something wrong.] But it was amazing, the way he spoke of various things, and then he's telling [me] in the car *ki 'Tu toh aise baithi hogi apni ungli pakad ke ki ye kab grammatical galti karega.'* [You must have been waiting, holding your breath, for me to make a grammatical mistake.]

all laugh

But what I am saying is that when a person is privileged, then he grows this much. And then there is Irrfan who's not privileged and he grew like this. That's what I find very commendable, which I keep telling my elder son [Babil].

SG: As partners, did you ever feel a sense of claustrophobia? Because you were both so much in sync.
SS: He said *ki, 'Nahi, nahi, hum saath kaam nahi karenge; hum bahut ladte hain!'* [No, no, we will not work together – we fight a lot.] All the time we talked about work, but actually, objectively,

---

* A 2016 Ron Howard film

49

it did not involve me, right? Because [they were] his films! He always thought I was very judgemental.

For me performance is very important, Shubhra, and he knew it. For me a film does not work if the performances are not working. I don't know whether Shailja knows or not, but he did feel that I had a keen sense of performance, and I was a much better judge of performance than he was.

He always said, '*Agar Sutapa ne bol diya ki ye take achha hai, Irrfan, toh woh take achha hi hai, uss mein koi shaq nahi hai.*' [If Sutapa has said that this take is good, then it is undoubtedly so.] I'm a horrible actor. It's so easy to critique something, it's so easy to give your opinion, but to do it in front of the camera is a completely different thing. My producers [Tony and Deeya Singh in *Banegi Apni Baat*] used to make fun of me: '*Apne husband ke liye sabse achhe dialogue likhti ho.*' [You write the best dialogues for your husband.] But Shubhra, it's not like that. *Maine sabke liye achhe dialogue likhe, lekin sabke bass ka nahi hai.* [I have written good dialogues for everyone, but not everyone can deliver them right.]

all laugh

I always used to get a surprise in the scene, which came as his interpretation – which is so interesting for a writer to watch.

SG: There was a time that he was getting impatient with television and he just didn't want to do anything with TV anymore. It was *The Warrior* which actually changed everything for him, right? Asif Kapadia's film?

SS: Yes. And Tigmanshu was actually the casting director for

The Warrior. Irrfan was thinking, '*Warrior … aur main?*' He was very thin at that time: '*Main kaise "warrior" ban sakta hoon?*' [How can I be a 'warrior'?] You know, I still have that black kurta which we thought was very lucky. For anything *main bolti*, '*Woh black kurta pehen ke chala ja tu.*' [Wear that black kurta and go.] So he went, but international projects do take much time, and I don't think even Tishu believed *ki Irrfan actually choose ho jayega*. But when I asked Asif this – he came home just one month before [Irrfan] passed away. I asked Asif, 'Why did you choose him?' I don't remember the exact words, but he said, 'I was looking [for] the soul of the warrior; I was not looking for the body of the warrior.' So that's where Irrfan got lucky.

SG: After that the floodgates opened, and in 2003 came *Haasil* and in 2004 *Maqbool*. I know that Tigmanshu and he were great friends from NSD. But how did Vishal [Bhardwaj] discover Irrfan?
SS: Through Gulzar saab or somebody – we knew each other. And Bobby Bedi [Sundeep Singh Bedi] was producing *Maqbool*. See, I don't think it's about discovering; it is about getting … 'reassured' is the word I would use for the industry. I think *Haasil* reassured many of them that he can be popular as well. Initially I think [it was supposed to be] Manoj [Bajpayee]. It's not that Irrfan was the first choice in *Maqbool*. Irrfan was the second choice and they stuck to it and the rest is history.

Tabu called the other day. And she said, 'You know, Sutapa? I just get so annoyed with God; why did he have to take my best – *itne saare log hain* – my best co-actor on screen. I mean, I will never do films with him, and I will never create that chemistry again with anyone else.'

SG: So was he excited about the film when he finished it?

SS: Oh, very much. Very much. He was very excited … and that was the most money he had seen till then. Honestly, I don't even remember how much it was, but he closed the bedroom door in Yugdharma – we lived in Yugdharma at that time. He said, 'You know what?' He showed me the contract and hugged me and we laughed. At that time, it was important for him to feel that he could become a good actor, but in India, if you get a good director, that's how you become a better actor, right? Otherwise, you keep doing *Kasoor* and *Thank You** and stuff like that. I think it was equally important for him that he was doing Vishal's film and it was based on a Shakespearean play.

III

SG: So, after *Maqbool* and *Haasil*, when the breakthrough happened, was it still a struggle for Irrfan to get the roles that he wanted?

SS: It was a struggle. But you know, interestingly, it's not that he wasn't getting roles. He was never the kind of person who would go to look for work. Work kept on coming, but not the kind he wanted. You keep making strategies – 'I will do this now and my market rate will go up.' And then, after a while, you say 'Fuck you', you know? You will only do films you like. But honestly speaking, for that you need to have a position in the industry. You need to have that stability in the industry to do that.

But yes, he got work galore after *Maqbool*. But thank god that he didn't make that mistake so many do. Irrfan knew for very

---

* A 2011 Anees Bazmee film

sure that he cannot be that kind of hero – *pedon mein ghoom ghoom ke* [dancing around trees] – '*Woh meri capability nahi hai. Woh mera forte nahi hai.* I should know what I'm good at, and I should look for that. Instead of trying to become a "popular actor". So, in a way, he got his clarity very, very quickly. Of course he did make mistakes. But there was no dearth of work. Then he became this 'thinking woman's heartthrob' or whatever they called it. That kind of 'hero'. I think in *Piku* he actually broke that definition *ki* he can become any kind of hero if he wants to be. He does not have to do what the conventional heroes do.

SK: I was also reflecting [upon] recently *ki* what made Irrfan come to us. When the whole world was at his feet, offering him roles. I think Irrfan came to us at a stage [when] he was also looking to widen his audience base in India. That's what I feel, and that's what his conversation was about with me when we spoke. Why can't we widen his audience? And why would he not be the central focus of a populist film? Being sensible also, but still being the central focus? Why would it always be an arthouse film, or a film for only the very intellectual people?

But what Sutapa and I were trying to do for Irrfan, I think, you know Sutapa has this intellect and she has the nuances down pat, and for him, I was probably a person who understood audiences. So, the combination of Sutapa and me, in that sense, felt to him that we would be able to come out with stuff which would make him [a commercial star] … and actually we were heading in that zone. So the last couple of films … I think it started from *Piku*. So whether it was a *Piku,* whether it was a *Hindi Medium**, whether

---

* A 2017 Saket Chaudhary film

it was a *Qarib Qarib* [*Singlle*], I think he was wanting to move towards a wider ...

SG: So, are there any performances of his apart from *Paan Singh Tomar* ... were there any films where you felt that he really was outstanding? What are your favourite performances?

SS: One of my most favourite performances is *In Treatment*. I love *Paan Singh*. I also think, as an actor's first film, *Haasil* was brilliant. As the first film, where he didn't know the language of cinema so well, even then, I think he delivered very good dialogues, very *taali-maar* [applause-worthy] types. In *Maqbool*, I really liked his performance.

I did tell him that in *Paan Singh Tomar*, 'You are brilliant, and I'm really happy this time.' In *Maqbool*, there are some scenes where I did feel he outdid Naseer bhai. He was much more subtle and effective in many scenes than Naseer bhai. And I think *Qarib Qarib Singlle* also has many brilliant moments which are very endearing.

SG: How did *Madaari* and *Qarib Qarib Singlle* happen? Did you always want to produce films?

SS: No, no, no, no! Not all the while. But beyond a point, you just realize you want to tell a story. Especially with *Madaari*, we wanted to tell that story very desperately. *Humara toh ek hi Shah Rukh aur Salman Khan tha, woh tha Irrfan Khan! Hai na?* [Our Shah Rukh and Salman Khan was Irrfan Khan, isn't it?] And we had Irrfan in the project! And it's also true that a Shah Rukh or Salman will not act in a film like *Madaari*. They will do some other film. In that sense, we were lucky that we had the actor who believed in the kind of thought process we had.

SG: I know this is a tangent, but when you talked about Shah Rukh, I was reminded that they have done Priyadarshan's *Billu* together. How was the experience?

SS: Yeah, he did. It was really good, actually. Priyan [Priyadarshan] is a very chilled-out guy. Very disciplined. *Matlab din itne hi baje shuru hoga, din itne hi baje khatam hoga; aaram se kaam karte hain, lambe lambe shots lete hain.* [The days would begin and end on time; we would work in a relaxed manner.] We stayed in a very small place, the same place where Priyan shoots every film of his. Shah Rukh was extremely warm with Irrfan. Even with my son. Everybody knows Shah Rukh is that warm person who makes everyone feel important.

SG: I also want to ask you about his Hollywood sojourn. What was it like?

SS: See, as far as the international scene is concerned, he's one of the actors who said no to 'Indian' roles. In the last two years, he got many roles which were Indian. And he told his manager, 'I want to be treated as an actor.' So, in *Jurassic World**, he's not an Indian. In *Puzzle*†, he's not an Indian! So that's what his contribution was in the international scene – they were not looking at a brown-skinned character. He said, 'When some black guy can play an Indian, why can't I play an American?' White American for that matter. He said, 'Hire me as an actor.' He refused many films. When he was called, he knows *ki* they want that brownie point ... *ek Asia se le lo, ek yahaan se le lo, ek wahan se le lo* and you make the project. Hollywood is also about projects like India is making projects, right? So you need to say,

---

* A 2015 Colin Trevorrow film
† A 2018 Marc Turtletaub film

'No! Treat me as an actor.' And they did, finally. The saddest part is that when he was sick, his agents were overloaded with work for him – and not as Indian characters but as characters in the film. Which he couldn't do … He was really getting offers from big projects as an actor.

SG: You're saying he was not just the stock brown guy. He was called because he was Irrfan.

SS: Yeah. Because it makes a difference. Tomorrow they will know there are actors in India: 'We will call them because they are actors, not because we want to put an Indian character in a script for our market in South Asia.' So, he was there as Irrfan, an actor, as a performer.

SG: So when people here were not giving him the attention he deserved, and when Hollywood called him, was it a feel-good thing for him?

SS: What he actually liked is if you work in Hollywood or the international scene, you will realize that the working method is completely different. And he enjoyed that. Like Tom Hanks, for heaven's sake! Who didn't have his spot boy accompany him. So that whole thing gave him a kick. He saw a real working atmosphere. Natalie Portman was walking with him on the street during Mira Nair's short film, *New York, I Love You*, and she gave him a co-actor's respect. So, you know, it's a different ballgame altogether. It's a very work-oriented atmosphere, which he loved. And that's why he wanted to do southern films. In the end he was dying to do a south film because that's where he felt people work for work, and discipline. And work is most important, not the paraphernalia.

SG: So he's actually never done any film from the south, right?

SS: When he was doing *Karwaan*, he was shooting in Kerala. And he was meeting a lot of directors, they were sending scripts and he wanted to produce some films. It was not to be …

SK: I felt it was a masterclass working with Irrfan. I also think that there was a great synergy which was beginning to form for the 'premium mass' kind of content. Which is where I always felt he should be … Sutapa was much more strict; she is more purist. I am more populist than purist. And for me, the audience is the most important. I have a knack for understanding *kis ko kya achha lagega* [who will like what]. Sutapa has the knack *ki* this is absolute and this is the best.

I really felt that after *Qarib Qarib* [*Singlle*], Sutapa and I were now probably, sort of, ready to actually be producers, but *yeh masterclass sirf aur sirf humare liye possible hua* because of Irrfan. *At least mere liye toh possible hua*. Sutapa stays with him, lived with him all her life. But my way of looking at stories changed from 2012 to 2017. These years we spent very closely in terms of developing scripts and doing stuff like that. And I think it was wonderful, because I had been in the business of storytelling for a long time, having done populist content and I think *Irrfan se seekha ki* how to approach things holistically. So I wanted to add earlier, that he was not only a generous actor … he was just generous in every which way. I can say this because Sutapa is the wife so she has another equation with him, but me being an outsider, you know? The generosity … why does an Irrfan Khan need to call me and say *ki 'Tum kuchh karo aur main karoonga.'* It's just generosity!

I mean who am I? I'm not a movie producer, I'm not anybody. I have not even written, or done anything so why should he say *ki*

'*Tum karo, main karoonga!*' There's no need. Even throughout the whole process … I would say that Sutapa is my day-time friend and Irrfan is my night-time friend. I wish I could have shown him *Churails**.

SG: When you were actually working with him, how did you separate the personal and the professional?
SS: In *Madaari*, we didn't have any heroines, so I don't know.

laughs

In *Qarib Qarib Singlle* … this is very difficult for me to answer, because it's been like this forever. Like, I know Shailja loves him. I know all my girlfriends love him. And I'm so used to that thing of sharing him.

SG: You were not jealous?
SS: I'll be very honest with you – I am so used to it. I have never been into this one-girlfriend, one-boyfriend set-up. Even in NSD we always moved around in a gang. We were always like this. And honestly, between all of us, I'm a little embarrassed to have this one-to-one. I mean, if I was young today, I would not publicly even kiss my boyfriend, because I find this is a very feminine, *nyaka* thing … in Bengali it's called *nyaka*. How to explain …

SG: Don't explain!
SS: We never had a *nyaka* relationship.

---

* A 2020 Zee5 web series

58

'Irrfan did become a star'

RAJAT KAPOOR

Rajat Kapoor – actor, playwright and director – has crafted a unique space for himself in Hindi cinema. In his directorial debut, *Private Detective: Two Plus Two Plus One*, Irrfan was cast as Inspector Khan, the first of many 'cop' roles he played. Also in the film was Naseeruddin Shah, one of Irrfan's gurus.

One of the few Indian filmmakers who use whimsy beautifully in their movies, Kapoor is best known for *Aankhon Dekhi*, *Mithya*, *Mixed Doubles* and *Raghu Romeo*.

SHUBHRA GUPTA: You've done theatre, you've done a certain kind of cinema. You are part of Bollywood and not immersed in it; you're in it and yet out of it. So I'm very interested in your perspective. You did this film [*Private Detective: Two Plus Two Plus One*, 1997] with Irrfan early on. It's a very stock Bollywood character – a police inspector. In retrospect, it's funny – if he hadn't got films like *Haasil* and *Maqbool* soon after, he would have got stuck in this inspector-type role, which he played so many versions of later, in his mainstream movies. When you chose him for that film, did he come to you? Did you go to him? Were you aware of him as an actor or a performer?

59

RAJAT KAPOOR: I wasn't. At all. Shubhra, this is '95. I don't know what he had done before that. Did he do some television before that already?

SG: He had just started to do some TV at that time.

RK: There was nothing – there was no Irrfan Khan, like that, at that time. We shot it in May '95, which means the auditions must have happened in February or March '95. I didn't know him at all. I didn't know Jeetu Shastri,* his co-actor in the film, also.

I didn't know them at all. Except for Naseer saab, everybody went through an audition. I met Irrfan and Jeetu at my little one-room office in a Santacruz colony. There was no money, of course, for that film; the budget was thirty-five lakhs. I think Irrfan's fee was either ten or twelve thousand. I think I was offering ten and he bargained and got it to twelve. And it was, what, five–six days' work for him. The dialogues were written by Kamal Swaroop. And I was a fan of his [Swaroop] because, again, we had worked in *Khayal Gatha* together – Kumar Shahani's film. But *Private Detective* wasn't really, in a sense, my film. I'll tell you what I mean. I was very influenced by Kumar at that time. Also Mani [Kaul], but I think more Kumar. And in my head, unconsciously, the thing was, how would Kumar do this? So it wasn't, in that sense, my film. I think I made a short film after this – *Hypnothesis* – and, with that and *Raghu Romeo*, slowly I found my voice. Kamal Swaroop was also hung up on Kumar's legacy. So the dialogues happened in a certain

---

* Also from NSD, who plays a cop as well; Shastri, who made a career of sharp supporting roles, passed away in October 2022.

way, which Naseer saab was very unhappy about. But I said, 'No, no, this is what I want.' So he lived with it.

But I remember that one scene with the two cops in the housing society – which I wrote at the moment of the shoot. And that line: '*Woh jiski bibi abhi taazi taazi mari hai, uske face pe koi shock nahi hai.*'[There's no shock on the face of the guy whose wife has just died.] And then Irrfan says, '*Das babu, pakode khao aur mast raho; case maine solve kar liya hai.*' [Das babu, eat pakodas and relax; I have solved the case.] Those I had written and those few dialogues were very different from the rest of the film. And you can see Irrfan's ease suddenly in that scene and with those dialogues. You can see he's found something that he can latch on to, rather than this very formal approach that the film had in the rest of the scenes. When we were dubbing, Irrfan started to change the way he said everything. And I remember telling my assistants, '*Yaar yeh toh sab change kar raha hai. Bahut acting kar raha hai!*' [He is changing everything. He is acting too much.] Irrfan said, '*Yaar, tumne wahaan pe acting karne nahi di; ab toh karne do kam se kam.*' [You didn't let me act there; at least let me do it now.] He said it very clearly. And he brought a certain accent – almost like a Haryanvi cop – into that. It was really his; I had nothing to do with it. I was very happy with what he'd done, of course. But then I was happy with Jeetu Shastri also.

You know, this is very funny, Shubhra, what you ask. I really feel that this is such a game of luck and chance, *yaar*. It's a game of dice. As far as I'm concerned, Jeetu Shastri could have been another Irrfan. Didn't happen. And he was terrific on stage. I've never seen Irrfan on stage, but I've seen Jeetu on stage. Because he'd done a one-act thing with Anuradha Kapur. He was phenomenal. He was a wonderful actor. That's the funny thing –

you don't know who's going to be what. And it's really ninety-five per cent luck. Of course, Irrfan was very skilled and he had a great talent, but I'm saying that he was not the only one. I meet a lot of actors; I know a lot of actors. You have many, many like that. And eighty per cent of them don't make it. They keep waiting for the right role at the right time and they disappear, or they give up. Like you said, Irrfan would have; like Tigmanshu said, if *The Warrior* didn't happen at that time. It's bizarre, why this happens. Why, suddenly, a role comes to you. Where you find yourself. Or where the role finds you. Where something happens between you and the character that becomes meaningful.

SG: When you were casting for this film, had you put the word out that you were looking for actors and that's how Irrfan showed up at your office?

RK: Yeah. Word used to get around. There was no social media, but actors were always looking [for roles]. At that time, there was no FTII acting course, so there were lots of actors from NSD in Bombay. And other actors, not from NSD but ... actors generally. So the word used to get around very, very quickly.

SG: When you met him that very first time, was there something that struck you about Irrfan, or was he just another actor looking for a role?

RK: I have no memory of the audition. Vaguely, I remember that thing about money, that little negotiation. But on the set, of course, I remember ...

SG: Did you reach out to him for any of your other films?

RK: I always wanted to work with him. *Raghu Romeo* was Vijay Raaz; it was fixed in my head, that's Vijay Raaz. *Mithya* I wanted to be Naseer saab when I wrote it.

SG: I was about to ask you. I thought he would have fit so well in *Mithya*.

RK: Yeah, yeah. I thought he would have too. I had written it for Naseer saab in '98, but we made it ten years later. Naseer saab then was a little too old for that role. And meanwhile, I'd done *Mixed Doubles* with Ranvir Shorey, and Ranvir was fabulous. But why didn't Irrfan audition for *Mixed Doubles* … I think we lost touch somewhere. But he was a big fan of *Mithya*, I know.

SG: How do you know he was a big fan – did he tell you?

RK: He told me, he did.

SG: And did he say, '*Tumne mujhe kyun nahi liya uss film mein?*' [Why didn't you cast me in that film?]

RK: No, no, he didn't say that. Because Rafey [Mahmood, cinematographer] was very close to him; Rafey had shot *Haasil*. And then my daughter, Rabia, and Babil were in the same class, and my younger son, Vivaan, and Ayaan were in the same class in school. Rabia and Babil are still great friends, and Ayaan and my boy are best friends even now. So it was not that we met very often – we met Sutapa [Sikdar] more often, at school functions and this and that. A couple of times I went to his house, for Eid with Rafey, and he was always very, very gentlemanly. He was very kind, very sweet, always.

At one point I was going to produce a film for Anik Ghosh. Anik was one year my senior at FTII. He had written a gangster film called *Lucky Boys*. And PNC [Pritish Nandy Communications] had said yes to it, and I was producing it. So we gave it to Irrfan. I met him and he said, 'I'm so keen to work with you that I read it in one day.' I was very touched by that. This was after *Mithya*, so I knew that he'd liked *Mithya* very much. But then that film didn't happen for whatever reasons.

I worked with him on another small film called *Apna Asmaan*[*] in 2006 or '07. Good-intentioned, but not a good film. I worked for a few days with Irrfan on that one. We also did *Krazzy 4*[†] together, in which again I had only two days' work with Irrfan. Another bad film. But during *Apna Asmaan*, I remember this: we were sitting in a car for a shoot and I think Kaushik [Roy, director] asked something about money, or ambitions. About one crore. And Irrfan laughed and said, '*Woh mere agenda pe hai, poori tarah.* [It is on my agenda, absolutely.] I am not getting it now but I am going to get it.' And he laughed, like really loud. It was very clear for him – an idea of money also, you know. I remember this very clearly, that he had – somewhere – his eyes set on that. In some ways, I think it's a validation of who you are. That, you know, I will not only make it as an actor, but I'll make it big on those terms. So he would continue to choose roles that would excite him but also this other idea of getting there, of being a star, was very clear in his head.

Irrfan did become a star, I'm sure everyone realizes that. He became a big star. Which has not happened to an actor like that, who came from outside, who did not fit – in your words – the mainstream Bollywood idea of an actor. And I think he could command a price that a big star would.

SG: When he began, there was a certain kind of Hindi cinema which was being made by the studios. Do you think in the last ten years Hindi cinema has shifted? Has there been some kind of a change, where there have been more films which are from the outside coming in?

---

[*] A 2007 Kaushik Roy film
[†] A 2008 Jaideep Sen film

RK: You know, these things people have been saying for the last twenty-five–thirty years. New cinema emerging, new this, new that. Nothing has changed. Nothing has changed and nothing is going to change in the long run. Same shit is being made. *Chaar filmein achhi aa jaati hain, hum log kehte hain ki change ho gaya hai. Kuchh nahi change ho raha hai. Abhi kya, kuchh release hi nahi ho raha; ab toh aur chakkar hai.* [Four good films come out and we say that things have changed. No change is taking place. At the moment there are not even any new releases – now things are even more complicated.]*

SG: Do you think the pandemic is going to change something fundamentally?

RK: I don't think so at all. This has been going on for many years and we are optimists, all of us. So we keep hoping that things will change. In the late nineties, we said, 'Oh, Hollywood studios are coming.' Now they'll make reasonable films. They did the same thing Bollywood is doing. Then, 'Oh, multiplexes are coming. New space for us, for independent cinema!' It happened for two years. Then, again, big films took over.

SG: Which two years are you talking about?

RK: I think around 2005–07. There was a time when films like *Khosla ka Ghosla!*†, *Mixed Doubles* and *Bheja Fry*‡ could become big. By 2008, it was finished. When *Dabangg*§ and these big films came, they started with 4,000 prints. Again, there was no space for indie films.

---

* The interview took place during the pandemic when theatres were closed.
† A 2006 Dibakar Banerjee film
‡ A 2006 Sagar Ballary film
§ A 2010 Abhinav Kashyap film

SG: So let me flip it around. You said Irrfan *was* a big star; he did end up being a star. Because he made it very clear that it was where he wanted to be. But he was always the 'other' big star. He was not part of the pantheon, right? So are there now enough people in this country who are invested in this other kind of cinema, where they can create a star out of Irrfan?

RK: There are not enough people like that, I'm sorry. I mean, if *Paatal Lok** comes and becomes a hit, then Jaideep Ahlawat will get some traction, you know. Or Pratik Gandhi out of *Scam* [*1992*]†. But if a Jaideep Ahlawat film comes, people are not going to run and watch it in a cinema.‡ So that kind of stardom, which will actually get footfalls in a cinema hall, is almost gone.

There's another problem, Shubhra. The face is a big thing but people will not go and watch that film if it is not of a certain kind. Saif [Ali Khan] can do *Being Cyrus*§ but *Being Cyrus* will not get the kind of people that *Hum Tum*⁵ or *Salaam Namaste*** will get. It's the whole package; it's not only Saif Ali Khan – which is an important thing – but it has to be that kind of commercial 'masala' film that will get people coming. Even Shah Rukh has to do what Shah Rukh does because that's what people want to watch him do.

SG: Sure. But still, I am looking at it from the glass-half-full kind of perspective. Where someone like Irrfan – a total outsider – is

---

* A 2020 Amazon Prime Video web series

† A 2020 SonyLIV web series

‡ An Ayushmann Khurrana–Jaideep Ahlawat starrer, *An Action Hero* opened in December 2022 and garnered a viewership.

§ A 2005 Homi Adajania film

⁵ A 2004 Kunal Kohli film

**A 2005 Siddharth Anand film

able to make deep inroads into the industry, enough to be able to get out there and say, '*Yaar, main hoon.*'

RK: How many Irrfans, Shubhra? How many Irrfans do you know, in the last ... Naseer saab would be another one.

SG: Rajkummar Rao, I would say. Ayushmann Khurrana is a big star, right? All of these guys have come from the outside.

RK: Correct. They're all good actors but ... my humble opinion is that Rajkummar or Ayushmann have found their slot. Or again, some things worked and then they found a few films and their character, and their idea of a persona within that. *Woh small-town chal gaya ek film toh chaar film woh hi chalta rahega. Woh hi limitation ho gayi, aap ki bhi, audience ki bhi.* [If one small-town film works, there will be four more films like that. That is the limitation, where both the actors and the audience are concerned.] Performance-wise. Rajkummar and Ayushmann have something very nice; they're very vulnerable, which is attractive and good to watch. But the moment that thing becomes an idea, you know, film after film ...

See, there is not enough work. Now it might have changed a little bit with web series and so on but even then, there is very little good work. And an actor needs a good script, otherwise it'll never sound convincing and true. How many films are like that in a year? Five films, three films? So it's not that there are not enough films – we make 1,500 films a year – but for an actor to prove his mettle, where are the roles? Where are the lines that ring true? *Aap ek bahut hi umda actor ko ghatiya line denge toh matlab woh actor ghatiya hi lagega.* [If you give a great actor terrible lines, that actor will seem terrible.] It's only maybe Mr [Amitabh] Bachchan who can rise above a bad script and still give a great performance. Most actors need a script or role or good dialogue to carry it with some degree of oomph, you know?

SG: I wonder if that's why Irrfan looked towards Hollywood, to get the roles. Or was it the money, or both?

RK: Yeah, why would he say no? I remember in 2010 or '11, we heard vaguely that Irrfan was considered for *Ocean's Thirteen**.

Or twelve or something. There was a big buzz at that time. There must have been something to it. And we were all very pleased, very happy for Irrfan. I was saying, wow, that's an international star who is actually getting proper roles there, not just walk-on parts. And he's getting them because of his talent. Because Ang Lee sees something in him. He was really making that on his own terms, but luck is a huge thing in it.

SG: You come back to that – the luck factor. I think once you know your entry point, then you can start going from there. And *The Namesake* also did something fantastic for him.

RK: One performance that I really admire of his. And I like that film also, very much – he was fabulous in that.

SG: When you think of Irrfan, what is the one thing that comes to your mind?

RK: I think it's … a mixture of arrogance and humility. Which is very nice. He knew who he was and what he was capable of. But along with that, there was a sense of absolute groundedness. He always met people with such affection, such warmth. I remember meeting him – maybe one of the last meetings – at Dubai airport. Vinay [Pathak] and I were coming back from our show – a play –

---

* A 2007 Steven Soderbergh film

and he was travelling to some place. Such warmth, Shubhra. After he left, Vinay was like, 'He is so warm, *yaar*, so good.'

SG: And that warmth was genuine …

RK: Genuine. *Bilkul. Bahut hi khoobsurat tha woh* – that bit in him [was beautiful].

SG: So where did the arrogance come from – a sense of 'I'm so good'?

RK: No, no. Maybe arrogance is not the … But the knowledge. Not in his behaviour – he was not arrogant in his behaviour – but there was an arrogance of the self, you know. I know my worth, I know who I am. That.

'Who else could you look at when Irrfan was on screen?'

SHYAM BENEGAL

Shyam Benegal, who shaped the parallel cinema movement in the seventies and eighties with such classics as *Ankur, Nishant* and *Manthan,* among others, was responsible for one of Irrfan's earliest forays in TV. He gave Irrfan a chance to appear in a short story on Doordarshan, as well as play a few minor characters in his opus *Bharat Ek Khoj,* one of Indian television's best series. These were small parts, but Irrfan left a mark.

————

SHUBHRA GUPTA: Do you remember your first meeting with Irrfan?

SHYAM BENEGAL: You see, my memory is now failing a bit, because this happened so long ago. In the mid-eighties sometime, I was preparing to do *Bharat Ek Khoj.* And I was doing a series of short stories. Doordarshan had decided to create different kinds of entertainment programmes. You know that period – nobody was watching Doordarshan, seeing it as a mouthpiece of the government. And among them there was one particular short story I remember. Must have been Chekhov. And I was looking for actors.

There was this young man who came to see me. I'd asked to see him; everybody told me that I should see this young man. When he came, I got him to do a couple of things – one of the short stories. He was absolutely first-rate [in it]. We used to get about three or four days to do a short story. Otherwise it wouldn't be affordable, at that time. He was so good that I gave him his lines and said, 'These are the scenes that you will be doing.' And so what I was supposed to do in two days, I did in a day.

He was so wonderful as an actor. But there was also something else I noticed about him. One of his arms, he was tending to hide it. And I'd keep saying, 'Listen, why are you hiding that arm?' He said that he had had an accident and his arm had just come out of the cast. It hadn't fully healed and the shape of the arm was also slightly crooked; bent, as it were. He was getting a little worried about that. I said, 'Forget about it, just be normal; it's okay if you have a slight problem with that arm.' Which, of course, healed very well later because he had it treated.

After that, I said, 'Well, because he was so good in that short story, I will use him in *Bharat Ek Khoj*,' which I did. Soon after, he became not only a big star in India, but a big star internationally, and was recognized all over the world as an Indian actor. After that, of course, I hardly ever met him – we would meet only in passing. Nor could I afford him! He had gone into a different league altogether.

SG: The big studios at the time didn't have a role for him because he was unconventional in his looks. He was a great actor, but they didn't know how to use him. So I was wondering whether that had something to do with the fact that it took him so long—

SB: Yeah, it took him a long time, because he came via television. Normally what happened with Indian actors was that they directly went into cinema. A lot of people in the film industry didn't care for television actors; there was this phase at that time. But Irrfan, of course, caught the eye of international directors very quickly. He was playing what they call character parts here. But he was playing main roles in the international productions.

If you got character parts, they would never choose you to play the main role.

SG: But even in some of his really big international movies – *Jurassic World*, *The Amazing Spider-Man**, *Life of Pi†* – he was never the lead.

SB: No, but they were key roles. They were crucial to the story. They were not sidies, you know? They were absolutely crucial to what was happening: the plot, the story, all of that. That's why he became a name in the Western hemisphere. People used to line up to take him.

SG: Really?

SB: Yes, because he'd become a very popular actor. And everybody knew who Irrfan was. Say, for instance, I was in New York or Toronto or Los Angeles or San Francisco – he was the one Indian actor everybody knew. They may not have known some of the top actors here – except maybe Amitabh Bachchan, who was known everywhere. But Irrfan everybody knew.

SG: That is an amazing thing, because he felt like he did not really get his due in Hindi cinema for the longest time.

SB: Which is also true. Because he didn't fit into any kind of slot.

---

* A 2012 Marc Webb film
† A 2012 Ang Lee film

SG: Naseeruddin Shah and Om Puri were also people that the West knew, right? They also went out there and the West came looking. But if I were to ask you to compare these three people? Irrfan has been on record several times to say that he was a huge fan of these two actors.

SB: Oh, he was. In fact, I think they were great role models for him. Although Naseer didn't particularly focus on doing work outside India. He did theatre work – National Theatre in London – very successfully. Om Puri became, out of all of them, the most known Indian face in Hollywood. Because Om was the most unconventional of them all. In India, nobody would have thought that he could be a star. But he did become an international star. Irrfan was more or less on that part of the spectrum.

SG: These were true actors; these *are* true actors. From the Balraj Sahni tradition – who fully embodied a role. They were not just playing yet another version of themselves; they took on the skin of the people that they played. And I think, after Naseeruddin, it was only Irrfan.

SB: And Om Puri – those are the three.

SG: Right. I think they paved the way for Irrfan – these two – and Irrfan himself paved the way for, say, someone like a Rajkummar Rao or … even an Ayushmann Khurrana, who's been playing these unconventional roles in conventional Bollywood. Looking back, if you were to say what was the significance of Irrfan, the actor and the performer …?

SB: The significance of Irrfan is that he belongs to a particular genre of acting. Which includes people like Om Puri, Naseeruddin Shah. They are totally unconventional. As far as popular Indian cinema was concerned, they looked at people and said, 'Is this a potential star or not?' Nobody saw these people as potential stars. But internationally, people saw them as stars. Because they were acutely talented people. Irrfan was hugely talented, there was no question about it. He could play any part you gave him. He's like a chameleon. [This] ability to change – he had that. Like the others we have named. These were actors who refused to be slotted and stamped.

SG: From what you've just said, they were considered stars in the West because of their talent and the fact that they could literally become any part they chose. But this is the same ability which led conventional Bollywood to be wary of a prodigious talent like Irrfan.

SB: They had to allow them, first of all, to show their wares as actors. But they didn't get that opportunity easily enough. What is that quality that makes an actor? The moment you come to the screen and everybody's looking at them and nobody else. Who else could you look at when Irrfan was on screen?

SG: You say that he was a star nationally *and* internationally. What kind of a stardom did he own, or wield? Obviously not like the three big Khans – which is why, I was told, that he dropped the Khan from his name, because he didn't want to be in contention with any of these guys. He knew that he was Irrfan and he did not want to always be compared.

SB: That was probably due to something numerological. When he came into the film industry, he came with a normal name like I-R-F-A-N. Then he added an 'r' and knocked off the Khan. Obviously, somebody must have told him that, for your career to go up, it would be better for you to do that. But who knows?

SG: He did do all kinds of movies, he lifted the material in all the really silly mainstream Bollywood films he was in. He did get a foot into that door, but it took him a long time to get all the way in. So I'm wondering whether mainstream Hindi cinema ever knew how to use him.

SB: Look, it's not like a director choosing to make a film. Because an actor is an actor. He will get to do the work that he would like to do. Also if the money is right for him. Then, of course, when he becomes a star, he becomes very conscious, so he limits himself to the roles that will [allow him to] retain his stardom for himself. I think he was working out a strategy for himself, like everybody else. But he was very much in demand as an actor.

SG: Was he?

SB: Oh yes. Like you mentioned, he played the policeman roles, he took different kinds of parts. But it wasn't as though he didn't have work. I mean, it was a question of how busy he would like to remain as an actor. It was a matter of choice. And anybody who has a choice of that kind, you must consider as being very successful.

If you are not having to keep looking for jobs, when you get the jobs constantly, and you're being kept busy all the time, you'll find you're successful. Some people are very choosy, but you can only be choosy when you are getting roles. You can't be choosy when not getting roles. So you either look for work or the work comes looking for you. You'd rather be in a situation where work comes looking for you. In that sense, he was successful, because he was not going looking for work, which he did early in his career.

SG: How would you describe Irrfan?

SB: I would describe him as a very, very thinking actor. A man who worked out his role [and] the graph of his performance. All these things he worked really hard on. He didn't just come here saying, 'Give me lines,' and disappear. Because with stars, they know that they're playing the same role in every film. So they come to the sets and say, 'Give me my lines,' while they're being made up. This used to happen with big south Indian stars. You know, the old days with NTR* and all – they would be doing the same roles, so they didn't really bother about anything. They'd come, sit in the make-up man's chair and say, 'Give me the lines,' and then perform and go home.

SG: One last question. Not having someone like Irrfan in the industry – what does that mean? Before his illness, he had started to get to the place where he could carry a film commercially on his own. Then, of course, he fell ill. And although he did *Angrezi Medium*†, he was, by that time, quite sick.

SB: See, it isn't as though the Indian film industry is short of actors – that's never the problem. But you have to have the right parts for them to shine. You can't just make them stand somewhere in your frame and expect things to happen for them. It shouldn't be like that. We do have a lot of talent and very capable actors. Apart from everything else, there are acting schools – National School of Drama and FTII – all of these various places.

He was an excellent actor, he got some very good opportunities. Everybody knew that he was a very bankable actor, because

---

* Legendary actor and filmmaker-turned-politician Nandamuri Tareka Rama Rao was active primarily in Telugu cinema.

† A 2020 Homi Adajania film

he was worth whatever you paid him – much more than that. Because the audience loved his work. He had this ability and that 'x' quality—

SG: 'X' quality?

SB: It's like, when you see people on the screen, your eye gravitates to one of them. He was the one that your eyes gravitated to.

If you saw him, you were hooked by him.

'He used to give his soul to his films'

TIGMANSHU DHULIA

Tigmanshu Dhulia – writer, director, actor, producer and Irrfan's close friend from their NSD days – was instrumental in getting him cast as the lead in Asif Kapadia's *The Warrior*. If that film hadn't come when it did, Irrfan may have left acting. And if Dhulia hadn't got around to making *Haasil* when he did, Irrfan wouldn't have got the Bollywood recognition he so desperately craved. He also made three other films with Irrfan, including *Charas, Saheb Biwi Aur Gangster Returns* and *Paan Singh Tomar* – a celebrated Irrfan film that got him the much-coveted National Award.

SHUBHRA GUPTA: Let's begin at the beginning, your NSD days when you first got to know Irrfan.

TIGMANSHU DHULIA: Those were my formative days as an artist. I was the youngest in my class, just nineteen years old – this boy from Allahabad in Delhi, in awe of everything. Then I met Irrfan there – he was my immediate senior. Irrfan was in third year and we were in first year; there was no second year. The closeness kind of grew because there were very few students. I kind of started liking him. It was distant, my attraction for him, when I saw him in a play called *The Lower Depths* by Gorky. I had never seen anything like it. Irrfan mesmerized. His eyes were speaking. There were fifteen artists on stage at one point but one's eyes were only on Irrfan.

Irrfan was a quiet person; he was very introverted. He kept to himself and Sutapa [Sikdar] was there with him, as his girlfriend – they were batchmates. Irrfan used to stay in the tiniest room in the hostel. In a corner. But I don't know what it was about Irrfan's performance, his entire personality, his aloofness, that attracted me. We both liked Robert DeNiro, we both spoke about movies. I had still managed to watch a few films in Allahabad, because Allahabad had that kind of scope for cultural activity. But Irrfan had come from Jaipur, where he hadn't seen much. From then on, I could see that he was eager for knowledge.

In his going, I've lost a very close friend; somebody with whom I could talk about anything. Anything under the sun. As they say, to be an interesting person, you have to be interested. And Irrfan was like that. He was interested in trying out new cuisines, new things. So he was maybe one–two years older than me. And when I used to direct him, there wouldn't just be an actor in front of me, it would also be a colleague. Irrfan would have definitely made a good film one day, if he had the time. He had all the qualities.

SG: As a director?

TD: It's not necessary for a director to have all these qualities; you may not know a lot of things. But because he was interested in everything, he would have made good films … with a fresh take. Not like us – we *toh* make filmi films, right?

SG: Right. So *Star Bestsellers* became your calling card, right? It was an amazing confluence: you, Anurag Kashyap, Sriram Raghavan, Imtiaz Ali, Anup Singh all came together and made some fantastic television, and branched out from there. So my question is this: if Tigmanshu – or Tishu as he called you – hadn't been there, would Irrfan have been there? Would his trajectory have been the same if you hadn't been there together?

TD: Even if I wouldn't have been there, Irrfan's destiny would have been the same. Because it's not like he only acted well with me. He acted well with many other directors, especially Mira Nair. [The] Namesake was a brilliant piece of work; it's magical. There are many other films; in one of them he played a sardar ...

SG: Qissa.

TD: Yes, Qissa, Maqbool. There were so many films in which he was brilliant.

SG: Let me take you back to Haasil. You have spoken extensively about your coming together for Haasil, and the fact that you dropped him off in Allahabad some days before the shoot to soak in the atmosphere. How did the role come about?

TD: When I was writing Haasil, Irrfan was not in my mind. Those days, it was very difficult to make a film. But magically, things that are supposed to happen will happen. I had first gone to Manoj [Bajpayee]. I thought if Manoj says yes then work on this film can start, a producer can be found. And then Satya* released, after which Manoj said that he will not play the villain as he was playing the hero now. I didn't pursue it beyond a point. Dost ko kya patana? [You don't need to coax a friend.]

Then I described the Kumbh mela climax† to Irrfan. And I said I just have to make this film, come what may. So I took

---

* A 1998 Ram Gopal Varma film
† The climax of Haasil is set in Allahabad during the Kumbh mela.

Irrfan along, arranged money through some *jugaad* and did the shoot.

There were two characters in *Haasil* – Irrfan's and Jimmy Sheirgill's. Irrfan [depicted] that Allahabad attitude and Jimmy Sheirgill was [based on] me. There were a lot of personal things in *Haasil*. So the *paurush* – machoness – that is typical of Allahabad, I put in Irrfan. That *dabangg* character – Irrfan let it seep into himself. For seven–eight days, I left him with the boys of Allahabad. I told him to go around, go to the hostel, pick up the lingo. And he was enjoying it; if he didn't, then that performance would not have happened. He was enjoying that atmosphere and the company of these guys. And we were working with friends so there was no pressure of working with some star. I mean, if Irrfan liked doing what he was doing, then he used to give his soul to his films.

Magical performance *hota tha uska*. Either the writer supplies the dialogue and you deliver it in a way that the audience is impressed. Or all it takes is the performance. When the performance is like that, not cushioned by good writing, then you call that performance great. Like Amitabh Bachchan's best performance for me is *Abhimaan**. It was not written for him – it was Jaya-ji's film – but you see his performance; it is so ... *sahaj*, you know, effortless. Seamless. Irrfan has given many such performances.

SG: Yes, he had the ability to surprise. And he broke away from that templated form of acting that we had seen until then. Irrfan was a pure actor; he got the *sur* of the performance and he just did that and nothing else. And he lifted bad material. He was

---

* A 1973 Hrishikesh Mukherjee film

so good in what were considered offbeat roles. Even *Life in a...
Metro**, for example – that is a role no one else could have done.
Isn't it amazing?

TD: Brilliant. It was outstanding.

SG: I think after that, he really became everybody's Irrfan. Before
Metro, only a very niche audience was watching him. For me,
there are three Irrfan films where I think he is superlative. *Paan
Singh [Tomar]* is the purest of his performances. There is not
a single thing he does that is out of gear. *The Namesake* is also
fantastic, and *Maqbool*. So, tell me about *Paan Singh*. Because in
the original modern dacoit film – *Bandit Queen* – in which you
were casting director, I know that you tried to get Shekhar Kapur
to take Irrfan. Why did Shekhar not choose him? Did he ever tell
you why?

TD: No, we didn't discuss it after the initial casting sessions. He
wanted a particular look. I wanted to cast Irrfan for the role which
Nirmal [Pandey] did – Vikram Mallah. But Shekhar-ji had an
image of Vikram Mallah. After pestering and trying to convince
him, I said, 'What do you want?' He said, '*Yaar*, it should be
someone who people see on the screen and say, "*Marega*."' [He
will die.] 'Long-haired?' I asked him. He said, 'Yes.' So I said, 'I
have a guy, he's my batchmate' – Nirmal was my batchmate – 'but
he is shooting in London.' I showed him a photo from hostel, and
Shekhar-ji liked him. That's how Nirmal got the part. Irrfan was
not physically fitting his imagination.

When Irrfan approached those real roles like *Namesake,
Maqbool, Haasil* ... I got to know only when we were doing *Paan
Singh* what he actually does to get into the skin of the character.

---

* A 2007 Anurag Basu film

I asked him. He says, 'Yaar, I grab a quality of the character, just one quality. I don't do twenty-five scenes in twenty-five ways. Every scene has a different emotion; you have to be angry in one, in another you have to profess your love, in something else you're talking to a daughter, in another you're talking to a brother. Every situation is different. In every situation, I focus on one quality of a character and then hold on to it throughout the film. So the audience is not confused and a seamless quality seeps into the performance.' In *Paan Singh Tomar* I had an assistant – he is still my assistant – his name is Hemant. He's from Morena, close to the Chambal area [where the film was shot]. He was very young at the time of *Bandit Queen*,* and then he came to Bombay. Then he got to know that I'm doing *Paan Singh Tomar* and I got his help for diction, accents, etc. If you look at Hemant now – he's been in Bombay for years – you can see a noble man in him, what good village teachers are like. There is a noble-*pan*, a wisdom, of a special kind. Irrfan just emulated Hemant. He said, 'I just channelled Hemant to play Paan Singh. *Bas*.'

SG: His performance is pure magic. But it wasn't smooth sailing with *Paan Singh*, right? I remember there were some delays in the release.

TD: There were these focus-group screenings and the feedback they got was that people said *ki* we like what we are watching, but who's going to come and watch this film? Who'll come to theatres? Based on the feedback, UTV [the producers] thought that there's no point releasing the film. The film got delayed by more than a year. That is the time I made *Saheb Biwi Aur Gangster*

---

* A 1994 Shekhar Kapur film

part one, because we had nothing to do. Then because they had sold satellite rights, they had to release the film. It was a very limited release. Once the word-of-mouth publicity got underway, we increased the prints.

SG: What made you get Irrfan for *Saheb Biwi Aur Gangster Returns*? The character was so unlike anything he had ever played before.

TD: Because he liked part one a lot. When we were planning part two, the gangster had to change, because the gangster in the first part dies. Irrfan said, '*Chalo*, I'll do it.' Let me tell you honestly – Irrfan's most difficult character is the one from *Saheb Biwi Aur Gangster Returns*. It's a very layered character; he's a bit cracked, a little *baudam*. And because he also has princely blood, we also had to show that. And he did incredibly well. In my opinion, part one is like a short story, like those of O'Henry, Oscar Wilde, Roald Dahl. Part two is a full novel.

SG: Looks like he enjoyed speaking those heavy-duty dialogues, very Amitabh Bachchan-type.

TG: '*Humari gaali par bhi taali padti hai.*'

SG: Haha, yeah. But you did not cast him in the film that you did with Saif Ali Khan in 2013?

TG: *Bullett Raja*. We all pleaded – even Saif. The role which eventually Vidyut [Jammwal] did. He wanted Irrfan to do that role. But he said no. There was another film we started. We shot for a week, and then the producer ran out of money. It was called *Killing of a Porn Filmmaker* …

SG: So was Irrfan going to be the porn filmmaker?

TD: Yeah, yeah. Then in 2005 I started another film. A big film, with Sunny Deol, Irrfan and Sameera Reddy. A whole lot of actors from England. It was a period film set in 1857. It was really close to my heart. Irrfan was playing a *pandari* – they are dacoits, mercenary soldiers for hire. And the coincidence is that, historically speaking, the place that the Britishers gave to these *pandaris* was the place where Irrfan comes from, near Jaipur. That film too we shot for a week or so; then it got shelved. Irrfan was doing so great in that film; those costumes and even those weapons we made were authentic, of that time.

SG: Out of the films that you've done with him, which is your favourite?

TD: I think if I consider Irrfan – only Irrfan, and not anyone else's contribution so much – I would say his best performance is *Paan Singh Tomar*, undoubtedly. But my favourite film is *Haasil*, because *Haasil* was much more than a film. *Haasil* made me, made Irrfan. *Haasil* was also not releasing for a year; we were just showing everyone the film, in the hope that someone would buy it. Vishal Bhardwaj had seen *Haasil*, and then cast Irrfan in *Maqbool*. Irrfan got *Maqbool* because of *Haasil*.

SG: In the film industry, I'm told, everyone's so busy with their lives and their career that nobody finds the time for friendship. But you and Irrfan did manage to spend time together?

TD: Yes, a lot. Only, I don't know why ... because of being a little busy, the frequency of our hangouts decreased. He had to do a lot of foreign trips, so we couldn't meet much. But yes, we used to meet a lot before that. We used to go out, roam in the jungles. We had our kids around the same time. Our wives got pregnant around the same time, and all our kids were born within a gap of a month or two. First Babil, then my daughter. Our kids even grew up together. Tenth, twelfth *tak toh* the kids even studied together.

SG: One thing that I've been struggling to put into words is: how is it possible to live in a world without Irrfan? In his passing, I have not seen this kind of overwhelming grief that so many people across the board expressed. It was like one of their own had passed. How does it feel to be without an artist of his calibre? You, of course, are a dear friend and you saw him through the really bad days towards the end.

TD: See, it's a very difficult question, so I'll start with his method. Irrfan's method when he was working was also how he lived his life. He was a good actor because his observation of life was very surgical, very meticulous. That is why you will not be able to predict what he will do next. Why? Because he is portraying a life. Irrfan's observation of life was so nice that his performance always used to look fresh, unpredictable; he used to rise above his character.

What is acting? Consciously you have to portray an unconscious behaviour. Because you are an actor, you are doing it with skill, you are conscious. But you have to portray that it's unconscious; I can check my phone and also tie my shoelaces at the same time. This behaviour can only be portrayed well if you have understood life, *na*? Most actors in India, who have never stepped outside Bombay, what have they seen of life? That's why, over the past ten years, you are able to see good actors because they are coming from smaller towns.

It's not that we don't have good actors, but somebody like Irrfan used to push me. See, I'm a writer as well. Every picture that I have worked on, I have written myself. The work starts there, with writing, because I'm not working on somebody else's material. I'm working on something I created myself. And if I have Irrfan in mind, I know that Irrfan will fit this character. Without Irrfan telling me, there's a push from behind, to write it well. And come up with a difficult character because you're giving it to Irrfan. You're not giving it to some normal, ordinary actor, who'll do a competent job, and if the performance gets lost we'll fix it with the background score. No, you're writing it for Irrfan. Now Irrfan never really pestered me to write like this. But your responsibility as an artist increases, in a healthy way. You're writing material for a great actor. He rises above the script. Since then I've worked with many new actors, the kind of actors that the world is fond of. But they're not at that level.

SG: What did he think about your performances? Did you ever chat about that?

TD: *Gangs of Wasseypur** was my first performance. I remember I hadn't seen it. I said, 'What will I do by watching it?' Irrfan went and watched it. Our offices were next to each other's, so he came to my office and said, '*Yaar*, you've done great acting in it.' I remember when he was producing the film *Madaari* – this is my regret – Sutapa and Irrfan had both come and offered me Jimmy Sheirgill's role. I don't know, for some reason – I didn't have the time or something – but I said I wouldn't do it. I don't remember if Irrfan and Jimmy had a scene together in the film. Us sharing the screen … it couldn't happen.

SG: Sutapa told me that even towards the end he was reading some brilliant scripts and how he was struggling with his pain

---

* A 2012 Anurag Kashyap film

but was always so positive. You were in touch with him during those days. That must have been so tough.

TD: I mean, I remember Irrfan every day. That said, if you want me to say it in a more profound and poetic way, as a good friend and an artist, I'll try and push myself. Irrfan was a good human being as well. I'll tell you one incident – you must write about this. We were about to start shooting for *Saheb Biwi Aur Gangster Returns*, so we went to the same location where part one was shot. [During] During part one, we had a very bad experience with some beehives. It was an old, dilapidated *haveli*, and there were these huge beehives. And the cook there placed the tandoor right below a beehive during lunchtime. When the smoke rose, the entire unit of bees flew out. They stung a lot of people, including me.

When we started doing part two, there were more beehives, and this time they were inside the *haveli* also. So I said, 'Yaar, remove this beehive. It's too dangerous. Irrfan and other actors were staying in the *haveli*, because there weren't any hotels. Next morning when I went to Irrfan's room, he was very angry. He said, 'Tishu, what have you done, *yaar*? I saw they had burnt the beehive; all the bees were lying dead. Thousands of bees were dead.' He was so upset. I said, 'I didn't ask them to burn it; I asked them to move it. I'm not an expert on the method of removing.' What bees do for the environment … Irrfan got so disturbed thinking about that. He had this quality; he was very close to nature. That's why all this reflects in his performance. Now these new actors that come, they want to become Irrfan. Irrfan did not want to become Naseer [Naseeruddin Shah]. He came to make his own destiny.

SG: So what about all the talk of Irrfan being a huge fan of Naseeruddin Shah and wanting to be like him?

TD: Who doesn't like Naseer bhai? If those films of Naseer bhai and Om Puri did not exist, maybe we wouldn't have been here. When we saw them on screen, we could feel that we can also do it. And the material we were seeing was so impressive. But Irrfan never said, 'I want to become Naseer.'

SG: Right. He became who he was. We all know that in his television days he was not very happy and wanted to break free. And I think *Haasil* and *The Warrior* set him on the path to what he really wanted to do.

TD: I think it happened with *Warrior*. He was a good actor from the beginning. He chiselled his skills as he grew, and he kind of experienced life. But he was a curious actor from the beginning, somebody who wanted to learn. What he lacked was confidence. And an actor who lacks confidence will never shine. Acting is eighty per cent confidence and twenty per cent impersonation. *Warrior* gave him that confidence. He saw his look on horseback, with a burning field in the background. I was the casting director for *Warrior* and, honestly, Asif [Kapadia] was *not* interested in Irrfan; he wanted to audition more. We made so many people audition and Irrfan auditioned some three or four times. Eventually, Asif decided that he's the one. I said, 'No one will do it better than him. Only Irrfan can do it.'

Warrior gave him that confidence. And Irrfan and Asif became very good friends.

SG: One last thing. If there is one thing that you had to remember Irrfan by, what would it be?

TD: *Awaargi. Bina kisi maqsad* [without any agenda], just head out and roam around with him. In the jungle. All you need is a cigarette in your pocket. *Bas.*

'A pure artist'

VISHAL BHARDWAJ

Vishal Bhardwaj – director, screenwriter, producer, music composer and singer – changed the language of Hindi cinema. He also gave Irrfan *Maqbool*, the crackling *Macbeth*-inspired gangster film. Maqbool is a hood. He is a killer. But more than anything else, he is a lover: his love for the beauteous Nimmi, played superbly by Tabu, transcends all else. Bhardwaj made two other films with Irrfan (*7 Khoon Maaf* and *Haider*), both memorable for different reasons.

SHUBHRA GUPTA: It's well known that when you started to cast for *Maqbool*, Irrfan was not your first choice. What made you gravitate towards Irrfan, and what was it like to work with him in that film?

VISHAL BHARDWAJ: I think it was destiny which brought us together, because some other actor was meant to be playing Maqbool. When I watched the trial of his film *Haasil*, I was blown away by his performance. Somewhere in my heart, I wished I had seen *Haasil* earlier. But by that time the other actor was finalized. Somewhere along the line, when we came closer to our shoot, we had some date issues with the other actor. Immediately I contacted Irrfan. He heard the script, loved it and came on board. It was destiny.

SG: The two of you coming together – tell me a little bit about that magic, that alchemy.

VB: Irrfan was a great actor. But beyond that, he was a very evolved human being. A very aware person. His views about relationships, his worldview about politics and religion were very evolved. And as we started working together, we gradually got close and became friends. *Itna khoobsurat insaan tha dil se* [He was a beautiful person at heart]; there was no malice within him. And to add to that, he had a *khatarnak* [deadly] sense of humour. He could find humour in anything.

When we started working together, I used to find it odd that sometimes he was so natural in front of the camera, it seemed like he wasn't even acting. So I had my doubts whether he had even come prepared or if he just walked in front of the camera without any preparation or homework. He always used to say that one per cent of what we do behind the camera translates into twenty per cent on camera. He used to be very subtle in his approach; he was so natural. Tabu and I used to tease him a lot because of a habit he had – sometimes he used to talk double-double. *Kaun-kaun, kya-kya*. So we would all talk like that amongst ourselves when Irrfan was around: *hum-hum, kaun-kaun, kya-kya*.

Irrfan could take a dialogue and make it his own, turn it into a rhythm. He didn't really sing a lot; he wasn't good at singing, but he was good at feeling music. I think he was one of those Sufi men. There was some Sufism inside him; he was born with it. So if Irrfan didn't work on acting in this lifetime, if he was in any other profession – politics or anything – his spirituality would have still come to the fore.

SG: You mentioned Tabu. How did this pairing come about? Every time they appear on screen, they just light it up.

VB: When I was working on *Maqbool*, the first people that I cast were Tabu and Naseer bhai [Naseeruddin Shah]. It was a transitional phase for Tabu, because she had begun a journey after *Maachis** and this [*Maqbool*] was eight–nine years after *Maachis*. So a different kind of phase had begun for her. Back then Irrfan used to do supporting roles, so I did doubt what Tabu's attitude would be, because she was coming from the mainstream, and he was transitioning from a supporting role to the lead. But the chemistry they had together – as people – they connected, you know? They connected very deeply. A lot of scenes, like the '*meri jaan*' scene – they both performed it so beautifully.

SG: Yes, that is a sublime scene.
VB: It didn't feel like they were actors – it seemed like those two characters were real in the scene. When they were crying during the climax, there was silence on the set. They connected as people. And we made a great triangle – we were so connected with each other.

Even when he was not well – we met only once when he was not well – the three of us, we met for three–four hours. After that, I only met him once, in London, and I think Tabu met him at his place. But the three of us met together only once when he was sick, and we were joking so much, it didn't feel like Irrfan was unwell. I think, to connect as people is essential. I don't think just by connecting with someone professionally you can do a good job. Unless you are connected personally, unless you have respect for each other, love for each other, you cannot create magic on screen. Magic gets created on its own when all these things come together.

---

* A 1996 Gulzar film

SG: Everybody I have spoken to has told me about your very special connection with Irrfan. Mira Nair said she was in touch on and off. Tigmanshu Dhulia and he were close friends from drama school, and they kept in touch. But I'm constantly being told how you and Irrfan had something really special together. So tell me a little bit about that.

VB: It was beyond explanation, our connection. And that's why, I think, I'm still affected when I talk about him, and therefore I was avoiding talking to you. Because I don't *want* to talk about him – I'm still very affected by his going away. I still get ... I start missing him. Give me two minutes.

SG: Please, take your time.

VB: Yeah, sorry ... So that's why I was not ... I didn't want to talk to anyone. I didn't want to talk about him. I thought maybe I was over it but I was wrong; I am still very affected by his departure. Because it was not just ... we never talked deeply about work, about acting or performance or scripts. Everything used to just casually happen on its own. Even during *Haider*, when I approached him. He was very busy in those days, and I told him that he should read it once. 'This is a very *zabardast* character – you'd be able to play him,' I said. Sometimes he didn't do parts simply because the role was very good. His intention towards every project was clear. He read it and told me that this script should definitely be made into a film: 'To this day, nobody has done anything like this on Kashmir, so I will do it.' I don't know from where he dug out those five–six days. On 26 January, we started the shoot in Kashmir. He was available only on those five–six days.

Once, during *Ishqiya* [2010], we had a small fight. He was supposed to do Arshad Warsi's part. When he didn't do it, I had a small fight with him over that.

And I didn't work with him for many years; then I approached him again. Because everyone was saying no to that character he played in *7 Khoon Maaf* – that masochist husband. I called him on the phone – I still remember, it was in Mussoorie. I said, 'Look, everyone is saying no.' He said, 'I will *toh* do it, because I have to make it up to you.' He did it just for that reason. And what he did in that, he did very beautifully. This was also his way [of saying] that this style of storytelling is so *khoobsurat* that I want to be a part of it. After that, he was upset with me again. His part in *7 Khoon Maaf*, no matter the length, was very poetic. The entire story had no dialogue; the whole part was done in only poems and songs. Finally, because the length was becoming a bit too much, his story was cut down the most, so he was very upset.

So when he came to do *Haider*, he said, 'My first condition is that you will release my entire story of twenty–twenty-five minutes on YouTube.' I wanted to do it but I could not find that cut.

He was great. I have never told this to anyone, that Meghna [Gulzar] was going through a very bad phase in her life, in her career [before the making of *Talvar*]. So he said that Gulzar saab must be feeling very low that his daughter is not able to do well. And this was a good script; he wanted to do it. 'If not for Meghna, I want to do it for Gulzar saab.' He was a great human being, and his selection was not only based on the role. He would look at the intention of the whole film and then want to be a part of it.

SG: Everybody used to offer him these very intense roles; did he really want to do the other kind of roles? Not so intense, so serious.

VB: Yeah, I think his comic timing was excellent, and this dance-vance of his. There was this *ajeeb* thing about him – whatever Irrfan did, it never felt fake. Nothing seemed false. So to me, it felt like even if he did the song and dance, which he did later—

SG: With AIB?*

VB: Yes, AIB and all those other videos he did – in those, he was so natural, he never looked fake. So he had this quality – *kuchh bhi de do, woh usko apna bana leta tha aur usme dhal jaata tha.* [Give him anything and he would make it his own and lose himself in it.] He made everything his own. Obviously, who doesn't want to do commercial cinema and who doesn't want to be a superstar? I remember, after the first time he saw the trial of *Haider*, he came to me. He had a very filmi entry in it. He told me, 'If you wanted to give me such an entry, why did you give me money?' Do you know that when we reached there at the time of the shoot, it was very cold? There had been a lot of snowfall, and we had gone high up for that shot. Dachigam village. The costume designers had given Irrfan white on white and I was not sure how that would look. But Dolly Ahluwalia [costume designer] – she's great – she said, '*Ghost ka feel aayega*, if [against the] snow he's wearing a white shawl and he's seen coming out of it.' And Irrfan picked up some snow and rubbed it on his glasses. Look at him – he comes and cleans his glasses, like this [*gestures*]. So he used to do these intriguing things. He was very spontaneous. Sometimes it felt – like I was saying earlier – as if he came to

---

* All India Bakchod, a Mumbai-based comedy company founded in 2012 – now disbanded – which collaborated with Irrfan on their viral spoof video 'Every Bollywood Party Song'

the set without any effort. But I started understanding later that he comes in after doing so much work and then leaves it all. He unlearns everything. He becomes a blank slate. No matter the preparation; if he has to do the opposite of it, he will do so. That's why he was great, that you do so much homework with so much dedication, method-*wala*, and then you come to the set and just leave it all behind. I think that's the quality even Naseer bhai has. He also comes with a lot of preparation, then leaves it all.

SG: Irrfan opened the doors to people like, say, Rajkummar Rao, Pankaj Tripathi. Like Naseeruddin Shah and Om Puri, who were supposed to be Irrfan's gurus, paved the way for him. I asked Naseeruddin if he thought Irrfan was a good *shagird*. He said that Irrfan was his own actor; he was nobody's disciple.

VB: Actually, he built his own school – the Irrfan school. Now there are a lot of people – Rajkummar Rao, Pankaj [Tripathi], even, for that matter, Vicky [Kaushal]—

SG: Ayushmann Khurrana?

VB: Ayushmann is still conventionally good-looking, a bit fair and handsome, which is required in Hindustan. But you see the rest – unconventional. This path was paved by Irrfan. Especially for Rajkummar Rao. This path is also opening up for Vijay Varma.

SG: Do you think conventional Bollywood knew what to do with an actor of his calibre? Barring a policeman or don, they didn't think of any other character for him for so long.

VB: Mainstream Bollywood will make a film for a star, not for an actor. They'll make a film which can make money. So I don't think mainstream Bollywood even has that intention, which is rightfully so, because it's a business for them.

SG: When he was looking to the West, it seemed to me that he was looking for something that he was not getting in Bollywood, which is why he was looking at Hollywood.

VB: I don't think so. Hollywood he was looking for because there he got a lot of dignity, in terms of work. Any role is perceived that way there; *bade bade star chhote chhote role karte hain.* [Even the big stars do small roles.] Brad Pitt and all also do small roles – like the part he did in that Tarantino film [*Inglourious Basterds*]. There they see it as a character, and if it excites them, they go and do it. Of course Hollywood was giving him a different kind of standing, so that's why he was doing it. I never saw him frustrated here; even when we were doing *Maqbool*, and post *Maqbool*, he was never frustrated about wanting or not wanting to do a certain type of role.

One day, he brought Uday Prakash to me. Uday Prakash is a great writer of Hindi literature. Irrfan used to keep asking him for stories – he kept in touch with him. There was this one very beautiful story – 'Tirichh'. Irrfan brought it to me saying, 'Let's make this film together – "Tirichh". I will play the part of the father.'

So this journey that Irrfan was on, it was for stories. So many times I have seen him talking to writers only because of their stories. He didn't even get down to the character; he was just all about the story. So he was above getting or not getting parts in Hollywood; I don't think he cared for it. He was beyond all that; he was a pure artist. He wanted to convey a good story. What can we discover within that story; the internal conflicts of a person.

SG: I spoke to Nikkhil Advani and he told me that all these actors used to look up to Irrfan. They would say, 'Give us a role like

Irrfan's.' I had asked him whether somebody like Irrfan impacted studio-led Bollywood. According to Nikkhil, all these young, upcoming actors were very impressed with his performances, and the way he approached everything. They wanted to become like him. They wanted the roles that people wrote for him. And it was only after *Hindi Medium* that Bollywood suddenly woke up to him and said, '*Arre*, he can also make money!'

VB: Yeah. He was very happy with the result of *Hindi Medium*. He was shooting in Delhi when he said, 'I want a favour from you. Can you write the climax of the film for me?' I knew Saket [Chaudhary, director of *Hindi Medium*] very well. I told Irrfan that Saket writes well; he might feel bad. To which he said, 'No, Saket and I both want you to write our climax.' So I wrote the climax, because they needed a certain style which they thought I would be able to write. He's great, *yaar*. We had a different connection, you know.

SG: When he came on set, did he always do something that you expected? Or was it something completely different? And did you see him grow as an actor, from the time you started working with him to later?

VB: In *Maqbool* we were exploring, but after that it so happened that we would expect him to do something, but still he used to surprise. He used to find some strange rhythm of his own. He would do some unexpected things, which were not calculated, and I think these came from inside him. Such a natural actor, and so dramatic. Never boring.

And how he did grow – I think I rate [*The*] *Namesake* as one of his best performances. The way he has played that old man's character – oh my god, it is so beautiful. God has been exceptionally kind to him – whichever character he did, he just became that and yet portrayed it in a new light. It never felt seen before, anything that he did. There was a certain freshness in his every approach. In every character, every line, every mannerism. He was not too interested in the physical side – that I need to become fat or thin. He would do things simply yet differently.

SG: When you think of Irrfan, what is the first thing that comes to mind?

VB: That habit of his – he would shut an eye and smile. I really liked that. I always recall that about him – anytime something good happened, he would shut his eye and smile. *Woh bahut, bahut khoobsurat smile hoti thi uski.*

'He made the ordinary extraordinary'

POOJA BHATT

Pooja Bhatt is a well-known actor and producer. Her debut production *Rog* gave Irrfan one of his early mainstream roles, in which he plays a policeman obsessed with a beautiful woman. In the film, Bhatt gave him a 'bombshell' to share the screen with. Irrfan also fondly acknowledged her father, the prolific filmmaker Mahesh Bhatt, as a mentor.

Pooja Bhatt's latest work includes the female-forward web series *Bombay Begums* and the psychological thriller *Chup*.

———

SHUBHRA GUPTA: You are a child of the industry, a legacy person. Irrfan had mostly done offbeat films with little-known directors at the time you and Mr Mahesh Bhatt offered him *Rog*. I was curious to know how these two worlds collided.

POOJA BHATT: We planned *Rog* as a firefighting exercise, to be frank. We said we've got to make a film which is kind of intimate with regards to its canvas. And we need three key players. I'd met Irrfan through Dad and, Irrfan, strangely, wanted to direct at that point, before he did *Maqbool*. We met him as somebody who came to us saying, '*Yaar*, I want to direct for you guys.' I had seen *Maqbool*; in fact, it had released on the same day as

Paap [her directorial debut, starring John Abraham], if I am not mistaken. And I loved Irrfan, because I thought he was a great guy, so pure in so many ways. He was a damn good-looking man, whom the industry was refusing to see in that way. They were like, '*Character actor hai, kamaal ka actor hai,* but he can't be a hero.'

And for whatever it is worth, my roots are in commercial cinema. I always wondered why it has to be one or the other; why can't you have the commercial framework and put the songs in and make it in a certain manner where it's lush and tactile and sensual, but tell a story that's off the beaten track? So I told my dad, 'Let's cast Irrfan.' My father was delighted; he said that would be amazing, because he would bring so much gravitas to this part.

I spoke to my partners and they just jumped at the idea immediately. Suhel Seth's casting was my dad's idea. Irrfan and Suhel, they played off well. And then I said, 'I want to cast a bombshell opposite Irrfan. Because normally, you'll put into Irrfan's arms another serious actor. You know, someone like Tabu, whom you've seen with Irrfan before. I said, 'No, I want to see Irrfan with this beautiful woman.' And then we found this South African model, Ilene Hamann, and I remember, we shot the film's poster with them – we had made Ilene sit at his feet – and he was a little shy. Because I don't think he saw himself like that, you know? And I'm like, 'Irrfan, you're such a beautiful man! We need to boost you up, man.' But then I could see that he was getting into it, you know? He was enjoying all of us looking at him ... it's all about the gaze, Shubhra. As an actor, I can tell you, when a director looks at you and believes that you are going to shine, you shine. And I think all of us were ... we were Team Irrfan. We were rooting for him. And when he sat there in that black linen shirt with this bombshell from South Africa at his feet, I said, 'This man is a star.'

We made *Rog* in a record thirty-six days and we made it for a ridiculous amount of 2.25 crores. Because I had good actors and we were focused. And I ended up making a hefty profit. If I remember correctly, I think it released on his thirty-eighth birthday – on the 7th of January, 2005. I remember telling him, 'Irrfan, you're not going to have time for me after this.' And he's like, '*Nahi, nahi, yaar, next film plan karte hain* – let's plan the next film.' I said, 'I'm just glad I've done my little bit to tell you that you are way up there with the best of the best and who the hell has called you a "character actor"? Who decides what works and what doesn't work?' And the rest is history.

Of course, *A Mighty Heart* came out after that. Then it took Angelina Jolie to make the whole of India realize that hey, you've got somebody smouldering and very attractive in your backyard; why are you bracketing him as this serious actor only and not looking at his raw sex appeal?

Irrfan shot his first love scene with me, by the way, for *Rog*. That was hilarious – I must tell you. He kept postponing that shoot, kept finding some excuse. Finally, I said, 'Irrfan, why are you postponing this?' He replied, *'Ek toh, yaar, mere ko storyboard nahi diya.'* [I wasn't given a storyboard.] I said, '*Storyboard nahi diya*? You want a storyboard for a lovemaking scene?' He said, '*Yaar*, I'm nervous; I've never done something like this before.' I said, 'Okay, now that we've put our vulnerabilities on the table, we can go about it the right way.' And I remember going in there, telling them both that this can take two hours or we can be done in half an hour. It's really about how comfortable you guys feel. And we were done in a matter of half an hour. And then he's joking and telling me, 'Can we do it again?' We used film in those days, so I said, '*Film kaun khareedne wala hai*?' [Who's going to buy the film?] He said, '*Mere paise se kaat do ek can of film.*' [Take out the cost of one can of film from my pay.]

He was very, very shy. Brilliant, but cautious about even daring to say out loud that he could replace the so-called commercial heroes out there. Because I don't think anyone had let him believe that, and I think *Rog* was that first step, really. My producers believed in him, I believed in him, my father believed in him. The whole team was rooting for him, so it was a very enjoyable experience after that.

I remember meeting him a few times, and we kept talking about those *Rog* days. It's bizarre to think that he is not here anymore and we are talking about him in hindsight. After he'd announced that he's got cancer, my father went to see him and he sang that song to him, '*Maine dil se kaha dhoond laa na khushi, nasamajh laya gham, toh yeh gham hi sahi.*' I think that song resonates as a kind of anthem about his life in so many ways.

For me, he'll always be that shy boy. Irrfan, with all his smouldering intensity, who'd ever think that he was so shy, like a little schoolboy, nervous about doing a lovemaking scene.

SG: I wanted to pick up on what you said. That the industry did not see him as this hero. Why do you think that was?

PB: Because I guess the industry has got old eyes, Shubhra. That's something my father has always told me – and I believe that very strongly – that we don't need new people, we need new eyes. And the industry has old ways of looking at things, in terms of this is what a hero or a heroine should be like, [only someone specific] can play the villain's character. Irrfan Khan, villain; Irrfan Khan, character. Irrfan Khan, hero? *Nahi, yaar.* The industry's references are the hit or the flop that's gone before. They're not navigating roads by today's map; they're navigating it by yesterday's map. And that was exactly the problem with Irrfan. I mean, while my co-producers said yes, there were people within the industry – even my uncle [Mukesh Bhatt] asked me – why Irrfan? So I'm like, 'No, he's right for this role; he's got everything going for him and he's got all those commercial elements. He just hasn't been given that opportunity.' So they were like, 'Okay, fine, but John [Abraham] *ko hi lelo.* Launch a new boy.' But I said, 'No, I don't want a new boy, I want Irrfan Khan. And he'll act for both people [him and Ilene], so there's no problem.'

SG: How did he react when you told him about *Rog*?
PB: I think he was a little taken aback when we told him we want to make this film with him in the lead and we are casting this girl called Ilene. But he kind of had this twinkle in his eye; he liked the idea. I think actors go through that phase, you know, where we really forget our worth. Or we've not woken up to it. It takes one person to ignite that spark.

SG: So there was *Rog*, and then he made *Life in a... Metro*, then of course he was doing all those Hollywood films. I remember writing in 2009 that he needs to come back to India, because he was doing *The Amazing Spider-Man*, which is nothing amazing.
PB: What you said is exactly what he said. I remember walking into the Marriott in Juhu once, with my father, and we bumped into Irrfan, who was standing there with some white production person, talking about some film that they were planning on doing in Hollywood. He was very fond of my father. Me and Irrfan, we had a different equation, but he loved my dad. He introduced

my father to that man with great fanfare and said, 'You've got to meet this man; he gives me so much. *Bhatt saab, film banaye saath mein* – let's make a film together.' So, my father being my father, said, 'I have no illusions, Irrfan, that I've got anything you need. The world is at your feet now.' He says, '*Bhatt saab, kutta jo hota hai, khud ke mohalle mein naam karvaana chahata hai. Bahar log jitni bhi tareef kar lein, mujhe ab yahan pe hit film karni hai. Yahan pe commercial film karni hai.*' [Even a dog wants to be known in his own street. However much the West may praise me, I want to do a hit, commercial film here.] He was very keen to come back into the fray and do a hardcore commercial film, after all of that Hollywood stuff was done. Because he wanted the man on the street here to kind of lust for him. He said, '*Mujhe ek mauka chahiye, bas.*'

The last film I saw where he was cast very well was Tanuja's [Chandra] film [*Qarib Qarib Singlle*]. I really liked him in that because if you know Irrfan, that role was so him, in so many ways. But even after all of that, recognition abroad and being part of hit after hit after hit, there were few people who actually cast him solo, as a romantic interest. As somebody who was the lover. Which is why I was keen that he be part of brand *Jism**, because I felt what I started with *Rog*, I wanted to take one step further and now kind of have him come back as an asset in more ways than one. Where it would not be an experiment anymore; he's established his credentials, not only abroad but here.

I was confident that this would put him where he rightfully belonged, where he would become a very good option for mainstream Bollywood.

But the old eyes never did go away. People, I find, do not give you your due and I think, in all fairness, there should have been

---

* A trendsetting Vishesh Films franchise

a queue outside Irrfan's house from within Bollywood to cast him in mainstream cinema. Where the story did not have to be offbeat. Because he would have been able to pull it off. He would make a very ordinary line seem like it's sparkling. And he would bring to it a certain degree of reality and depth that was missing in the average actor.

SG: So why did this line not happen?

PB: Not enough female producers like me. If you have to name ten of the most attractive men on the planet, Irrfan Khan would be one of them. I really think he's damn hot, *yaar*. He's a sexy, beautiful man. I genuinely believe that Irrfan Khan is one of the most attractive men to have walked the planet, because he's not even aware of the kind of impact he has on you. I just thought that Irrfan was such an exciting package, because here you could tell a story and then you have a credible actor. He made the ordinary extraordinary, and there was a certain degree of gravitas and depth that he brought to the most mundane roles.

SG: Right. So how did he actually come to meet Mr Bhatt?

PB: I think they go back to the Plus-channel* days. I'm not sure exactly when my father met him but they interacted a few times. I remember me and Manoj [Bajpayee], my father and Tanuja were flying to Calcutta just after *Zakhm* had released, in 1999. And we were getting the Calcutta Critics' Award there. On the plane, we were planning a film. You know the film *Dad*, with Jack Lemmon? It's three generations of men – we wanted to do a film like that. And I was asking Manoj, '*Direct kaun karega*?' Manoj looked at my father and said, 'Irrfan.' So my father said, 'Irrfan is

---

* A leading media company from the nineties, which produced content for television and cinema.

directing?' Manoj said, 'He wants to direct and he'll be a damn good director.' Manoj and Irrfan were friends. Then we called him. We met and spoke about doing projects together. At that time, he was a little unsure where life was taking him, whether it was down the acting track or into direction. And when we planned *Rog*, we just called him to the office and it was the most simple conversation. *'Irrfan, hum yeh film plan kar rahe hain.'* [We are planning this film.] He had that twinkle in his eye and that smile on his face. And even the talk about money was over in a matter of minutes – simple.

SG: And what was the shoot like?

PB: We were working at breakneck speed. We used to kind of work really hard and, every evening after we packed up, it was a given that I had to put two bottles of Old Monk on the table and they had to be cracked open and then Irrfan would get nicely hammered, because his [threshold] for alcohol was zero. I mean, I would drink him under the table most of the time. But the rum had to be consumed and then we would recap the day.

The last time I met him was at an event; I think it was in 2016. I met him after really long – there was Tigmanshu and Irrfan and all of us. We spoke about working together again. I remember holding him around his waist – he's much taller than I am, of course – and pottering out with him because the more whiskey I drank, the straighter I walked. And with him, the lesser he drank, the more unevenly he walked. So I remember propping him up and taking him out. And saying bye to him and giving him many kisses and hugs, and that was it, that was the last time I saw him. I haven't seen him after that. That was the last time I drank also … I was pretty devastated with the news of his passing, even though we knew that it was inevitable. But you know, you always hope for a miracle.

SG: So, as an actor, as a producer, as a creator, what do you think this world is like without Irrfan?

PB: You know, when he passed away, I was at my farm. It was bang in the middle of the lockdown. I was very upset because when I went online, I saw some truly wild comments from a few people. People whom I forgive because I don't think they even understand what they post. To the effect of, oh, one less Muslim in the world. I was so heartbroken. I actually wrote on Instagram that if this is the world he left behind, I don't want to be part of it. And I literally looked up at the heavens and said, 'You know, God, this is the world that we have managed to create, where even a virus that puts us in our place has not taught us basic fucking humanity. Then take me, because I don't want to live anymore. And I swear, Shubhra, on anything dear to me – see I'm getting gooseflesh talking to you – it was a hot, muggy day. Out of nowhere, clouds came and rain fell and this wind blew and … and I just got this feeling that it was him saying, 'Relax'. And that was, in a strange way, my goodbye.

I think, post Covid, somehow we seem to have become more polarized and, for whatever it is worth, the magic of the film industry was that it was always goal-oriented. It didn't matter what your religion was as long as you make me money. But the world we live in today, the industry that we are inhabiting today, is not the same. This *has* permeated the film industry.

But I don't think Irrfan's religion got in the way. What got in the way was the fact that he was too ahead of his times, in more ways than one. He was unusual; he was not your cookie-cutter hero in that sense. He was unconventional. His unconventionality – which was his asset and strength – which the West lapped up, we didn't have the eyes for. And like I said, it took *A Mighty Heart* for a lot of people to look at him and say, 'Oh my god, that's Irrfan!'

Because he's in the same film with Angelina Jolie, suddenly he's very hot. Earlier, he was not. So it was just the fact that people are unable to see beyond their references and that's the only thing that prevented more people from queueing up. Otherwise there's no reason why they didn't, because he was accessible – we didn't have to go through twenty secretaries to reach him, even after he had started working abroad. You could get an audience with him; you would know immediately – yes or no. He was pliable with money. He would understand where you're coming from; he would tell you what his base requirement was and, if he felt it was worth his while, he would slash his price in half. But then for certain movies, he knew, 'Yeh main paise ke liye kar raha hoon,' [I am doing this for the money] and rightfully so – then he wouldn't compromise. But the only thing that prevented a line of filmmakers at his door, so that more movies that were far more refined than Rog could be made, was the fact that they didn't quite know what to do with him.

SG: What is the one thing that comes to your mind when you think about Irrfan?

PB: Innocence. I think he was a child. He was a little shy boy who was too coy to kiss Ilene Hamman. I had to go there and say, 'Listen, Irrfan, the first lesson my father gave me when I was filming Sadak* was that if you're going to feel awkward, the whole world is going to look at it as something awkward. Just kiss the girl, for god's sake!'

I remember him once getting very drunk – I had eight dogs then. He said, 'Don't look after your dogs and your puppies! You have to look after us. You have to look after me, you have

* A 1991 Mahesh Bhatt film

to nurture me!' And I was like, 'Irrfan, where is this coming from? We have to shoot tomorrow morning – go home.' That's the equation we had with each other. There was nothing that I couldn't say to him; I didn't feel as if I was walking on eggshells with him. He opened up to me a little slowly, but there was a deep affection that we shared and not one where we would be in touch regularly on the phone. But whenever we did, there was a genuine spark. He was one person with whom we would shoot eighteen hours; then we would spend six hours drinking.

You asked me this before: What is the world like [without Irrfan]? I don't know, sometimes I think that … the way the world is going, I don't think the world deserved him, you know? He went, Rishi Kapoor passed away the day after that. There are a lot of people leaving us, and with the world being what it is – so polarized, so full of hate – I don't think we deserved him. Which is why sometimes I also feel that he came like a comet. His star just went through the roof and then … it was gone. But there was so much that happened to him in that limited period of time. It could have been spread out over twenty-five–thirty years as well. But he achieved all of that in such a condensed time period. I think that somebody up there knew that he was a special child and gave him all of that and more and then said, 'Listen, your time's up, buddy, because this place is getting very messy and you need to get out of the room before it gets really ugly.' He was not somebody who liked too much confrontation. He preferred not to be in ugly situations. Some people thrive on it, as we all know. He did not. He had this one make-up man who'd been working with him for years. He was very low-maintenance as a hero. Didn't need to be nurtured in that sense, you didn't need to suck up to him. Just … a normal guy, *yaar*. Which is such an anomaly in this industry.

Maybe if he acted like more of a diva and had thrown a few more tantrums and not been as nice as he was, probably he would have got a lot more work. When you're too nice, somehow people feel you're too accessible.

But this would have been a great time for Irrfan to be around. This is a time when he would have done so much more. But well, he still did a lot more than most people have done in thirty–forty years.

'I can't think of a single thing
he could not have done'

NASEERUDDIN SHAH

Irrfan regarded **Naseeruddin Shah** – actor, thinker, iconoclast – as his guru. They worked together in one of Irrfan's earliest films, *Private Detective: Two Plus Two Plus One*, and then, in *Maqbool*. Irrfan also 'very graciously' agreed to act in Shah's directorial debut, *Yun Hota Toh Kya Hota*, a film the latter says he is 'very embarrassed about'.

———

SHUBHRA GUPTA: How well did you know Irrfan? Did you know he was a great admirer of yours?

NASEERUDDIN SHAH: When I first tried teaching at the National School of Drama, it was a couple of years after his batch. I think this was the batch of people like Tigmanshu Dhulia, Nirmal Pandey, Sanjay Mishra and some others. Quite a few of that class have been illustrious alumni of NSD.

But I did not know Irrfan at all, nor had I heard of him as a student at NSD. I was unaware that he is so fond of me and tries to emulate my work or whatever, but I would think that he was more like Om [Puri], during his NSD days at least.

Over the years, I've kept in touch with NSD and there are

several actors whose performances – when they were students – are hugely celebrated and imitated. And those were the most showy actors. Like Pankaj Kapur, Manohar Singh, Om Shivpuri – these were the gents whose performances were talked about in hushed tones. Om [Puri] was not, though Om gained a lot more from the three years at NSD than I did.

And I suspect Irrfan must have been a personality like Om. Because Irrfan is from Tonk, which is a tiny little place near Jaipur. I knew Tonk because I spent my childhood in Ajmer. And that's the first thing I discovered about him when I first met him. He was here, in fact, rehearsing with Ratna [Pathak Shah] for this film *Jazeere* which Govind Nihalani did. I walked in and found him sitting and he walked up to me and introduced himself. I said, 'Oh, you are Irrfan – I've heard of you.' I mean, I knew he was acting in the film but I hadn't heard about his work. I saw his performance in that – quite an incomprehensible film – but I thought he was very, very confident. I was astonished, in fact, at his level of assurance.

The next thing I saw him in was *The Warrior*. Asif Kapadia took me to a screening in London and I was totally blown away by Irrfan's performance because that was not the intensity I was expecting; I thought he'd be this mild kind of guy. There was a lot of craft evident in the way he performed that part; there was a great deal of emotional truth. And, of course, he looked quite amazingly photogenic. So that is when I first got in touch with him. As I said, we didn't really spend too much time together. But when we did meet, I tried to get him onto the stage, but he was not keen.

SG: I was going to ask whether you did try to reach out to him for a theatre performance.

NS: Yes, I did. He came to see some of my work in theatre and I would always say, 'When are you coming back to the theatre?' And he would say, '*Haan, theek time pe, Naseer bhai, theek time pe.*' [When the time is right.] But he never did.

I, in fact, offered him a couple of parts. In the Ismat Chughtai series, I wanted him to do some of these stories but he had this weird reluctance about playing an elderly man. It's a pity that he never came back to the stage. I have a feeling that he was probably too internal an actor to be effective on the stage. Which was a great attribute as far as his film acting was concerned; I'm not so sure about the stage.

SG: But when I spoke to Mira Nair, she said that the first time she saw him was at NSD, when she had gone looking for actors to cast in *Salaam Bombay!* and she saw this 'tall, lanky boy' with eyes that really spoke to her and said he was the only one who lifted off the stage for her. So I'm wondering whether he did have that internal quality – was he always this person who kept everything inside of him?

NS: I really can't say. I think he was skilful enough an actor to be able to understand the different requirements of the theatre and the camera, and I think the play she's talking about is probably something called *The Narrow Road to the Deep North*. It's a Japanese play that he kept talking about later on in his life.

When I did get him though, he said *ki*, '*You know, Naseer bhai, meri ammi aapko bahut bad'duayein deti hain.*' [My mother curses you a lot.]

So I said, 'Why?' [He told me] she said, '*Tum uss Naseeruddin Shah ki tarah banna chahte ho? Khuda uska bhala kare.*' [You want to be like that Naseeruddin Shah? May God bless him.] So I said *ki*, '*Yaar, mera salaam kehna unko.*' I think the day will come when she will stop this and give me a few blessings instead. But I think that was really sweet; I was a bad example to emulate.

And then, of course, there was *Maqbool*, in which he was cast by default. Kay Kay [Menon] was supposed to play the part but couldn't for some reason. He pulled out, so Irrfan was on. This was serendipity, really, that Vishal [Bhardwaj] zeroed in on him and he was absolutely marvellous.

But Irrfan did have a peculiar savvy about how he wants to be perceived. I thought his performance in *Maqbool* was excellent in the first half; in the second half it wasn't that effective and I told him so, and he said, 'Yeah, that's my mistake. I tried to make the character a winner.' I said, 'Big mistake. Macbeth is by no means a winner; there's no way you can make Macbeth lovable. He's a bastard and he deserves what he gets in the end.' I don't know how many people agree with this, but at least I felt that. But otherwise, the gravity that he would be able to bring to his presence, the stillness which is rare among Indian actors particularly – he knew all these things; he was not performing by fluke. The man knew his onions and that was very evident. I've never seen a weak performance by Irrfan.

He'd also done a very small part in Rajat Kapoor's first, a movie called *Private Detective* ... before he started on his journey. It was a terrible film and I was in it, and Irrfan was there in a small part. But he would make an impact in anything that he appeared in, however brief it may be. Whether it was this or the tiny part he did in *Salaam Bombay!*, he was always the real thing.

And then I got to know him a little bit when I was making my film [*Yun Hota Toh Kya Hota*], which I'm thoroughly embarrassed about. I really wanted him to act in my film and he was nice enough to agree, although the part wasn't all that much and got further butchered in the editing. It was my fault really; it was a terrible piece of writing. You can't have a protagonist who does nothing, which is what Irrfan had to do in that section of the story. And most of his scenes got chopped because I felt they were not adding anything, but Irrfan never once complained, he never once held it against me. He just took it in his stride. Which I'm very, very affected by.

SG: I saw it again a couple of days back. I had forgotten all of those lovemaking scenes, especially when he kisses Suhasini Mulay's feet. To have Irrfan do that stuff was quite new.

NS: But I think women really found Irrfan very, very attractive, and he carried a great deal of sex appeal. Those eyes and that sort of altogether kind of attitude that he had – I don't think that Irrfan suffered the slightest bit of insecurity, like all of us actors do. I don't think he was ever awed by anyone. And you can see evidence of that in the film he did with Mr Bachchan. He was not at all, in any way, awed by the presence.

SG: You're talking about *Piku,* right?

NS: Yeah, it was an amazing ability the man had. You know what Robert DeNiro said about Mr Marlon Brando? That he has a sense of truth in his instincts, in his reflexes. I think Irrfan had the same quality. And I'm certain that he worked at it. As I said, he had this thing about wanting to be liked; he wanted to be a popular star – like all of us did – he wanted to be attractive and he managed that. He didn't want to do elderly parts before he was actually old enough to do them. I think, again, because it was a question of how the audience would perceive him. So he was very aware and I really think that if he'd lived on, he would have been one of the very big names in Hindi cinema. Possibly internationally. A performance where he partly failed was when he tried to assume an American accent or Canadian accent in *Life of Pi*. He was ill at ease there.

SG: You were one of the first people to have a sense of what is going on in the West – you and Om Puri. A lot of people reached out to you and you did a lot of international cinema. But Irrfan was going to be a breakout star, because he was doing *Life of Pi*, he was doing *The Amazing Spider-Man*, he was doing—
NS: *Jurassic World*.

SG: They may have been blockbusters, but they were not *his* movies.
NS: I didn't see those movies. The first *Jurassic World* and the first *Spider-Man* were enough for me. So despite Irrfan being in [the later ones], I didn't bother to sit through three hours of rubbish just to see Irrfan for two minutes. I think they were parts not worthy of him, and he did them for the lucre, like a lot of us do. He was very good in *Slumdog Millionaire** and one other – I forget now.

I'm saying it would have been just a matter of time before he started getting those featured parts. The story would have repeated itself the way it did here; from tiny parts, walk-ons, one scene and you blink, he kind of worked his way up to what he finally got. I think the same thing would have happened in Hollywood. Though, of course, being brown, being Indian, all that may have gone against him. He's not a Riz Ahmed or a Dev Patel, you know.

---

* A 2008 Danny Boyle film

SG: Back when you and Om Puri were getting all those roles, were you also getting constrained by the fact that you were brown and Indian?

NS: Yeah, absolutely. After *Monsoon Wedding**, I was offered this monstrously budgeted action movie with Mr Sean Connery which I immediately – not immediately, but after they improved my part – I said yes to. One hell of a lot of money involved and I wanted to meet Mr Connery because I'd always adored him. I didn't, however, hallucinate that this would mean crossover by any means. It never would have happened, even if that film had been a success, which it wasn't, or if it had been a good film, which it wasn't. The only parts I got offered after that were, again, of maharajas or the Indian domestic or people with *pagris* and *dhotis*.

So I turned all of them down and accepted a couple of very small movies, which were shot in New York, which no one ever saw. One was about 9/11 called *The Great New Wonderful*, and one was *Today's Special*, where I play a taxi driver in New York or something. They were very small movies, and I got the part in *The League of Extraordinary Gentlemen†* because of *Monsoon Wedding*, apparently. But again, it was the Indian maharaja. I was actually asked by the script supervisor if I could speak in an 'Indian' accent while we were reading. So I said, 'You mean Peter Sellers, right?' And she said, 'No, no.' So I said, 'Tell me what you mean by an Indian accent because there are a hundred and one accents in India. And this is the way I speak English, this is the way I imagine Captain Nemo would have spoken, so this is how I'm going to speak.'

---

* A 2001 Mira Nair film

† A 2003 Stephen Norrington film

But I think Irrfan would have covered more ground than I did. I think he didn't have such a massive ego as I have. He probably would not have hesitated to audition. Because it is a custom; apparently even actors who are well known are asked to audition for parts over there. I find it offensive; I have a bit of a thin skin. But I think Irrfan would have got much further than I had. And quite simply, he was a highly skilled actor.

SG: So do you think Hindi cinema has evolved at all? I would say that there are some changes that have happened; some storytellers are now trying to do stuff out of the box. There was a time you did what began to be called 'parallel' films with Shyam Benegal, etc., and then you crossed over to the other side. You have gone on record many times about the 'lack of honesty' in that kind of parallel cinema. And about the fact that mainstream Hindi cinema, despite all its problems, knew exactly what it wanted. Did you find yourself at ease – to use your words – in the kind of movies that you did?

NS: To answer your question, Shubhra, do you think it's changed in any way? As far as the ... what shall I call them ... the 'different' kind of filmmakers are concerned, certainly there's been evolution. You watch the craft of a film by Anurag [Kashyap] or Vishal or [Vikramaditya] Motwane, the wonderful filmmaker who made that—

SG: *Udaan*.

NS: *Trapped*, or his other movies also. There's Homi Adajania; there are many of them. They are far superior to the filmmakers of the seventies in terms of craft, in terms of savvy.

What they were saying was very valid, very powerful, but the craft was weak. I think these filmmakers have transcended that barrier and really come to grips with the technique and the art of storytelling also. And none of them are making films on borrowed plumes; they're making films about things which matter to them. Where commercial cinema is concerned, they're deluding themselves that they have made a great deal of progress. All they've done is improve the photography and the editing and that does not exactly make a good movie.

But what I will say to their credit is their ability to accommodate actors like Gajraj Rao. The one who was in *Badhaai Ho** – fabulous actor. Or Pankaj Tripathi, who is the flavour of the season. Marvellous actors. It started with actors like Nawazuddin Siddiqui and Rajkummar Rao and Ayushmann Khurrana. They were not the chocolate boys. I really think these actors would not have appeared, had actors like Irrfan not appeared in the interim. They had the tradition of Irrfan to fall back on, just like Om and I had the tradition of Balraj Sahni and Motilal and Yakub to fall back on. I don't think we would have had a chance, had Motilal and Balraj Sahni not been around. It's like a domino effect. So that ability to accommodate these kinds of actors who normally would not have been given the time of day by commercial filmmakers, and for them now to be cast in central parts, that is a sure sign of progress.

SG: Were you in touch with him in those last days?
NS: I was in touch with him. He, in fact, sent me a message from London, saying, 'Knock knock, Naseer bhai.' So I called him up at this London number. I knew he was ill. And we chatted of this and that and we laughed and talked. And then I said, 'How are

---

* A 2018 Amit Sharma film

you feeling now?' and he said, '*Ab kya karein*; how many people have the opportunity to see death approaching? I'm lucky. I can look at it objectively and see it approaching and it's fine with me. I wanted to do more with my life but never got the chance; I don't hold that against fate.' It was very, very moving, and the courage was quite unbelievable. I have never seen that in my life.

Then I said, 'But physically, how are you?' He said, 'At times, the pain gets so bad that I can't even describe what it's like. And I wonder at this frail body of mine. How can it contain so much pain?' We spoke several times but never once did he say, 'Why me?' Never. And then his last movie was done with Homi [Adajania], who is a fun guy. I used to keep in touch with Homi and ask how Irrfan is doing, and he would say, 'I joke with him all the time; I say, "You bastard, if you die before my film gets completed, I'll be up shit creek."' So the man was able to face up to the facts. Incredibly brave. I really miss him, even though we weren't close friends or anything.

SG: I asked Mira Nair whether there was anything she thought he could not do as an actor. And she said no, she couldn't think of a single thing that he couldn't do.
NS: Absolutely. I can't think of a single thing he could not have done. I can see him singing songs, I can see him romancing the most beautiful girls. I really felt he was a complete, all-round actor. I never saw him sing a song. I wonder if he would have been able to do that; I *think* he would have.

SG: You mean lip-sync, that all Hindi film actors do?
NS: Not just the lip-syncing. But the narcissistic 'aren't I beautiful' kind of stuff, which I was asked to do on occasion and failed

miserably at. I think he would have done better. Bollywood has such a fixed idea of what a romantic hero should look like. I think Irrfan would have transcended it. He was skilful enough and attractive enough to do that. You've got to have a great deal of self-love of a certain kind in order to do those things. I think Irrfan had it. Sorry, you were asking something.

SG: I was going to ask about faith. About how Irrfan wanted to drop his surname and be credited just as Irrfan. How much was his faith important to him?

NS: I think the film industry, despite all its hypocrisies and double standards, did always have a place for all people. If you look back at the history of the contribution of Muslims to the film industry, it's enormous. Mohammed Rafi never felt the need to change his name, nor did Talat Mahmood, nor did Mehboob Khan, nor did K. Asif. There were Parsi leading men, there were European ladies who were starring in the silent movies, there were Maharashtrians, UP-ites. Then when movies turned into talkies, they needed Urdu-speaking people, so there was the whole influx of Muslims who could speak Urdu. And that space has not yet shrunk; the existence of the three Khans at the top testifies to that. They don't have any religion as far as the audience is concerned. Salman is worshipped equally by people of any faith. I don't think Irrfan removed the Khan from his name in order to be not branded as a Muslim; he probably didn't want to get in competition with the existing Khans. I didn't think he wanted to be lumped with them.

SG: But there has never been any discrimination, as far as you've seen, with you or Irrfan?

NS: I haven't felt my being a Muslim to have been an obstacle in any way. In the film industry, whatever faith you may belong to is immaterial, provided you can deliver the goods. There's one god that is worshipped in the film industry and that is Mammon. You may belong to any religion – doesn't matter.

SG: What was it like to be part of the same screen in *Maqbool*?
NS: That casting was a masterstroke, and I take credit for it. Because Vishal wanted me to play the father – the gangster, in other words, the king who gets killed in Macbeth. The part played by Pankaj [Kapur]. And I said, 'Look, I've played this kind of thing before. I don't want to do this part.' And I suggested Pankaj. They said he's too short. I said, 'Look, you just shoot the guy in close-up and you see the power he transmits. Short is going to look fantastic when he's surrounded by these towering henchmen and he's the one in command.' Luckily, Vishal saw the sense in that but then he said, '*Aap ka kya?*' So I said, '*Hum dono* [Om Puri and Naseeruddin Shah] *yeh role karenge.*' [The two of us will play this role.] Om was supposed to play Banquo – the part which Piyush Mishra did – and Pankaj and Piyush were supposed to play the two cops. So I said, 'Here, you shift things around, get Om, and I'll persuade Om.'

SG: And what was it like to direct Irrfan?
NS: It was the easiest thing. He would get it like that. [*snaps his fingers*] I don't think I ever had to tell him anything, except what exactly he has to do in the shot. And I just left the rest of it to him. If I'd say, 'Look, I'd like you to be a little sadder, even perhaps tearful in this scene,' he'd be able to deliver it like that. He had his own technique and I don't know what it was, but he had his own way of doing it. And it was a delight. The way he absorbed direction, and the way he would better the instruction, so to say. I'd say, 'Look, you've got to come in and react with shock because you're seeing this dead body here for the first time.'

And he would – seemingly without effort, without preparation – be ready always. I never saw him sit in a corner and brood and get into the zone and all that shit; he'd just come out with it right away.

Acting with him in *Maqbool* – I'll never tire of telling this story – there were just two or three occasions when we were together. One is the beginning of the film and we're just watching. Another scene is where he comes and shoves a pistol in, my face in the prison and I had to act suitably terrified. But the one I remember, though, was when Banquo's body is brought in, and it was a wonderfully written piece where, instead of Banquo's ghost appearing, Irrfan kneels near the body and, the body opens its eyes. So they were doing that shot of Irrfan and I'm standing behind him. And he knelt over the body and, in a second or two, he fell over backwards. So I kind of thought he'd toppled over. And he said, 'Naseer bhai, please, *yaar,* what are you doing?' So I said, '*Bhaiya, tu gir gaya tha.*' [You had fallen down.] So he told me, '*Main gir nahi gaya tha, main acting kar raha tha* – I was acting. Please don't support me when I fall – I want to fall.' It was so utterly real, and no big song or dance about it, you know – that was the great thing about Irrfan. He did not make his process public; he did not make an issue of it, like a lot of us do. Like I often did, early in my career.

SG: How will you remember him? What is the one thing that comes to your mind when you think of him?

NS: His eyes are the most memorable, absolutely. Fantastic eyes. They spoke a million things; they were transparent when they needed to be, they were hard and cold when they needed to be. And his gentle nature. I think he was a very gentle person by temperament.

PART II
2006–2013

'He took us on a journey of really high craft'

MIRA NAIR

Mira Nair's celebrated body of work includes *Mississippi Masala*, *Monsoon Wedding* and *The Reluctant Fundamentalist*. From offering Irrfan a promising role that was crushingly whittled down to a single scene in *Salaam Bombay!*, to giving him the gift of *The Namesake*, in which he delivered one of his best performances, Nair has covered both ends of the spectrum. She speaks of Irrfan with great affection, offering glimpses of the special relationship between director and actor.

Nair's latest is the BBC miniseries *A Suitable Boy*.

SHUBHRA GUPTA: Let me start at the beginning. When you walked into the National School of Drama and saw him for the very first time, what was your reaction? How did you respond to this actor called Irrfan?

MIRA NAIR: Well, I was casting *Salaam Bombay!* – it was 1986, I think – and I'm a Delhi girl, and National School of Drama is an exalted place that I definitely would go to. I wanted to even study there. So though I had come very strongly from a *cinéma vérité* tradition, *Salaam Bombay!*, which is about street kids, was always going to be street kids playing themselves. But I wanted to mix it; I wanted to go to the National School of Drama to see if I could interweave it.

I knew that Chillum was going to be Raghubir Yadav. I hoped that Naseer [Naseeruddin Shah] was going to be Baba, but it was Nana Patekar, who was very good, and Anita Kanwar. These people I knew could blend with the real kids. So the question in my mind when I went to NSD was: is there a young actor who I should look at, who could be a street kid? I remember talking to Ram Gopal Bajaj – the venerable teacher – and he allowed me to basically roam the classrooms. I walked into a basement and they were doing a workshop, like a play demonstration – I think it was Beckett but I was not certain. I saw about sixteen–twenty young people engaged in the process. And I was struck by Irrfan, because, first, he was extraordinary-looking in that hooded-eyed, quiet, intense way – what I call his praying-mantis looks; he was all angular and had a face, as we all know, of all times. You know, it can be an old man; he can be the youngest person. He looked interesting, he was listening with great care and not showing off or not being outward. He was the only one, frankly, who struck me. I talked to him after the class, and it was easy. That's all I recall, that it was very easy to communicate with him. And I said, '*Yaar, main experiment kar rahi hoon – pehli picture hai.*' [I am conducting an experiment; this is my first film.] I wasn't, like, selling myself. I was just saying that I'm doing a workshop with street kids that hopes to become a movie. Will you join me? *But yeh sab school-vool chhodna padega* [you will need to leave acting school] because you'll have to stay with me in an empty flat, and with whichever kid doesn't have a place for the night, and we are just going to go into this zone for many months. Anyway, that's what I recall, Shubhra. I don't recall any interim period of any dithering or discussion. Next thing I recall is that we – he,

Raghubir [Yadav] and I, and the cinematographer Sandi Sissel – were all sharing a completely empty flat in Bombay. I had just got some *chaddars*; I don't even think beds! Maybe two beds. And the only other important [person] was Dilip, my brother and sister-in-law's cook, who was donated to me from Delhi and came and cooked for us. That was our household for about a solid three–four months.

I rented a space and we were there for close to six weeks. Barry John, the director of the Theatre Action Group, was the director of the workshop, with essentially twenty-nine street kids I had picked from a bigger circle. And Irrfan, Raghubir, and only *much* later, like four weeks later, came Anita and Nana. So this was the group, and we worked from about 9 a.m. to 5 p.m. every day, and went from a series of theatre exercises and dance and debate to just becoming of the street and learning from them as much as we taught.

But Irrfan had to become part of this fabric and very much did. Except in one thing, which he couldn't help, which is that he was almost six-foot-three and the kids were all malnourished and reached only up to his waist. As we kept working, it became clear that Irrfan, visually, was so distinct that he could not play Salim, who was one of the street kids. And it was a terrifyingly sad realization: what could he do in *Salaam Bombay!* then? He was so much a part of us, and so copacetic, so simpatico with my direction. I mean, not my direction but the direction that the film was taking; the play, the casting, the rehearsals, everything that was going on that would become *Salaam Bombay!* He was really seeing so clearly and feeling like a part of the whole group and this very organized but mad effort. And then I started bringing the cameras into the rehearsals – which was like five weeks later – and taking the kids into a lift set, teaching the sort of discipline of what it would be to shoot. Then it became absolutely clear that he just didn't fit into this world – actually, physically and perhaps in any other way. The only part that he could do was the scribe, which was a brilliant scene into which Sooni [Taraporevala] fit a whole story. And he played it to perfection, without any rancour. Just [said to me like a] real friend, 'You owe me – *aap bhoolna mat*; don't forget.'

And *kabhi nahi bhoola*. But the point is, casting is everything and I can only think of him when it's right. If you look at my movies since *Salaam Bombay!*, I don't think there was any role that Irrfan could have actually played, except Ashoke Ganguli [his character in *The Namesake*], which came along fifteen years or so later. For me, he was always Ashoke Ganguli. It was like relief: *baba, aa jao, Irrfan bhai*. And he came. There was no audition, nothing, *kuchh nahi*. I arrived in Bombay and I was meeting people because, for me, he was *in* but I hadn't met him. Anyway, he came in a good linen shirt and just sat there languidly. We had met several times in the fifteen years as friends, but not as working people. It was very easy, so I gave him the role and he liked it. I think he had read the book between my phone call and our meeting. I said the screenplay will be based on Ashoke and Ashima, even if the book is about Gogol.

What I didn't know was that he had never been to New York, which was a boon. He had never been to America. And Ashoke had also never been to America, in the early part of the story. So it was perfect. Irrfan was like a sponge. A very quiet sponge. For him everything was new in the most beautiful way. He had an appetite for his character. He said, '*Ashoke bhi aise hi aaya hoga, yaar. Usne bhi nahi dekha hoga yeh sab. Thand mein kya pehenne ka …*' [This is how Ashoke would have arrived. He wouldn't have seen all this before. What to wear in cold weather ...] As you know, the film goes from his arrival as a young bridegroom almost to his death. So Ashoke gets more acclimatized and Americanized in the course of his becoming older and, for that entire continuum, he had Jhumpa's* father to observe and really, if he wished, to even live with. But we didn't live with them; we saw them maybe three–four times before we were filming. These were leisurely times – a weekend, a long day, Sunday meal. Not *fatafat* meetings. So Irrfan could do what he does best: observe quietly, engage if he needed. And he really did engage; he was not a formidable, inaccessible chap at all. It was like being with a friend, who saw everything but didn't actually judge. Took what he needed, in a way, but very much a student of life. But what he did best, also, for his art, was sift life; he sifted what was important from what was not important, always.

When I knew you and I were going to talk, I thought, what is it about Irrfan? Right from the beginning, I felt that he thought he was good, that he was special, not to be frittered away. Even when he may not have had anything, he was never desperate. Maybe he had those moments, but I've known him since he was just in his first month of thinking that he could be an actor. Without showing off, without speaking about it, innately he knew he had something to offer and he was not going to fritter it away, be wasteful. That was remarkable. And I know he went through about seven–eight fairly arid years. But I don't ever recall that he was any different from that period in the beginning when he knew he had something to offer. That makes him a great actor, because ego doesn't obfuscate him.

---

* Jhumpa Lahiri, the author of *The Namesake*, on which the film is based.

SG: Right. It was a hard grind, from that time when he didn't get the role you promised him in *Salaam* ..., and the time, after that arid period, when he got that much-awaited break. He got *The Warrior* and that gave him some hope. And then in 2003 came *Haasil* and after that *Maqbool*. Did you see any of these films?

MN: All of them, all of them. I went to the opening premiere of *Warrior* in London. I was with Asif [Kapadia]; I don't know if Irrfan was there – I can't recall. But I was just blown away, transported by his strength and his charisma. For Irrfan, that was the eye-opening film that made the world, and India also, aware that he existed in that powerfully charismatic way of an actor. And then I saw *Maqbool* and *Haasil*.

SG: You said that in the fifteen years between *Salaam Bombay!* and *The Namesake*, you were in touch with him. Tell me a little bit about that relationship where you didn't have to be in the same room, but you were connected.

MN: Yeah, it's very ... hard; it's a little difficult because when I think of that, I [realize] that he's really gone. I always believed, exactly as you say, that even though we were not together, it was easy access. He would write to me, send me two lines about a book that I should read. Or when we would meet. And it was only really related to *The Namesake*, but that was quite a hit, so we had a bit of a tour with it. We had Los Angeles premieres, we had Rome, we went around the world with it. So I have wonderful and very easy memories – nothing overtly special. Like, on the way to a showing, we'd stop to see a bookshop and he'd prowl around *ki*, '*Yaar, yeh kitab lena tha tere liye.*' [I wanted to buy this book for you.] He was like that, he was very much into the *nasha* of finding a melody that he loved, or a book. Now *toh* they say it's global-vobal but those days, very few people – especially those who had just always lived in Bombay – had those kinds of tentacles across the world, looking for good work, good things. He was always that way. Whether he watched something on VHS or through a video, he was always in pursuit.

And I think, as he got more fragile, he began to look for that nourishment again. Last I met him – which I certainly did not think would be the final meeting – he looked worse for the wear; I remember he looked pasty from the chemo. But he had all that *shaukeengiri* – in him still. My friend rode up on a bicycle, and Irrfan just jumped on the bicycle and said, '*Yaar, ek block ho jaye* – let me go around one block.' He was not jumping up and down with energy; he was feeling the treatment. But that *shaukeenpana* – whatever it was – he needed that, Shubhra. I think, before that, he was fearing that it was all over, that maybe he'll never feel that *nasha* again or know how to seek it. But then, whatever little I saw, quickly resolved into this. Not quickly, I'm sure. Sutapa [Sikdar] and the family had so much to do with it; he always felt so supported and loved. Also, he was doing the right thing by then, with the kids being in school in London. But it was hard to hear him be so wonderfully philosophical and open about the fact that it was not forever, you know? He knew it. That's amazing to witness. It wasn't front and centre, but it was the elephant in the room.

SG: So *The Warrior* may have been the film which got the world to look at him, but it was *The Namesake* which took him much further. He became this guy that everybody started to look out for.

MN: Yes, and want.

SG: Yeah, but I will also say this: I thought that the films that he did in the West – not yours; yours I don't consider a 'Western' film – but *The Amazing Spider-Man* ...

MN: *Life of Pi*.

SG: Yeah, *Life of Pi*. I really did not think that even Ang Lee got him fully. The film is what it is, but nobody got him the way desis did, even though it was fantastic for him to be out there and become this crossover character.

MN: Yeah, but there is one difference in the Western canon of his: after *The Namesake* was *In Treatment*, an HBO series. They totally got him in that. And he got it – he was amazing. But it was extremely related to *The Namesake,* and the way he had got the *dhun* [tune] of Ashoke Ganguli so well. I don't know the answer to your question, Shubhra, but the thing is that the task of a director is to make the actor bloom, to protect the actor as well. So it is important for the director to find their way into the actor and unlock [their qualities] or ask to make it happen. With the West, generally – and I have some experience of it – when you cast a big actor in these tent-pole movies, they tell you from the beginning, 'I am going to come to the set with the character sussed.' Like Johnny Depp told me with *Shantaram*. I mean, *he* didn't tell me that; other people around him told me that you just receive, baby. I don't work that way, but that is the style. They come all sussed. And maybe they expected that of Irrfan, that he must be in a state of readiness to receive what he would get from the director. So often I've seen it, Shubhra, there's very little communication between the two. I'm not saying Ang is like that – he is completely not like that – but one never knows what goes on between the director and the actor. I remember Irrfan calling me during *Life of Pi* to speak about some lines in the voice-over. Because we speak the same language, literally and otherwise! So just to take away the ... unknown fear, just to make it easier, to make it bloom a bit. A lot of directors don't have that type of patience or access. I don't know what happened in those movies, but there was a lot of sink-or-swim, do what you have to do, I think.

SG: I've been grappling with this question for a while now. Lots of people say that of course he was a star. But as far as legacy Bollywood was concerned, they did not think of him as a star; they always thought of him as a 'character actor'.

MN: Yeah, that's Bollywood for you. He knew he wasn't going to be the conventional hero, singing and dancing. I don't think he ever wanted that, and he certainly knew that he was not that. I don't think he came to Bombay with hopes of being a hero which were dashed to the ground. I think he actually just felt so propelled to act that it led him out of Jaipur into the National School of Drama. Because he had to act. And I don't think it was in a showy way, even in the beginning. You know, when young people say I was performing for my parents and all, I can't imagine him having done that. He came to it as a craft and as a study.

I didn't see him [when he was] in the arid zone, after *Salaam Bombay!* and into the television scene. I was in touch with him, but not seeing him. So I don't how he felt. But I don't think he ever thought that he would become the chocolate boy of Bollywood. Or that he lusted to be a star in that way. What he wanted to do was what he was doing, in the last fifteen years of his life, which is to do the best international films, but also that lovely comedy routine he did, that was just so fantastic. ABC ... what was it called? ABD?

SG: AIB? The All India Bakchod guys.

MN: All India Bakchod, that's it! That was brilliant. So what I'm saying is, Irrfan was at his happiest in those years, when he did *The Namesake*, *Life of Pi*, but also did Bakchod and [*Life in a...*] *Metro*. *The Namesake* and also, to some extent, *The Lunchbox**, later, I find to be very rigorous films for him. *Sab kuchh theek tha uske liye* – they were perfect for him. Everything was at his level. I feel that he is very nourished in *The Namesake*, by great performers, the way it's shot, the way it's sculpted.

SG: So how did you think of Tabu?

MN: Well, to be honest, it was Konkona [Sen Sharma] for a long time. And then two or three weeks before we were going to shoot, Konkona had to go and do Aparna di's [Aparna Sen] film, and I couldn't believe it. But that too must have been a blessing because it was always a problem to think of lovely young Konkona as the mother of Gogol, you know? I really wanted to cast Bengalis – that was the thing. That's why I didn't go to Tabu in the first place. But then, as these things happen, we had already cast Kal [Penn] and cast this family. I don't remember what propelled me but I'm sure it's her ability to always just become the character. Tabu is scintillating in that deeper way. But also, I was very influenced by Ritwik Ghatak and [his film] *Meghe Dhaka Tara* while making *The Namesake*. You know, Supriya [Choudhury], her eyes and the way he shot her, Soviet-style, and the close-ups – I did all that in *The Namesake*. And Tabu recalls those faces. Supriya's also in *The Namesake*; she plays Tabu's [Ashima's] nani. So Tabu belongs; even though she's not Bengali, she looks like that. And I loved her in *Viraag*. *Viraag*?

---

* A 2013 Ritesh Batra film

SG: *Virasat?**
MN: *Virasat*, yes. You know when she does that comic thing – I loved that. She can be a serious Bengali Soviet face, and she can be a total mischievous imp. And she just got out of everything that she was in to be in the film! I was amazed.

SG: How were they together?
MN: While shooting, they were beautifully distant. They lived in the same building in Times Square – different apartments – and I know that they preferred to be driven to work in different cars. I thought that was very lovely because Ashoke and Ashima, especially in the beginning, really did not know each other. And of course, Tabu and Irrfan really knew each other, but I liked that they kept their distance to help the Ashoke–Ashima story. So they were never pally-wally, no friction; they were at arm's length but in the most comfortable way, so that when they were together, we had that slight frisson of not knowing each other. They were very easy together; they would feel very comfortable, but at the same time, they wanted to be sure if they were doing it right. Not always querying, because by the time we were shooting, we were very well prepared with all those things – accent and dialect-building. We didn't overprepare at all, because I wanted to keep it easy. But they were very happy to give it everything. And the patience with which we worked: it was quite detailed, almost microscopic. Both of them were really engaged in that process, making it excellent. Always a keenness *ki* is it right? And throughout, taking joy in doing it as beautifully as possible. That was definitely the vibe all through the shoot.

---

* A 1997 Priyadarshan film

SG: I just saw *Migration*,* where he plays a tiny little role of a gay man. Is this the first time that he plays a gay man?

MN: That's right.

SG: He's not 'effeminate'; he just transforms into this gay person. Tell me a little bit about that.

MN: Well, *Migration* was inspired by the endless facades that we live with, as well as AIDS as the great leveller of any class. In that generation of twenty years ago, how many closeted-gay husbands do you know? How many people are married who are in the closet? Who have children, and their wives suffer. So the idea of camouflage, that you don't appear 'effeminate' or fake; it's all hidden – Irrfan understood that. Irrfan loved the *doobna* [immersion] – the journey itself. He never thought of it as just a five-minute role and asked that he be given three more lines. But also, he did feel very protected with me; that '*Whatever tu kar rahi hai, achha hi hoga yaar.*' [Whatever you are doing must be good.] There was never going to be anything pedestrian or *fatafat*. Or exploitative. It would, hopefully, be real; some risk-taking in cinema, we hoped.

SG: From your perspective – somebody who's an insider-outsider, who knows India so well, a Delhi girl and a global girl – how do you look at Irrfan in Bollywood? Do you think he made a difference? Did he really break the mould in some manner?

MN: I definitely think he makes a difference anywhere, frankly. In Bollywood more particularly Naseeruddin Shah and Dilip Kumar before, and Guru Dutt before that, Waheeda Rehman as well, have shown us that it was possible to be a great actor within

---

* A 2008 Mira Nair short film

the commerciality of the time. But with Irrfan, what was really fab was that he also brought comedy to it. He was like Balraj Sahni meets – not quite Johnny Walker – at least Asrani. He could do *Paan Singh* [*Tomar*] with *Metro* and, of course, *Piku*. He made himself belong and took us on a journey of really high craft. Sometimes the films weren't always as high-crafted, but he was always. But that's what Irrfan did differently from the high-calibre actors that entered Bollywood, and stayed that way; he showed us that he could do anything. And what he didn't want to do, he didn't do. He isn't prancing around trees and singing because I don't know if he could do that.

SG: So he then opened the doors for people like Rajkummar Rao – is that what he did? What did he actually manage to do, as far as shifting the needle is concerned?

MN: There was Irrfan and then there was streaming – the incredible television series that were coming out, pretty much in a confluence. Irrfan's presence sort of opened the door for the absolutely high-calibre actors, like Jaideep Ahlawat, Rasika Dugal, who are not going to ever have to question that they can retain their calibre and yet be a part of strong commercial Indian filmmaking. Which is beautiful. Irrfan is part of that journey; that journey is going to become ever more fluid and expansive.

SG: Last question: when you close your eyes and think of Irrfan, what comes to your mind?

MN: Fun. You know, intensity, *woh sab hai*, but he had an ability to see, have humour. We shared a way of seeing through things with love. Seeing through things with love – that's Irrfan.

'His talent couldn't be held down'

SOONI TARAPOREVALA

Sooni Taraporevala, Mira Nair's long-time screenwriter and collaborator, was a first-hand observer of the heartbreak Irrfan went through when his role in *Salaam Bombay!* was reduced to a blink-and-miss scene. But because it was Irrfan, he left an impact, and it is, she says, one of her favourite scenes in the script.

Taraporevala, who also wrote the screenplay for *The Namesake*, is equally known for her directorials *Little Zizou* and *Yeh Ballet*.

––––

SHUBHRA GUPTA: I've heard that all of you had lived together in a little flat, doing three months of rehearsals with the street children for *Salaam Bombay!* Can you tell me a little bit about that time?

SOONI TARAPOREVALA: Actually, Shubhra, I wasn't living in that space because I'm from Bombay, so I had my own home. That space was really for people who were not from Bombay, like Irrfan. But of course we were in and out all the time. The workshop was amazing, because I had never been to one like that before and Barry John [who conducted the workshop] was just stupendous. Irrfan was part of that, as was I. I have a unique credit in that film, as screenwriter and still photographer, which I am really proud of.

So I have a lot of photographs of the workshop, and one in particular is one of my favourites – it's in *Home in the City: Bombay**: a black-and-white picture of an exercise. I don't remember the exact exercise, but everyone had to be blindfolded and there's a picture of Irrfan with Sarfuddin – Sarfu, one of the kids – both of them have blindfolds on and it's one of my favourite pictures.

Irrfan was always a part of the workshop but he was, of course, older than the kids and he wasn't a street kid. Towards the end of a workshop, Sandi Sissel – the cinematographer – came to town. I think Mira [Nair] might have been a little nervous about, you know, hinging the entire film on a bunch of street kids and, for her, it might have been a comfort factor having someone like Irrfan anchor the group. But then, Sandi saw it with new eyes and said, 'You know, I signed onto a film about a group of street kids. And with Irrfan, with all due respect, it becomes like juvenile delinquents, because it changes the nature of the story.' He was just so much older and stood out so much because he was lanky; the kids were all much littler. Fortunately for the film, but unfortunately for Irrfan, Mira did a rethink and told him that he couldn't be part of the gang. And he was so totally devastated. I still remember that so clearly – feeling so conflicted because I knew it was best for the film but I really, really felt terrible for him. I comforted him as best I could – I mean, we were friends then – and I told him some stupid cliché like one door closes, another opens – all that kind of stuff. And he very sportingly agreed to play the letter writer, which is a nothing scene, but he played it so brilliantly. It is actually one of my favourite scenes, even in

---

* Sooni Taraporevala, *Home in the City: Bombay 1977*, New Delhi: HarperCollins India, 2017.

the script. And then I didn't hear of him or see much of him till I got an invitation to go see *The Warrior* at the British Council auditorium. He was there, and when I watched that film, I knew he had got his break and was going to be on to great things. I can't profess to know Irrfan really well, as the other people you've spoken to have, but I know that he had a deep feeling of gratitude and respect towards Asif Kapadia. Because I think Asif really gave him his big break in life. And I have another connection, later, with that. I was approached to adapt *Last Man in Tower**[*] by Aravind Adiga, and Irrfan is the one who initiated that and Asif was going to direct. Ben Rekhi [the American filmmaker], who has since become a close friend, was producing it. So I wrote two drafts, but Asif was busy with his first documentary and was kind of going off on another path. And then Irrfan had second thoughts, because he said, 'I don't want to play old, because if I do, I'll be typecast in this industry for the rest of my life.' Ben was particularly disappointed because it was Irrfan who had started us on this journey. I went to meet him at his house, I tried to convince him, but he was kind of on the fence.

SG: I want to ask you, from your inside-outside vantage, why did mainstream Bollywood not know what to make of this man?
ST: I don't think Bollywood really – I'm sorry to use that term as a shorthand for mainstream Hindi cinema – I don't think they're very much into good acting. I don't think that's part of the brief of what they do and so, a fantastic actor can be admired from afar, but what do we do with him? We don't want fantastic actors; we want over-the-top actors, we want loudness, we want everything that Irrfan is not, actually. That's my take on it. One thing I used to hear about naturalistic acting: 'He's not even acting! What is

---

* Aravind Adiga, *Last Man in Tower*, London: Fourth Estate, 2011.

he doing?' So that kind of mindset, that acting is something that is obvious, that a person is acting – Irrfan was just the absolute opposite of that. And he did not have the world of movies – alternative, independent cinema – to really support him. Yes, he of course made some great films, but maybe in another country he would have been a huge star because there would have been many more such movies that he could have been in.

SG: He did actually in Hollywood. I mean, he did go off and make movies there; but from my perspective, I think those films were probably great for his CV, great for him to get a sense of how Hollywood works. Their pay cheques must have been really fantastic. But in terms of giving him his due, I don't think even they had a handle on what to do. You know, you do a two-minute bit and you lift it, because you're Irrfan. But you don't really get to do something which is a headline part. He's also in the film, but he's not front and centre.

ST: Yeah. But you kind of excuse Hollywood, because, I mean, those are American films and even now, the roles for Indian characters are very limited in American films. But when your own country doesn't know what to do with you, that's a different matter, you know. I was so pleasantly amazed and surprised about the tsunami of really sincere, deep-felt sorrow at his passing. Which was, for me at least, a little at odds with what people did with him when he was alive. I mean, how he was used in films. So I think there was a recognition of how great he was; maybe there was a little guilt about not giving him his due when he was alive … I don't know.

SG: Do you remember, while you were shooting *The Namesake*, how he approached the role, for example? Mira talked about how he and Tabu had never been to America before, so for them it was more like an opening up of their universe, and both did a great job of being Bengali because they spent time with Jhumpa Lahiri's folks. I was wondering if you had some memories of the time when you shot that?

ST: Of course, Irrfan being married to a Bengali helped. I wasn't there for the America shoot; I was only in Calcutta for about two weeks. I shot a few stills, and Irrfan was always very zen on set – very calm. I have stills of him with things happening all around him, and he's just sitting calmly. I never really discussed the character with him, but I know that in lesser hands, Ashoke Ganguli would have just disappeared into the background. Because he is so gentle, not a loud character. It takes an actor with great confidence to play someone like him. And he disappears! His role is not that large and then he disappears halfway into the film. So only someone like Irrfan could have played him, and played him so well that he became the heart and soul of the film. Because, you know, objectively, if you read the book, Gogol is the main character – and we changed that. We made the older generation as important, if not more important than the younger generation. And out of the older generation, Ashima's character has much more to do, and Ashoke is really like the silent rock, and only someone like Irrfan could play that and make him so memorable.

SG: It's the little things that he does: a little nod there, a look here, subtle and powerful.

ST: Yeah. I call him a poet, but in the medium of cinema. Just like poets can evoke a whole world with the conjunction of a few words, that's what he did; he could evoke a whole world with a glance or a look. That was the beauty of his art. He could distil an essence in a glance. It's something that can't be taught.

SG: I feel he would have done such a great job of just being a romantic hero. Because he had, like you said, the soul of a poet. And only towards the end – in *Piku* – was he allowed this space. He was this quirky guy who could also be romantic rather than just a full-bodied romantic.

ST: Absolutely. Those eyes, yeah. And that smile, absolutely. But this is one of Bollywood ... mainstream Hindi cinema's shortcomings, as to who is considered a romantic hero or heroine and what they have to look like. For instance, our main character in *Salaam Bombay!*, Chaipau – played by Shafiq [Syed], such a brilliant actor – never got a chance in Hindi cinema because of the way he looked.* It's sad that we are so short-sighted. And I don't think it's the audience, it's the gatekeepers who make these decisions.

In all the chats about the films that got made, I forgot about the films that didn't get made, and how helpful Irrfan was. I had written a kind of very large, expensive sci-fi movie back in the day, I think 2015 or 2016. And I had approached Irrfan and he was very responsive; he would always reply to messages. He sent me a book that he was thinking about adapting – *The Mirror of Beauty*† – that didn't go anywhere. And [he was working on this] project which was called 'Three and a Half'. He called me on set – he was shooting for a thriller with Aishwarya Rai [Bachchan] ... I forget the name.

---

* A few years later, Shafiq Syed was reportedly found working as a rickshaw driver in Bengaluru.
† Shamsur Rahman Faruqi, *The Mirror of Beauty*, New Delhi: Penguin Random House India, 2013.

SG: *Jazbaa.**

ST: Yeah, yeah. He called me there. He had read the script and he was really encouraging. That was the time I think he was doing *Piku*; he had invited me to the preview and Kangana [Ranaut] was sitting behind me and he introduced me to her. He attached himself to the project and so did Kangana, but it didn't go anywhere. He introduced me to Anup Singh also, because he thought that he would be a good contact to have for the financing.

SG: You saw him at a time when he was just about coming into the industry. He wasn't the Irrfan that he became later, someone that people were starting to reach out to and create roles for. When you're looking back at his journey, what is it that strikes you about it?

ST: I guess what strikes me is that there is some justice in the world. Between *Salaam Bombay!* and *The Namesake* were many, many years. But once he got his break, he was off like a comet. So life is unfair sometimes but there is also justice in the world, and talent will out – that's what I get from Irrfan's journey. His talent couldn't be held down.

But till the end, he never played a star with me, or I don't think with anyone. I'm sure he was like that with others also. He had no starry *nakhras* about him, which was very, very gratifying. And he was also always, constantly looking for things. Like, you know, this book that he gave me to read and he wanted to adapt, nothing came of it. But I think he was always searching for things. It wasn't like he was sitting back and things were coming to him.

---

* A 2015 Sanjay Gupta film

I think Homi [Adajania] would be really good to talk to because Homi lost his father when he was quite young, and he lost his sister more recently. Homi has had an experience with death and dying, but he's still such an amazingly rambunctious, crazy personality. At that point in their lives – Homi's and Irrfan's – they were a perfect fit and I feel like it was someone up there who put them together for Irrfan's last film. I don't think, besides Homi, he would have ever had this kind of camaraderie with anyone – [as Irrfan is] someone who's been through what he's going through; that's the way I feel.

SG: Yeah. Because by then, I think he knew. Not just the fact that he had had the diagnosis and that it would be a struggle, but I think by that time he knew this wasn't something he would be walking past. He kept hoping but he also looked at death coming. A lot of great actors never stop looking and observing.

ST: Observing? Yeah, all the time. He was very encouraging of people who were struggling or trying to make it. He was never that closed-off kind of star who tends to say, 'Speak to my manager.'

SG: When you think of Irrfan, what is the one thing that comes to your mind?

ST: His eyes and his languid half-smile.

'Woh yaad rahega zindagi bhar'

ANURAG BASU

Anurag Basu – director, producer, screenwriter – made *Life in a… Metro* with four parallel tracks. One of them belongs to Irrfan and Konkona Sen Sharma, and it pretty much takes over the whole film. Monty is a thirty-something man of deep inexperience, desperate to make a connection with a woman, and yet, even in that desperation, there is a gentleness and humour to him, an ability to laugh at life's quirks. Monty was a breakthrough for Irrfan, allowing him to travel from the intense to the light-hearted with ease.

SHUBHRA GUPTA: Irrfan's whole trajectory changed with *Life in a… Metro*, and the audience started to see him in a completely different manner. With Monty [his character in *Metro*, Irrfan became mainstream, in a manner of speaking. Tell me about *Metro* and about working together in TV before that.

ANURAG BASU: Irrfan was very upset I didn't cast him for *Gangster* [which released in 2006] because we had done a lot of work in television together. I think my best work with Irrfan was on television, which is not out there. So I said, '*Yaar*, Irrfan, if I cast you, it will fall in the same *Haasil* space; it will be like an extension of what you have already done, and I want to do something new.' When I wrote *Metro*, from day one, I saw only Irrfan in Monty's role. I imagined only Irrfan playing that character. *Uska jo dialogue ka metre hai* – the role was written with him in mind.

Sutapa [Sikdar] played a big role in convincing Irrfan. Irrfan was not very happy with the narration. I called Sutapa and said, '*Thoda Bengali mein samjhao*.' [Persuade him in Bengali.] I played the Bengali card with Sutapa. *laughs* The first day, after the first take of the first scene we did, Irrfan was completely convinced. He was happy playing that character. It was done very quickly; we shot for ten days and it was magical.

I have done a lot of work with Irrfan. He always knew his work from the very beginning actually. Even when we were in television, he always knew his work and he kind of guarded his skill. Because we tend to put actors in boxes. He never wanted people to do that. So he said no to a lot of projects, and we used to wonder why he is saying no. *Lekin usne bacha ke rakha apne aap ko bahut dino tak*. [But for the longest time he preserved himself.]

Before Irrfan, people used to see mainstream actors differently: North Indian, *gora chitta*, six-pack. After Irrfan came, people started appreciating acting differently, even in mainstream films. And that effect can be seen now with Pankaj [Tripathi] and Nawaz [Nawazuddin Siddiqui]. *Nahi toh yeh Pankaj, Nawaz dus saal baad aate* [they would have arrived ten years later], had it not been for Irrfan. This legacy is created by Irrfan. Other actors are benefiting from it now.

SG: Naseeruddin Shah said almost the exact same thing. Tell me about how you came to know Irrfan?

AB: I was directing a show called *Tara*, while Sutapa was writing *Banegi Apni Baat* [both Zee TV shows]. Irrfan was a part of *Banegi Apni Baat*. That time the television clan was very small; we all knew each other, we were friends, we used to go to each other's places, party with each other. Irrfan was not very keen on doing soap after soap. He was doing very little work. Then television started doing one-offs like [*Star*] *Bestsellers*, *X Zone**, *Mano Ya Na Mano*† – that's when Irrfan became very keen. Through those short films, *hum apni cinema ki bhook mitaate thay* [we used to satisfy our hunger for cinema]. For us, it was like doing mini-films.

We did a show called *Saturday Suspense*‡ and another one called *Thriller at 10*§. I think Irrfan was just doing TV while waiting for something great to come along.

I remember doing one scene so well. Irrfan [his character] is looking for his pump because he is having an asthma attack. First he looks inside his car in the car park. Then he enters the drawing room, and then the bedroom. It was a ten-minute shot, and I told Irrfan that I don't want to cut and shoot it; I want to do it in one go. 'I'll follow you with my handheld camera.' And then Irrfan began. He started with the car, he came inside, and by this time, his wheezing had become [more intense] and, by the end of shot, I was so scared. I was wondering if I should cut it there. I've never seen any actor, ever in my life, do something like that: his eyes were red, the eyeballs had moved up and it was

* A 1998–2000 Zee TV show
† A 2006 Zee TV show
‡ A 1997–1999 Zee TV show
§ A 2000 Zee TV show

so real. I have never seen any actor perform like that. There was this complete silence on the whole set; everyone was stunned. He's that kind of actor. 'Kar lete hain' [Let's do it] – that's what he said. Other actors would have prepared for three–four days before doing a take like that. His was impromptu. I said, 'We'll do it,' and he said yes, and then we did that shot. He was brilliant, yaar; he was amazing.

He was the favourite actor for all of us. You know, Bestsellers was only thirty-two episodes. There were also a lot of one-offs which Zee and Sony were producing at the time. We were all directing those mini-series – they were about forty-five minutes, fifty minutes, sometimes one-hour long. One week, one story – that kind of stuff.

I was doing another show called Ajeeb Dastaan. Irrfan did a lot of episodes for Ajeeb Dastaan also. We used to do all those amazing stories by Manto, Maupassant, Roald Dahl on that show. We did some of our best work together; I would even say the same thing about directors like Sriram Raghavan.

The other day my assistants were praising Andhadhun*. So I said, 'You know, he [Raghavan] has done better work in television than in Andhadhun, story-wise.' We have all done our best work in television. We were young at that time; we were all full of ideas.

SG: When did you first meet Irrfan? Do you remember your first meeting?

AB: I remember the day I first met him clearly. There was this show that Annu Kapoor used to anchor – Antakshari. I was there as a guest. There was a Star team, the Banegi Apni Baat team and another team. Suddenly this guy got up and started protesting: 'Yaar, cheating ho rahi hai; this is bakwaas.' Ekdum straight face,

---

* A 2018 Sriram Raghavan film

creating a ruckus on the set. We all became serious; we didn't know Irrfan. We found out later that he was joking, you know? It was hilarious, and that image of Irrfan has stayed with me. I think he was always bohemian by nature; that reflected in his acting. He loved people who were bohemian and he connected with them.

SG: Bohemian?

AB: *Haan, matlab fakeer mijaaz ke log.* He used to mingle with everybody but he needed his own space, on every set. Some beautiful corner with a little tree – Irrfan would go sit there.

SG: Tigmanshu Dhulia said to me that in drama school NSD, he had this tiny room – the smallest room – which was in one corner, and he would be there all the time. Or he would be in Sutapa's house, reading. Or talking about movies or just hanging around.

AB: Yeah, I completely relate to what Tishu said. Actually, on my set also, I remember, Irrfan *aise dikhta nahi tha saamne*. [You wouldn't find him in front of you.] He'd put his chair in a corner, and he'd read something, or talk to somebody. And we had fun. He used to fly a lot of kites. Irrfan used to call me: '*Patang rakha hai kya aapne?*' [Do you have the kites?] I said, '*Haan, rakha hai apna patang gaadi mein.*' [Yes, my kite is in my car.] I think we were shooting for *Metro* in January/February. While the set was being lit, we would fly kites.

There is this scene where Irrfan and Konkona are on a rooftop. We reached the location a little early on the day of the shoot. We said, '*Chalo chhatt pe patang udaenge; phir shooting karenge.*' [Let's go fly kites on the roof; then we'll shoot.] Where I'm sitting right now is also a flat with a terrace. When Irrfan first came here – I think the last time I met him was in this very office – he sat and talked. Then he said, '*Ek din aata hoon – patang udaenge yahan khade hoke.*' [I'll come one day and we'll fly kites from here.]

SG: Let's return to *Life in a... Metro*. Was Konkona always supposed to play opposite Irrfan?

AB: Irrfan was always in my mind. Konkona happened later, actually. I think there were two castings I was totally sure about when I was writing *Metro*. Irrfan and Kangana, whom I was working with on *Gangster* when *Metro* was taking shape in my mind. Everyone else's casting happened slowly.

SG: There's this fantastic scene between Konkona and Irrfan, in which she says that she really didn't like that he was staring at her chest. It was amazing the way he did that and managed to not appear crass.

AB: The first scene in the restaurant, Konkona was a little awkward, because of what Irrfan does. I told Konkona that we have this scene because it will connect with another scene later – that second scene where they are sitting and talking on the beach. But I think *uss pehle scene mein* their foundation was set.

See, I am notorious for not writing scenes. After that scene, I had a structure in my mind. I had scribbled some lines. Irrfan said, '*Chalo ek gaadi mein jaate hain; scene banate hue jaate hain.*' [Let's go in the same car and plan the scene.] It was in Madh Island, by the way, where they are sitting by the sea. So we wrote the scene while on the road. Irrfan made a big contribution to it.

SG: I think in that scene you can see the heart and the soul of Monty.

AB: Irrfan was a bit like him. He used to appreciate beauty. If a girl was going past, then Irrfan's *gardan* [neck] would surely turn.

I'll also tell you a secret about Monty. In the beginning, he was meant to be Debu, a Bengali guy. Because Irrfan has had a brush with several Bengalis in his life, he knows the essence of how they think and talk. Then I was shooting and thought that this should be the climax [in which Irrfan rides a horse]. So I said, 'Irrfan, can we do that take again?' Because we Bengalis don't ride horses, this can't be the climax. So then we tweaked the character. This is why the scene became a bit magical. You know, the side of Irrfan we try to tap into in *Metro* is the Irrfan I always knew – full of life. I think that's the reason I saw him in that character.

SG: That's why so many people suddenly became aware of him in a different way. Before *Metro*, he was niche. *Metro* was a hit, and that changed things.

AB: It happened with *Haasil*, if you ask me; not with *Metro*. There are very few characters which can be remembered for a very long time. I will put Irrfan's character in *Haasil* with Gabbar and Mogambo [two of Hindi cinema's most memorable villains] and all these classic characters. *Woh yaad rahega zindagi bhar* – I'll remember him all my life.

SG: If I am not mistaken, Irrfan told Tigmanshu that this character is like a Gabbar Singh; people will remember. But despite his villainy, he's still someone that I feel for. I feel for him because his being provincial holds him back. The reason I was so struck by Monty – and I still think it is a very difficult role to play – is that he's from nowhere. You can make out that he's an Allahabad *ka launda* in *Haasil*. But you don't know where Monty is from. He lives in Bombay, sure, but where is he from? One can't tell from his accent; he's a wannabe, he admits that he's thirty-five or thirty-seven. He's never been with a woman.

AB: Maybe because he was switched from being a Bengali to a Punjabi, he became a nowhere man. The character became unique as a result. Because his name was Monty but he continued playing Debu in it – that's the magic. I think he caught the *sur* in the second take, and we improvised so many things completely.

SG: I've always thought that he's one of the few actors who was never predictable. And when he teamed up with you, who also likes working on the fly, it must have been quite something. Stepping forward a little, how is it that you didn't work with him again, or did you do anything else with him after *Metro*?

AB: Before *Life in a... Metro,* he was really upset with me because of *Gangster* – really, really upset. We didn't speak for a long time after that.

I knew his attitude towards me changed a little bit. Then *Metro* happened. After *Metro*, there was no scope [of casting Irrfan] in *Kites* [2010]. I really wanted him to play Saswata's [Chatterjee, who played Jagga's father] character in *Jagga Jasoos* [2017]. And he was almost finalized, but Irrfan was also busy doing these international productions, *so* Jagga *mein raita phaila tha dates ka*. We couldn't manage the dates; it was unfortunate. Irrfan was the first choice; he loved it too and wanted to do it. With Irrfan's presence, the film would have been something else altogether.

And then we were planning to do another film. He wanted to play Monty again in some different form. He said, '*Main* Qarib Qarib Singlle *bhi uske jaise hi karne wala hoon* – I will play my character along the same lines.' That's what Shailja [Kejriwal] and Sutapa told me. He wanted to extend that character in another film. Then there was an amazing script, the *Metro* sequel. Not a sequel in the strict sense – there were two stories rather than four. We were discussing that, actually, before he was diagnosed.

That was the last meeting we had. I also discussed *Ludo* [2020] with him, but I was not sure if I would be able to cast him. But he loved Pankaj's [Tripathi] character. Pankaj's lines I wrote with Irrfan in mind because I thought Irrfan would do it. This is my trick as a writer: if I want to make any character different, I think of Irrfan playing it.

Even now. I know Irrfan will never be able to play it but if I think Irrfan will do it, if I picture him playing that character, it automatically becomes unique.

SG: You said he was very busy because he was doing all those international films. If you ask me, I don't think he did anything spectacular in any of those films. He was just a cog in a very big wheel. What do you think was going on, when he was saying yes to all those films?

AB: I think it was just … stepping stones to get to an international pinnacle. This is a process one has to go through. He did this in the Hindi film industry also. It took time for a *Haasil* or a *Metro*. One needs to do all these other films to arrive at this space. I think he was going in the right direction; it would have happened very soon.

Who was that *Reluctant Fundamentalist** ka actor who later got nominated for an Oscar?

SG: Riz Ahmed.

AB: Yeah. So Irrfan would have also got a nomination very soon. Riz Ahmed has done so many films like the ones Irrfan was doing. Finally, he got a film which brought him that close. I think that film was just round the corner for Irrfan.

---

* *The Reluctant Fundamentalist* – a 2012 Mira Nair film

SG: Not just internationally, Irrfan's presence meant something to the Hindi film industry. Why do you think it took Bollywood so long to get to the point where they could start thinking of casting him?

AB: The reason is Irrfan was also protecting his … He could have done *chhote-mote* character roles. But he said no to a lot of films. He knew his worth and he waited for a *Haasil* to come along. He did small films in between, but he also said no. Actors like Irrfan from NSD will immediately get nice character roles which will have a presence but will not create any mark. I'm sure he must have got a lot of films like that. I think he waited for the right opportunity, the right film. Things started changing from 2000. *The Warrior* came in 2001. *Haasil* was 2003. *Maqbool* was 2004. That's when the change began.

SG: So is there something about him that will always stay with you?

AB: A lot of things. I really love Irrfan and Sutapa both, actually. I remember their one-bedroom in Malad – Evershine Nagar. I still remember the view from that window; it used to overlook the mangroves. There were no other buildings. It was in a proper corner. I've been to that house, his Madh Island *ka ghar*. I sincerely believe Sutapa was Irrfan's strength. Irrfan was Irrfan because of Sutapa. A lot of his decisions about scripts and films were based on her suggestions. When he was diagnosed – because I had gone through the same thing* – I thought he'd fight; it would go away. He also didn't take it very seriously …

---

* Anurag Basu was diagnosed with leukemia in 2004.

SG: You also went through some very difficult years, but you overcame it.

AB: Correct. That's why I was always hopeful *ki yaar, yeh bhi kar lega*. [He will also overcome.]

SG: Did you speak to each other?

AB: We spoke, yeah. But I was in touch with Sutapa more than with Irrfan, throughout the treatment. I spoke to him before he went to London.

SG: I'm told he would talk about being able to watch the impending thing coming at him. I don't know what it takes for someone to be able to say that.

AB: Yeah, Sutapa told me. In between the treatment, she came to Bombay twice and we spoke at length. She was saying the same thing to me. He was smoking cigarettes. He wasn't supposed to but he didn't quit it till the end. That's Irrfan.

SG: What is the one thing that you will remember him by?

AB: Laughter, *yaar*. *Ek toh hansta nahi; jab hansta tha, hansi rukti nahi thi*. [First off, he would hardly laugh; when he did, his laughter wouldn't stop.] His laughter was infectious; you could hear it from a distance. It was a very peculiar laughter, very uniquely him, like everything else.

SG: Everybody speaks about his eyes and how magnetic they were … but you remember his laughter?

AB: Yes, when he would laugh, he'd have tears coming out of his eyes within two seconds. He would laugh and laugh and laugh. You usually don't see Irrfan like that. He was very intense. That is why when he would laugh, it was really adorable. There's a very soft side to Irrfan which I really love. Everyone knows his intense side. But he had a *sufiyaana* side. Even though he didn't understand it, he used to like listening to *baul* songs. He used to come to my Saraswati *pujo* and demand folk songs. We used to play folk songs for Irrfan when he would come for our *pujo*.

SG: He really played a great Bengali character in *The Namesake*. Did he get the cadence from being at the *pujos*?

AB: No. Sutapa was there. I think Mira [Nair] also; she studied in Kolkata, she knows Kolkata Bengali culture very well. The way she shot Calcutta in *The Namesake*, none of us Bengali directors could do it.

SG: Yes, the film is wonderful. But I'm just wondering if you regretted not working with him after *Metro*.

AB: *Bahut regret hai.* The frequency with which we used to work in TV never happened in films. I always had him on my wishlist after *Life in a... Metro*.

'He set the bar so high as an actor and as a human being'

KONKONA SEN SHARMA

Konkona Sen Sharma and Irrfan's love at second sight in *Life in a... Metro* was the best thing about the film. Sen Sharma, the National Award-winning actor (*Mr and Mrs Iyer*, *Omkara*) and director (*A Death in the Gunj*), worked in several other films with Irrfan, but none as memorable as *Metro*.

SHUBHRA GUPTA: You've done several films with Irrfan. Tell me about your experience working with him.

KONKONA SEN SHARMA: Of course *Talvar* and *Life in a... Metro* are the ones which are known. I've also done *Yun Hota Toh Kya Hota*, which was directed by Naseer saab [Naseeruddin Shah]. And there were many others, obscure ones, which we did in the early years. I had actually forgotten some of these, but now that I'm talking to you, let me note them down. One was *Dil Kabbadi**, which was based on a Woody Allen film – with Rahul Bose, Irrfan, Soha Ali Khan and me. There was a film called *Meridian* [*Lines*]†, about reincarnation, which didn't

---

* A 2008 Anil Sharma film
† A 2013 Venod Mitra film

release. *Deadline** is about a kidnapping, with Sandhya Mridul, Irrfan and me. And *Right Yaaa Wrong*†, with Sunny Deol, Irrfan and me.

SG: That's quite a lot of work.

KSS: Yeah, I moved to Bombay in 2005. I came here to do Rajat Kapoor's *Mixed Doubles* and, right before that, I probably did *Yun Hota Toh Kya Hota* with Naseer saab. I was very much in awe of Irrfan because of *Haasil* and *Maqbool*. I was a huge fan already and I wanted to work with him. In *Yun Hota Toh Kya Hota*, I remember we hardly had any scenes together. We all had to travel to the US, so we may have met outside of shooting a little bit, but nothing very much. I remember that Irrfan had really liked my work in *Yun Hota Toh Kya Hota*, so I was beyond thrilled because I considered him such a fantastic actor. And I really didn't think it was a great performance, but I was very, very thrilled because he was really high up in my world. I was just in love with him at that time, you know? As an actor. And, of course, Naseer saab – so it was really wonderful.

Because I was also kind of new to Bombay between 2005 and 2008, I was working a lot and trying to find interesting work. Somehow, a lot of those films from that time didn't really go anywhere; they were not great films. But I remember thinking if Irrfan is in the film, it must be good and I must do it. First we did *Meridian* and, at that time, I don't think either of us was very well known.

There was a series of films at that time which I said yes to, thinking, 'Oh, Irrfan's in this film so it's going to be decent.' And

---

* A 2006 Tanveer Khan film
† A 2010 Neeraj Pathak film

that didn't always happen. Because I think Irrfan himself, poor fellow, was trying to find interesting work to do. As a result, to be honest, both of us did a few duds at that time. Not that I want to disrespect any of the films we did when it gave us a certain experience. It paid us, it enabled us – me, certainly – to stay on in Bombay and continue to do work. But I remember him and me sometimes laughing, thinking that we are doing these films hoping for the best. And I told him, 'Irrfan, I'm doing it because you're in it. Even then you're not convinced of it.' And we were both laughing, saying, '*Arre, yeh toh karna padta hai kabhi kabhi.*' [One has to do such things sometimes.] So, you know, there was always a lot of ease in our communication.

SG: Do you remember when you first met him?
KSS: No, I don't. I don't because I ... why don't I remember? It seems like I've always known him. Because even though we never got to know each other very well, it was always the sense of [us being] from a similar world – there was some shared kinship. And I'm anyway a very shy person, so I don't easily make friends. At that time, we used to occupy a world where I think neither of us was very well known but he was obviously known for *Haasil*, *Maqbool* and a few other things he had done by then. So he was acclaimed, known to be a good actor but he was nowhere near where he would go.

And I was also known to a certain extent for *Mr and Mrs Iyer**, *Page 3*†, etc., but I had also not done that much work. So it was a nice time to know each other because I feel like there was very little pressure. There was this ease and comfort, where we had the ability to laugh at ourselves, sometimes be aware of the

---

* A 2002 Aparna Sen film
† A 2005 Madhur Bhandarkar film

limitations of the work we were doing, knowing that we were not necessarily doing the kind of work we wanted to do. But there wasn't any bitterness or crazy ambition. Maybe it was there in him – I don't know. I couldn't sense that. With both of us, it was a journey: '*Theek hai, yeh kar rahe hain; dekhte hain kaise hoga.*' [We are doing this now; let's see how it turns out.] That is the kind of equation I had with Irrfan.

I remember when Anurag Basu came over to narrate the story of *Metro* – he really did not do a good job of that narration. I think he was developing the script and getting confused between some character names. And I told Anurag, '*Arre*, you're not telling me properly.' I really miss those days and those people because there was a sense of not taking yourself seriously. I mean, you had respect for the work, but it was like making the best of what you have, knowing that other things are also important – relationships, work equations. We all did our work properly, we all came on time, we were sincere. But there was no insecurity, that I could tell. Whether in myself or in Irrfan. There was no angst, you know? For me, it was like being in a film school or something. Just going out, doing work, knowing sometimes that this is not the be all and end all of everything, knowing that this was not exactly the kind of work we were looking for, but hopefully we would get there. This sense of making the best of things and still enjoying ourselves?

I remember when Anurag gave me the narration, he said, 'Irrfan is doing it,' so I said, 'Great, then *toh* I'll definitely do it.' Almost blindly. I think Anurag himself had only done *Gangster* at that point, which I hadn't seen. In between, when Anurag said Irrfan is not being able to do it because of dates, I said, '*Arre* Anurag, I only want to do it if Irrfan is doing it.' And Anurag was also laughing because Anurag was of the same ilk.

We'd be shooting and then suddenly, he'd say, '*Arre*, today I really feel like cooking some mutton.' And then there was a whole conversation about where to find the mutton, where to cook it, when to eat it – we have to finish this scene quickly. That was the attitude. It was not that angsty insecurity or ambition. And there's nothing wrong with ambition; I'm just saying that I did not sense that. And there was this thing of … nobody's *that* busy, you know what I mean? I remember, Irrfan at that time, was into some numerology. And he changed the spelling of his name. There was some numerologist that he had called on set and I said, 'Even I want to meet him.' *Matlab bahut hansi mazaak.* [A lot of fun and games.]

SG: Sounds like fun.

KSS: It really was. And it was so easy, relaxed – that was my sense of working with him. You know, we all have to do all kinds of work to establish a career. Sometimes you do work which is brilliant, sometimes you do work which is okay. You cannot always think that the work I am doing is the best and the most brilliant work. So there was this self-awareness also. Without disrespecting the work or the people we were working with. I remember during *Life in a… Metro*, I told Anurag, 'Give him a stupid name, *na*, like Monty.' Because he's supposed to be a fool, that character. And even those scenes [with Irrfan] in *Metro* were so fantastic – whether it's screaming on top of the building, whether it's on that beach in Madh Island, that scene on the beach Irrfan and I did. It was a short scene, shot, I think, over five different days.

SG: There is a scene right in the beginning between your characters which is amazing. When he looks at your character's bosom and it is non-creepy. He's talking about his age and saying he's never seen a woman before and he looks at the cleavage and you don't feel, 'Ugh'; you don't feel creeped out. Which is an amazing thing.

KSS: Amazing. It's also Anurag. Because they have this sensibility, where the intention is not to titillate or manipulate; it is to show a man who is repressed or has not been exposed to have a deeper understanding of the character. That is what comes through. Both Irrfan and Anurag bring this across beautifully. With a lot of respect, integrity and sensitivity.

SG: I didn't know that came from the director. Because to be in that position as a female actor – and I know it's acting – but a gaze like that can make you very …
KSS: … Ah, uncomfortable.

SG: Yes, uncomfortable. Here, it seemed you were pissed off for other reasons, not for what he did. That scene, it's never left me.
KSS: I remember when we were shooting these office sequences, a very close aunt of mine had passed away that morning. And both Irrfan and Anurag were so amazing and understanding; I remember Irrfan said, 'Don't worry, we'll figure out the dates – just go.' These were the people they were, the people they *are*. So I have a lot of respect for both of them. I never actually interacted with Shiney [Ahuja] or Kangana [Ranaut] or Shilpa [Shetty] as much. Shilpa, I think, a little bit because she played my sister [in *Life in a… Metro*], but my main work was with Irrfan and Anurag.

I remember one scene in which I dropped a prop [a pen]. Immediately, Irrfan dropped his, on purpose. It was not in the script. And Anurag just went on rolling. We both started laughing. He was such an actor – any little thing goes wrong, and he would incorporate it into the scene … I don't remember any tension on the sets, ever. Especially on *Metro*. You can often, when you're working in films, sense another actor's insecurities or whether they are trying to …

SG: Upstage?

KSS: Yeah, maybe upstage, maybe establish that they're important. That was never there. And then the work is so much easier. I never saw any self-importance while working with him. And I'm so happy that I worked with him so early in our careers. We never really worked together later, except for *Talvar*. And when we met on *Talvar*, it was exactly like earlier. So easy, simple: 'Come, let's have a drink. *Arre*, we have five minutes.' This was the attitude. '*Ek chai pee lete hain.*' '*Arre, kaisi hai maa?*' '*Mangoes bheje hain Sutapa ne.*' [Let's have some tea. How is your mother? Sutapa has sent mangoes.] 'Come, let's have a cigarette quickly.'

SG: What you're telling me is very useful because it says something about both your working styles – easy, relaxed.

KSS: I think the agenda was to kind of respect the environment, respect the work and do it *aaram se*, easily. *Matlab, hanste khelte kar lenge. Isme kuchh tension nahi hona chahiye.* [We will do it without getting stressed. There's no need for tension.] There was a sense of we *toh* know each other from so long ago. There was a comfort that *I* always felt, I can't speak for him or how he felt. But I always felt a certain kind of kinship, that we are from the same world, we have the same kind of values. Cut from the same cloth. I used to find a lot of joy and comfort in that, because I had so much respect for him. And even more so because he wore his talent with such ease and never made anybody feel uncomfortable. In fact, he just made it easier for other people.

SG: When, as an actor and a fellow traveller, he was looking to the West, was it because he wasn't getting the kind of roles that he really wanted to do here? Or were they reaching out to him because they had heard of his talent?

KSS: I wouldn't know, Shubhra; I've actually not worked in Hollywood. I remember when he started doing work abroad, I was so happy. Irrfan's journey is so gratifying, because here's somebody with so much talent who got the recognition that he deserved. I mean, of course, he should have got so much more. He should have gotten the world, as far as I'm concerned, because he's one of my all-time heroes. And one has to do all kinds of work in a career. Sometimes, because, *chalo*, it gives you a certain kind of recognition or sometimes you work in Hollywood and get some recognition here, you're taken seriously here. Sometimes you do a project for the money, sometimes you do it because it's a great director, or it's a great role. You have to do all kinds of films in a career, isn't it?

SG: Sure, sure.

KSS: So I was very happy when he actually started getting that kind of fame and recognition. That is what you want to see, you know? Because we actually have seen, very often, people who don't have that kind of talent getting that recognition. Which is also fine, but when it happens to somebody you actually have so much faith and and belief in – somebody who inspires you – it's the happiest of journeys. Then that led to other great work and, towards the end of his career, he was absolutely booming, rip-roaring. If he had only done small indie films – great roles – he may not have got that level of fame and recognition abroad and then over here.

SG: Funnily enough, I thought he made a great lover and that he really did not get the romantic roles that he should have.

KSS: That's true! He could do anything; he would have been a great lover, a great villain, an inspiring hero. What is it that he could not do? Everything he could do, because he understood human beings, he understood himself, and how to portray those human beings; he was not judgemental. He brought those characters out. He had the kind of presence where you miss him. I remember, in [*The*] *Namesake*, when he's not on screen, you miss him after he dies. Even today, so many times when you think of casting for a role, you think of Irrfan. You miss Irrfan. I would have loved to have had him in a film that I make.

SG: That leads me to my next question: when you were casting for your film, *A Death in the Gunj*, did you think of him?
KSS: No, I didn't think of him. Firstly, he had become very busy and a very big star by then. And the kind of people I needed I already had in mind.

SG: What is it like to be a filmmaker in today's world and know that Irrfan is no longer there?
KSS: It's so sad, *yaar*. So many times when we are thinking of actors, we think of Irrfan. He set the bar so high as an actor and as a human being, and through the choices that he made, the integrity in his career. He's very inspiring, with what he's achieved, how he's gone about it. Irrfan, Naseer, Tabu – these are my heroes.

SG: As an actor, you're constantly honing your craft, as I'm sure he was. Is there something that you learnt from him?
KSS: I don't know that I consciously learnt anything concrete. But there are things which I admired about him, and those were things I like to think I was practising anyway and it was just wonderful to see somebody of his stature practise. Like he never drew attention to himself on set, wherever I worked with him.

Even when you're waiting between takes. And there are a lot of actors who do that. Irrfan would just do his work and then he would blend. I really have a lot of respect for that, where you do your work as well as he did, and then when you're between takes on set, you're just … being. You're letting everybody else do their work. You're not creating a fuss, you're not drawing attention to yourself, you're not making a big hoo-ha about anything. I really like and admire those qualities. There's a respect for the work that everyone else is doing. There is not a sense that I am the most important person on the set. Never saw that. Loved it. Did his work brilliantly and then let others do their work. And you know, I think it is a quality to which we don't give enough importance.

SG: What is the one thing that comes to your mind when you think of Irrfan?

KSS: Let me think. There was a certain ease, casualness … he put other people at ease as well. For somebody with such a great talent, to not draw attention to himself, to not take himself too seriously … so that, whatever it is, I know that I can go and talk to him. It was just always so easy.

I'll really miss Irrfan. It was nice to remember him like this.

'There was a lot of compassion in him'

KAUSHIK ROY

Kaushik Roy is a seasoned advertising professional who cast Irrfan in the lead role in his 2007 drama *Apna Asmaan*. In it, Irrfan plays the father to an autistic son, a character inspired by Roy's son Orko, whom Irrfan observed closely during the making of the film.

———

Shubhra Gupta: How did you zero in on Irrfan for *Apna Asmaan*?

Kaushik Roy: After writing *Apna Asmaan*, I bounced it off a few people from the industry. Their advice was to take somebody who's got box-office appeal. Initially I was a little confused – somehow, I couldn't see a box-office star actually do something like this. My other fear was that there was no budget and these people were going to ask for a lot of money.

At that point, since I was part of the telecommunication industry, we had Vodafone as a competitor. And then there was Irrfan, who had been used by them very, very effectively. Interestingly, the CEO of Vodafone Mr [Asim] Ghosh met me once and almost apologetically said that they [the ad firm Ogilvy] had chosen Irrfan. He spoke in Bengali: '*Amra akta dada khujchhilam*.' You know, who speaks in a way that others listen to him – basically a guy next door. Since I knew Ogilvy very well, I reached out: 'Will you get me a lead or let me speak to Irrfan?'

So that's how I got his number. I was told that he's shooting in Dubai. Obviously you don't call up anybody in Dubai because, in those days, it was going to be very expensive for him. So I sent him a text and he replied at lightning speed. He said, 'Send me the script and I will get back to you.' He had sent me his email, so I mailed him the script, and then he said, 'Call me.' So I called him. He said, 'Yeah, I've read the script, I like it very much, I will do it. You come and meet me when I am back in India.' When we met, there was a little more discussion and a little more of Irrfan Khan, the person. And I realized he was the guy next door who sat and rolled his cigarettes. Once in a while, his two kids would appear. The younger one was very small; the older one would come and sit and listen to the conversation. It was all very casual. And then Sutapa [Sikdar] would also step in and offer tea. So what I found was like, you know, they are people like us. Film people [tend to be] very different. You have to go through some secretary or manager or something. So it was a very different kind of experience – sitting and chatting. He said, 'I liked it very much, but you've written it in English. You need to write in Hindi.' So I went to my Hindi writer in advertising and it turned out to be a disaster. Because he's a *shuddh* Hindi person, Irrfan looked at [the script] and said, '*Yeh toh ekdum barbaad kar diya* – you have completely ruined it.' He had first said, 'The reason I liked your script was for the humour and those little dialogues, the way the character speaks, etc. This *toh* won't happen at all.' So our biggest stumbling block was how to write not good Hindi, but the Hindi that he thinks is right. And I realized his sense of dialogue was very, very good. His dialogues were so beautifully in his head – he would get them across so effortlessly.

For a filmmaker with very little money, working with him became a delight.

At that stage – I'm talking about 2006–2007 – he hadn't got enough recognition. And I'll tell you about the day that really broke my heart. When we were about to release, I told one guy to get me the poster which has Irrfan Khan's face on it. He came back and said, '*Sir, Irfan Pathan ka toh ek bhi photo nahi* – there are no photos of Irfan Pathan [former Indian cricketer].' It was heartbreaking for me that there are people who haven't heard the name Irrfan Khan. I think there was a kind of an anger in him – an anger [that made him determined] to take on the world, to challenge everybody, to prove that he could do things, deliver his lines in a way that nobody has been able to.

I later also realized that he was a very good observer. Before the film started, he understood that I had written it from a very different perspective because of Orko [Roy's son, who paints beautifully]. So he met Orko, who of course started believing that Irrfan Khan was his best friend. If there was a shoot, Irrfan would say, 'Where is Orko? *Orko se mujhe milna hai* – I want to meet him.' He would shake Orko's hand and give him a hug and all that. So what happened was that he internalized the whole story in his own way – he had a formula. He wanted to see the family; he observed me, Orko, Nina [Roy's wife].

In an interview after the film was done, he said something very interesting. He told this *Bombay Times* reporter that it wasn't difficult at all 'because I was just imitating Kaushik *da* ... I realized that even when you have a certain kind of pain inside, you can project yourself as a happy man, crack jokes, smile, laugh.'

So anyway, when he said he was just imitating Kaushik Roy, I realized that this man had a method which was very different. My observation is that he always tried to play a part which was *not*

Irrfan Khan. I'm saying this because we suffer from one problem in this country, where the biggest stars play the role of that star. I mean Shah Rukh Khan is Shah Rukh Khan and Salman Khan is Salman Khan. The way he walks in one film is the same way he has to walk in the next film. They never change; they always remain the star. The audience in India has defined what Salman Khan is meant to be. So he can never be a different person; from film to film to film, he has to remain Salman Khan.

Whereas Irrfan Khan had this ability to change completely. That is a very, very different Irrfan Khan in *Qarib Qarib Singlle* – the way he behaves, the way he talks. He must have done that after looking at somebody and deciding, you know, I am going to be this person. This ability to become another person is the hallmark of an actor. An actor is not supposed to be delivering himself or herself on screen but that personality he is enacting.

See, I haven't done enough in this business, but I can say one thing for sure: we got Irrfan at a time when he was the hungry man who was always wanting to prove that he was better than the rest. There was this scene [in *Apna Asmaan*] where he breaks down and cries. I could see that there was no hesitation in doing that. When you cry, you're not supposed to look beautiful or handsome. Your face actually turns rather odd. And so, when he cried, he looked like that person – who was not looking great, who was all broken.

There is one other scene I always use as an example. Those days, you had to be very clear that the shot has to be less than four minutes, because that's the size of your reel. So this is about three minutes and forty seconds – almost four minutes. It's a scene where he explodes for the first time. And I could see how much he enjoyed this scene, how very complete an actor he was.

SG: Did you get to know him at all, beyond just your professional relationship?

KR: Yes and no. I think I got to know him quite well and I found him to be a very kind person, in the sense that there was a lot of compassion in him. At the same time, there was a shield. You know, it wasn't like he would want to sit and have a chat or something. It was his wife who was always very friendly. Sutapa would start a long conversation. Whereas Irrfan would do everything right; he would never lose his temper. In small-budget films like ours, things happen – delays, etc. He would never show his temper or behave badly. Yes, we met outside the film once, at Cannes, where he would be on the red carpet for *A Mighty Heart*.

SG: And you were there for your film?

KR: I was. So yes, I had one meeting [which] had nothing to do with my film. It was about his film: Irrfan Khan, the Hollywood star, who's just finished a film with Angelina Jolie and would be walking the red carpet. He was obviously very excited and he made sure to speak about his tuxedo.

SG: Living with a differently abled person is a whole other experience. And Irrfan had no experience of this before, I'm assuming. So after he observed you, Orko and Nina, he managed to play his part as if he had always done it. Like it was his life.

KR: Yes, I think his method was perhaps observing me as a father. On his first day of shoot, when he arrived on the set, he wanted to make sure that Orko would be there. I think he wanted to see Orko with his parents, to be able to sort of observe that whole thing.

My feeling is that Irrfan was a very gentle person. His gestures were very soft. I used to see his fingers – they were never taut or stressed. He always looked like somebody who's flowing through life.

There is this thing I learnt many years back: that maternal feelings are not necessarily the domain of mothers. You can be maternal even as a father. I think he had that very maternal kind of personality. Every time I would go to his place, he would be engaged with his children, in spite of having all these film schedules, which are treacherous in terms of the number of days you're meant to be away from home.

But more importantly, he was a great actor. I think he had a very difficult role [in *Apna Asmaan*]. In a sense, the mother's role was almost straight. She's obviously hassled and suffered all kinds of humiliation, and she always has this thing about making her son perfect and normal. But in Irrfan's character, there was this guilt, this pain. There was something about him that tried to make it look like everything was fine. He was able to do it because of his gentleness – and his compassion.

Irrfan was also this curious person who wanted to know the lives of other people – a human quality that made him such a great actor.

SG: What is the one quality that you will always associate with him?

KR: His wit; he is … was, whatever … a very witty person. I feel that if you don't have a sense of humour, you cannot enact roles. So he was this very quiet, witty man with a sense of humour which made him special.

'One of the finest actors the Indian screen has ever seen'

PRIYADARSHAN

Irrfan always wanted to work in the south. One of the few films that he managed to do was with the very prolific **Priyadarshan**, who has worked across several Indian languages. In his 2009 film *Billu*, Irrfan plays the lead in a Krishna–Sudama-flavoured tale of two friends who branch off in very different directions: one becomes a very famous actor, the other is a barber who stays back in the village. Shah Rukh Khan plays the famous actor in three songs-and-dances and a handful of scenes. The rest of the film belongs to Irrfan.

SHUBHRA GUPTA: I was interested in how you cast *Billu*. Was Irrfan your first and only choice?

PRIYADARSHAN: See, I met Shah Rukh about a guest appearance for a film. He asked me, 'What is the story?' I was supposed to do a bigger film with Shah Rukh at the time, but the script was not good. So I said, 'Shah Rukh, we can do a film in which you have nothing much to do. But it's very impactful.' When he listened to it, he told me, 'Okay, good, I can work only for ten days. And who's the other guy?' I did not even blink; I said,

'Irrfan.' He said, '*Arre*, why didn't I think about it!' That's how it happened. Shah Rukh said, 'He's absolutely right and I've never done a film with him.' So next thing you know, he's arranging a meeting with Irrfan!

I met Irrfan in my hotel room. I narrated the story to him; he went down without saying anything. Ten minutes later, he called me, 'Sir, I'm in the lobby. Can you come down?' He was doubtful about the climax. He said, 'Sir, I'm a little shocked at the climax. But okay, I will do it.' That was how we started.

He used to come to me and ask, 'Okay, I have planned Billu in my mind, so I'll be having a certain kind of body language, a certain kind of hand movement, like a barber – my right hand will work faster than the left, because I will be cutting with the scissors.' I just kept quiet. I knew what I was going to make. With every actor, I'm very clear about that. Some actors are very, very self-centred, some are methodical. I had seen a few films of Irrfan before. What I liked about him is his simplicity, and he can be accepted as a person I see next door, whether in the village or in the city. But I was very sure what I was going to do; whatever contribution he gives, I thought, it will be fine. Then we started shooting.

Now, I don't know what happened; on the second day of the shoot, he told me, 'Priyan sir, I'm not going to do anything; you tell me what to do, I'll do that.' I asked, 'Why?' And he said, 'I thought of this character in a different way but the way you are explaining it to me, I think is the best.' So I said, 'See, that is where an actor succumbs.' This is very important when it comes to Irrfan. Amrish-ji [Amrish Puri, who starred in Priyadarshan's *Muskurahat*] knew that some director from the south is coming and making this film. Every time he used to say, 'Okay, one more take.' Then he said, 'No, one more take', then 'one more'. So I'm ...

177

bored, because I don't have patience. I know what I want from an actor. So Amrish-ji told me, 'You choose.' And I said, 'Sir, are you trying to impress me as an actor? Your first take was good; why you are trying to impress me?' The moment I told him that, he was okay. Then I did six films with him, and he never asked me one question. When I told Irrfan this, he said, 'Yes, we actors are very insecure. If the director knows what he wants, then we'll leave ourselves to the director.' After that, he left himself to me.

Last time I met Irrfan was at the MAMI* party in [Mukesh] Ambani's house. I am not the person who goes to parties or Filmfare functions or anything. My film happened to be at the festival, so I went. I just thought I'll stay for five minutes; then Irrfan came to me. He was completely lost in the crowd. He stood with me for a long time. He said, 'Priyan sir, the film did not do very well but still I feel very good. Many times, people call me not Irrfan; they call me Billu.' That was the biggest compliment I ever got from him.

I tell you – I don't consider myself a great director. I always have a lot of respect for people who have done a better job than me. But at the same time, I have made every kind of film: comedies, serious movies like *Virasat*. I have made films like *Kaalapani*, I have won three national awards. As a producer, director, everything. Now these things don't matter to me because every time – because we are talking about Irrfan –my job is to see that my casting is right.

One time, Irrfan said, 'I have one request. I want to do a Malayalam film, if possible with Mohanlal.' I said, 'Okay, why?' He said, 'I am a big fan of Mohanlal. You have done so many films with him. I have seen his movies, I have seen his subtlety,

---

* Jio MAMI, the Mumbai film festival

I've seen him do so many kinds of films. I have never seen a hero who has done so many variations, and I would like to do a film with him.'

Eight months after the MAMI party, when I called him, he said, 'Sir, actually I have some health problems. I'm going to the US; if I come back, I'll meet you.' The words 'if I come back' hit me very badly. I asked, 'Why "if"?' He said, 'I have a serious issue with my health.' He did not tell me what it was. It disturbed me. Then later I came to know that he has this problem. So this is my little bit of relationship with him.

SG: Do you remember, off-hand, which films you had seen of his before you cast him for *Billu*?

P: I don't know. I have seen so many of his films; I don't particularly remember. Because every day I sleep after watching two films; that is the entertainment of my life.

SG: Lots of filmmakers that I speak to say they never watch anybody else's movies, they don't watch their own films, they don't watch any films. And you watch two every day!

P: Yeah. And every Friday, if possible, I go to a theatre to watch a movie. See, I make a lot of brainless films, so I would like to go to a theatre and see how people react. I'm not talking about intellectuals and critics; I'm talking about ordinary people. That is why today I'm sitting on ninety-five films in thirty-five years in five languages. It's as simple as that. And I've come across actors with attitudes, I've come across actors who are superstars, but Irrfan, he's one person I never felt is an actor. I feel he was one of the production boys who is hanging around and just saying his dialogue, because he is as simple as that.

SG: But if, say, he had played Shah Rukh's role, and in Irrfan's role you cast somebody else, do you think that film would have worked?

P: No, it would not have worked at all. Because the film is inspired by the story of Krishna and Kuchela. Kuchela goes to Krishna. He's so poor and he goes with a little bit of rice to meet his old friend. What do you call Kuchela in the north?

SG: Sudama. Krishna and Sudama …

P: Sudama, yes. In the south, we say Kuchela. So it's the story of Krishna and Sudama and Irrfan is Sudama and Shah Rukh is Krishna.

SG: Do you think Bollywood gave him his due? I mean, because he kept struggling.

P: It's a very interesting question. Once I was talking to Irrfan and he said, 'Sir, I struggled a lot.' I said, 'Listen, I also struggled a lot; I almost got jaundice, went back and continued my psychology studies; then I got a break.' He used to tell me all his struggles. One day I told him, 'Directors cannot be beggars because they really have to use their minds. But actors are beggars; they cannot choose. What comes your way, you should take it. All actors in the world are beggars. If somebody gives you a good film, your pocket is full.' So he said, 'That's exactly what I believe, because I tried to plan my life and I tried to get it but I didn't know how to get it.' At one moment, he said, 'I'd left it, sir. Then I thought I'll go back to theatre. But things changed in my mind; I took up everything that came my way.'

Don't consider Irrfan an average superstar; please consider him an actor. He is one of the finest actors the Indian screen has ever seen. He cannot carry a song and dance, okay. The typical

Bollywood hero Irrfan can never become. But in his acting people found something new that they had never seen before; that is what made him him. They thought, 'Okay, he's one of us.'

SG: So basically you're saying that mainstream Bollywood had no idea what to do with this fantastic actor.

P: But he has been accepted by the mainstream also, as a man who has proved himself. Come on, what are you talking? After all, he's one person accepted by Hollywood also. Where Hollywood is standing, Bollywood is nothing.

You can write it – no problem.

SG: Was it because he did not look like a chocolate-box hero and did not sing and dance – do you think that came in his way of becoming a really big star?

P: No. In the first place, I don't agree that he was not a big star. I believe that he was a big star. Because if you consider the films that he has done, he has more hits than any other … You know, in cinema, what works is statistics – that's what you learn in Malayalam cinema. If you make a film for a hundred rupees, and the film collects two hundred rupees, it's a superhit. But when you make a film for a hundred crore and the film collects a hundred and twenty crores, I don't consider it a superhit. That way, Irrfan's films always made money for his producers. That means he is as big as any superstar. That is why he has survived. The industry is all about business. Nobody takes an actor and makes a film unless and until they are very sure that we are making money. See, with Aamir, with Shah Rukh, with Salman or Akshay Kumar, people know the market, okay? With Irrfan, they don't know the market, but still they believe that we'll not lose money.

SG: So if he were alive today – and it is so sad that he is not because he really would have changed so many things – do you think this would have been his time?

P: Yes. You know why? All the big stars in this country – I hardly know two people who have been recognized internationally. One is Om Puri, the other is Irrfan. Because they never considered him a star; they considered him an actor. There's a huge difference between actor and star. So naturally, you know, the Indian industry has been jealous. Even a C-grade actor, if he goes to Hollywood, it's great news in all the newspapers. This is our complex, basically. Many people went there just to prove that they've been accepted in the world. Irrfan did not do that. He was selected. They *called* him. There's a difference between being invited and asking to go there. I think if he was alive, we could have been proud that we have a very good international star.

SG: When you close your eyes and think of Irrfan, what is the one thing that comes to your mind?

P: His simplicity. And we both enjoyed smoking cigarettes together. Most of the time [while shooting], we used to exchange our cigarettes, that was our thing. We had a competition between Shah Rukh, Irrfan and me to see who could smoke more cigarettes.

SG: And who won?

P: All of us were in the same boat.

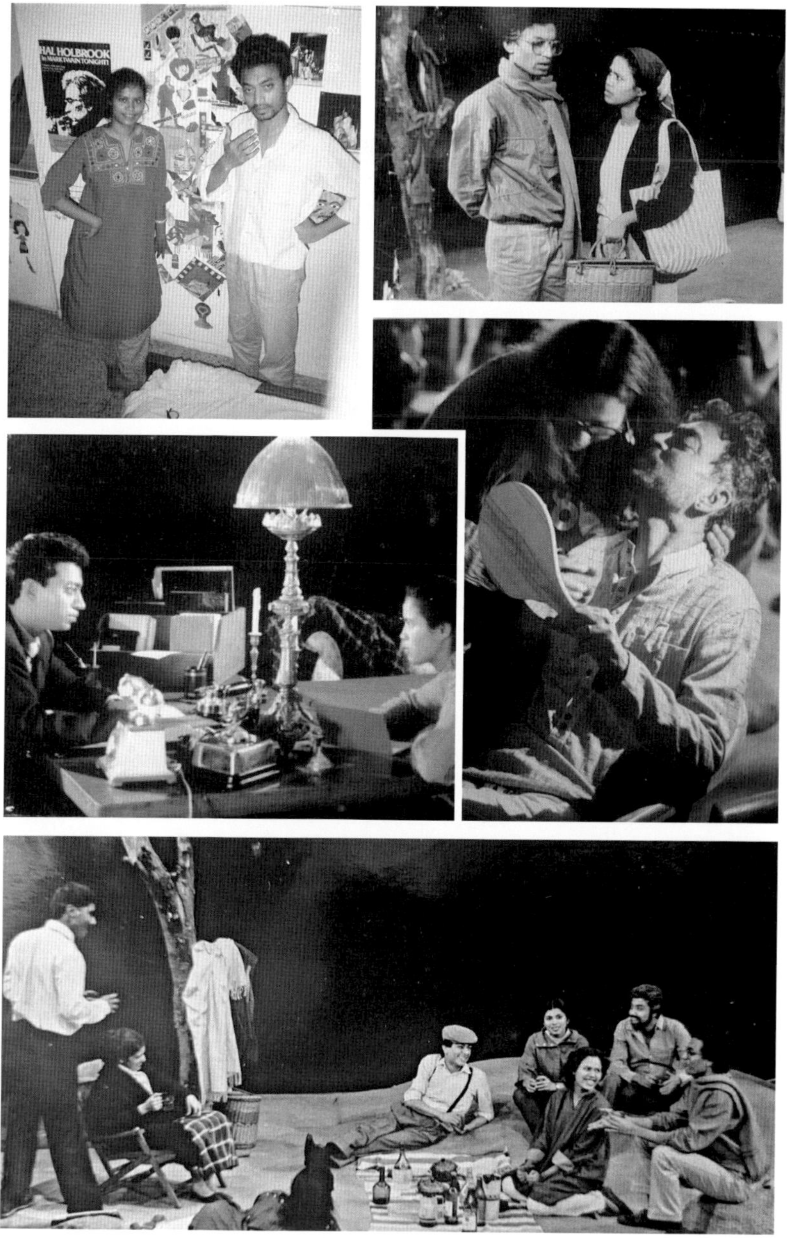

Irrfan and Sutapa, over the years

Behind-the-scenes from the sets of Mira Nair's Salaam Bombay! *(1988), featuring Irrfan with child actor Sarfuddin*

Irrfan and his co-star Tabu in a still from Mira Nair's The Namesake *(2006)*

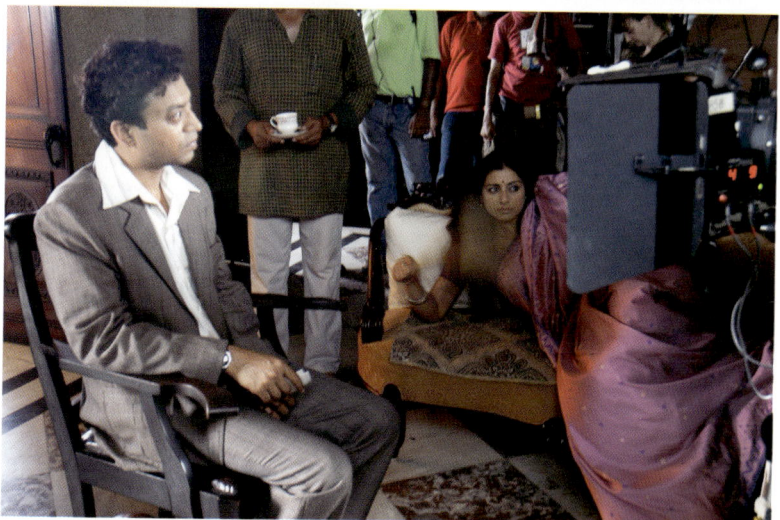

On the sets of The Namesake

Irrfan inspects his look during the filming of Qissa *(2013)*

Irrfan prepares for a scene with director Anup Singh

A still from Qissa, featuring Irrfan with co-star Rasika Dugal

Irrfan's character Umber Singh in Qissa

Left to right: Irrfan, Anup Singh, Tillotama Shome

A still from Qissa, with co-star Tisca Chopra

Irrfan with his Qissa *co-star Tillotama Shome*

Behind-the-scenes from the sets of Qissa

Stills from Nikkhil Advani's D-Day *(2013)*

Irrfan with co-star Arjun Rampal and a make-up artist on the sets of D-Day

A still from D-Day
Clockwise: Irrfan, Huma Qureshi, Aakash Dahiya, Arjun Rampal

Behind-the-scenes from the sets of Qarib Qarib Singlle *(2017)*
Left to right: Parvathy, Tanuja Chandra, Irrfan

Irrfan draws a massive crowd while walking to the shooting location for
Qarib Qarib Singlle *in Gangtok*

Behind-the-scenes from the sets of Homi Adajania's Angrezi Medium *(2020)*
Clockwise: Irrfan with Ranvir Shorey, Deepak Dobriyal, Kiku Sharda

Irrfan with director and friend Homi Adajania on the sets of Angrezi Medium

Stills from Angrezi Medium
Above: Irrfan with co-star Radhika Madan

On the sets of Angrezi Medium
Above, left to right: Deepak Dobriyal, Irrfan, Homi Adajania,
Kareena Kapoor Khan, Dimple Kapadia
Below: Irrfan and Homi Adajania

Above: Irrfan on the sets of Angrezi Medium
Below: Irrfan and Homi Adajania

Irrfan enjoys a light-hearted moment on the sets of Angrezi Medium

'An experience junkie'

SUDHIR MISHRA

Sudhir Mishra, veteran director and screenwriter, best known for *Hazaaron Khwaishein Aisi*, *Khoya Khoya Chand*, *Dharavi* and *Is Raat Ki Subah Nahin*, always wanted to work with Irrfan but didn't have a part for him until he made *Yeh Saali Zindagi*, in which he cast Irrfan as a lovelorn mobster. As someone who knew him well, Mishra has had a rare vantage into both Irrfan's personal and professional life.

———

SHUBHRA GUPTA: You knew Irrfan quite well.

SUDHIR MISHRA: I mean, we were neighbours, no? We lived in the same building for some time, so we met by accident a lot of times, when he was leaving or coming back. We would hang around when he was working out and I joined him, or when he was sitting in the garden, he would say, 'Come and have a cup of tea.' We were meeting almost all the time. Yeah, I knew him quite well, I think.

And he let me into his life – he was very warm and trusting. He was greedy, wanted it all; very inquisitive, very curious. He was always trying to be more than he was. He was always trying to discover something ephemeral. He never cared about his own performance much, you know? He never talked so much about himself as about the whole film, about other characters. So he was almost like a co-author. But then he also wanted to be a star!

SG: Did he?

SM: Yeah, yeah. He would get angry that he was not, that lesser actors were bigger stars. But he had the capacity to understand that everything is not possible, and he mostly made the right choices.

He's a very interesting, complicated, fun guy, you know? Most people make him out to be very boring. He was always looking for something, always wanting to increase the realm of his own experience. The limitations of his background ... he was always trying to cross. Yet he was very rooted. It's quite interesting the way he was always questioning his background.

SG: What was that background that he was trying to question?

SM: Wherever he came from: Tonk, Rajasthan; small-town, feudal background. He spoke about it fondly but critically. Not critical in a bitter way, but just amused, you know? When I think back, I never knew I would miss him that much, frankly. I often think of him. I wasn't missing him that much when, say, I hadn't met him for six months or something. But when he fell sick and now, when he's not there, it's kind of strange, you know? Strange that you're living and he's not there.

He was at the top of his game when he died. It was as if he had suddenly found himself totally. That confidence. And I almost worked with him at the end. He asked me to help with a project called *Gormint*, which Amazon was producing and the AIB [All India Bakchod] boys were writing. They asked me to do two episodes and to work on the script. That was the last thing he shot. They didn't complete it; he was supposed to go for the shoot in Punjab and then he discovered his illness. He thought he had jaundice, he went to the hospital and then one thing led to another. He looked really in fine fettle, as they say. Totally there. Not dull at all, very excited about it all. He was brilliant in it; I hope they release it. Because he's done about fifty days of work in there, and it's very good.

SG: Going back to what you said about Irrfan wanting to be a star. Some people say that he couldn't be bothered; he was okay with where he was – he was so confident.

SM: People who say that didn't know him. I think Tishu [Tigmanshu Dhulia] knew him really well. Vishal [Bhardwaj] and Shoojit Sircar knew him really well. There's a boy called Kabir, who's making a film with Kangana [Ranaut; *Revolver Rani*] – Sai Kabir – he knew him very well. Also Vipin Sharma, the actor. He was very nice with most people, but he let in only very few people.

And I don't mean this in any way – he just wanted the films that *he* was working in to be bigger than they were, and he was exasperated by the limits of what we could do. And the budget constraints. He wanted it to be wider, for more people to see it. It's not that he couldn't be bothered, but he couldn't be bothered to do crap because of it. He wanted a lot of things. He was like a soaker. That's the best way I can describe him.

SG: Like a sponge.

SM: Like a sponge, for experience. Always willing to take a risk for an experience. Even when it was uncomfortable, to go some distance in all sorts of ways. Not all of which I can reveal. But he was always looking for something to increase some part of the brain or touch a part of the brain that has not been touched.

SG: Let me take you back. When did you first meet him?

SM: When he came to see my first film in Uphaar [Cinema] in Delhi during the International Film Festival. My film, *Yeh Woh Manzil To Nahin*, was opening and their acting teacher, Ram Gopal Bajaj, had brought the whole class, not only him – he was in the third year at NSD.

My film also had Manohar Singh, who was their NSD Repertory head. B. M. Shah was the ex-director of NSD. Habib Tanvir [who was also in the film] was very connected; so was Pankaj Kapur. It was almost like an NSD ex-students' ...

SG: Reunion.

SM: Reunion, yeah. They'd all come to see the film.

SG: So did he come up to you or was it the whole group?

SM: I just remember a boy, who said, '*Achhi hai*.' I wouldn't have remembered him if I had not met him later. But then I remember meeting him properly when he came to meet me when I was casting *Dharavi*. And unfortunately, by then, I had already cast the whole film.

I remember very clearly this striking young man coming to my office in Bandra. After that, I made *Hazaaron Khwaishein Aisi*, *Is Raat Ki Subah Nahin*; he had done *Haasil* at almost the same time. Then we started meeting a lot. I always wanted to work with him, and then I had a part for him in *Yeh Saali Zindagi*. I didn't cast him as the typical gangster. I thought it'd be interesting if he played a romantic kind of gangster.

And he was very strange in the way he was interested in the other actors; he would always point out, '*Sir, woh bahut achha hai – dekho, dekho*.' [S/he is very good – watch] In cinema, every scene has been done, right? But he was always looking for some way to add something to scenes which have all been done before, even if it's not something I've asked him to do. What is original but that?

The thing with an actor like Irrfan: there are two or three things playing on that face – there's an ambiguity, there's no certainty. He's vulnerable. I really loved working with him. Sometimes he's difficult, you know? Like once he told me, '*Sir, yeh kya kar raha hoon – samajh nahi aa raha hai.*' [What am I doing – I don't really understand.] So I said, 'Why the fuck should I tell you how to act it out?' He said, 'This one scene, just tell me because I just want to look into your eyes.' He cared about the final effect. There is something called a pure cinema actor – Irrfan was that. He didn't care how he arrived at it, as long as the impact showed, as long as the scene worked. Even if he was in the background and the other actor was doing, supposedly, the main thing. But he knew that if he was in the right part of the frame, then it was working for him as well. This is very unique.

I remember him saying, '*Sir, dekho,* Hindi Medium *aake dekho; woh Deepak Dobriyal kamaal hai.*' [Sir, watch *Hindi Medium*; that Deepak Dobriyal is great in it.] He was constantly talking about Deepak. Always I've heard him talk about someone else, something else.

SG: Why do you think he did that?

SM: Because he was soaking it in; he was getting things from people. He knew that there are limitations to his experience, his frames of reference. He was very open in that way. Very giving, and he was very taking at the same time. He wanted to do his best and he wanted everyone else to do the same. He would get very impatient if he thought the director wasn't paying attention. He wanted it to work, you know? That's why he worked with Anup Singh, he would work with Tishu. And sometimes, he would not work with all of us! None of us could lay claim to Irrfan. At least I couldn't.

Sometimes, for instance, he would do something in Hollywood because it would allow his films to go across. He actually cared a lot for the smaller films he did, and he wanted them to travel a lot more. Often he did things so that he himself – and those films – could travel. And he was very conscious of the fact that as Indians, we haven't gone where we should have. As a filmmaking community, why do we fall short? He was a little upset with others and himself. I don't think he was totally happy with us, for instance.

SG: Who is 'us'?
SM: The tribe that we were, the ten–twenty filmmakers who we thought would cross over.

SG: Change the world?
SM: We haven't – why? It was a question which he asked. He could be uncomfortable; he was not cute. He confronted you. Tell you things which you didn't like to hear. Not that it carried over the next day at all. But in that sense, he was part of our generation, where we argued but forgot about it the next day.

Irrfan went at a time when he could have really done something. It would have helped Indian cinema more. I mean, that's an irreparable loss. His going has caused a gap. Some films will not get made, some films will get delayed, some films will have to be rethought. Those films will be lesser because he's not there.

SG: Looking at him from the time that he came into the movies – he did many years of television and, by the end of it, he was sick and tired of doing TV.

SM: Yeah, he was almost going to go when he got *Haasil*.

SG: Why did it take him so long to reach a *Hindi Medium*? I was told that because it broke into this '100-crore club', legacy Bollywood started to look at him seriously.

SM: Bollywood always looked at him seriously. From *Haasil* onwards, *Maqbool*, specially, and then *Paan Singh* [*Tomar*], I don't think anybody took him not seriously. Even some stars would say, '*Achha actor le lo. Irrfan ko lo na, yaar; humse nahi hota yeh.*' [Take a good actor. Why don't you cast Irrfan; we are not cut out for this.] I mean, it was almost like a *muhavra* [idiom], you know? But becoming a 'bankable star', as they say, that happened now. Which is quite unfortunate, because there were a lot of films that would have happened because of him.

'Why' is the question, you know? See, he didn't work for a kind of storytelling. Surely *Dilwale Dulhaniya Le Jaayenge*** is not possible with an Irrfan. He was meant for another kind of cinema which was itself not happening that much at that time. That was why.

Even a film like *Paan Singh Tomar* was held up for two years before it was released. The belief system of the moneybags in Bollywood at that time was the other kind of film. They pretended that they only made it for the money, but they actually also believed in that.

That point – eighties and nineties – was the loafer's point of view, no? The serial chaser's point of view. That Irrfan wasn't,

---

* A 1995 Aditya Chopra film

and many of us didn't fit in and he didn't fit in. Many actors lost their way; Irrfan still was gutsy and stood his ground and stayed where he was and owned his craft. When the opportunity came, he delivered. He improved himself from the boy who came from NSD to the person whose growth was just fantastic. There were two people who had that growth. One was Om Puri. Amazing graph; from where he came, to what he was when he passed away. It's a mind-blowing journey, if you know the background. And now, Nawaz [Nawazuddin Siddiqui], which is another amazing journey; remarkable self-confidence and evolution; a person who is working on himself, not satisfied with just some success. And Irrfan was the same, never satisfied, so that was quite a mind-blowing trajectory. And therefore, he was ready when the moment came. He worked on himself; he worked on his health a lot! He was given to extremes now and then, but most of the time, he was eating right, he was exercising right. He was staying fit because an actor has to stay fit, right? I was surprised by what happened. When we worked, I often had his food that came from his home. He was really eating well, so I was very shocked when this diagnosis came.

SG: On another note, why did he go to the West? Or did the West come looking for him?

SM: The West came looking for him. Basically, once an actor goes there, they get to know a certain kind of casting director – it also works like that. I don't know if he agreed with all the films he did in the West. He liked a lot of them; he liked, for instance, *The Warrior*. He liked the Anup Singh type of films. He loved Ang Lee, as a person. He liked Danny Boyle, as an individual. I forget the name of that one TV series [*In Treatment*] he did with that Irish actor [Gabriel Byrne] – that he loved doing. He liked doing a lot of that stuff but I think even then, he wasn't blown away. In the sense that he kept his self-respect intact as an Indian when he was working in the West. He didn't go and settle down there. He wanted to, in a sense, take his own homegrown cinema outside. He thought it was an interesting cross-pollination. Even [in the West], there was that search for something. He loved working with Mira [Nair]. I think *The Namesake* is one of his best performances.

SG: Om Puri is another actor the West really liked. And Naseeruddin Shah.

And from what I've been told, he had a great deal of regard for both. Their kind of persona and the films they chose made way for someone like Irrfan. And Irrfan himself made way for people like Nawazuddin Siddiqui, Rajkummar Rao ... What was his impact as an actor in Bollywood?

SM: He changed the whole trajectory. I guess Naseer, Om, Irrfan – and Pankaj, to an extent – were arrogant enough not to want to be ... in quotes: 'just Balraj Sahni'. Meaning just the secondary part, the good friend. Indian cinema relegated Balraj Sahni to the secondary parts. I mean, he only got his due in the beginning with Bimal Roy and in the end in *Garm Hava**, right?

They were very conscious of the fact that they should not be treated that way. So they fought for their place. Which is what made them rather difficult to work with for the popular boys. They wanted an idea of a script, they wanted to know what they were doing. They paved the way for some, like Naseer and Om who went on to do [Shyam] Benegal's films and other films like that. And all those films paved the way for someone like Aamir

---

* A 1973 M. S. Sathyu film

[Khan] to say that I will only do one film at a time. That culture which had gone away with Mr Dilip Kumar came back for people like Aamir – to do one film at a time, working seriously on his part. So I think a lot of younger, popular cinema boys are very influenced by these guys. Even, let's say, Imtiaz Ali, Ashutosh Gowariker, all these boys are no longer disdainful of the art film or parallel cinema. In fact, if you see Ashutosh's work, like, say, *Swades* [2004], it is very influenced by Benegal, I think. So that kind of acting, that kind of attention to character, that kind of casting – that all of us did following Mr Benegal. And then it was around in the atmosphere. Irrfan and all, I think, have an impact which is beyond their obvious impact.

A lot of popular directors have seen Irrfan, admired him, wanted to cast him, but he's not big enough for them to fulfil their other dreams, so they go and cast somebody else but they use the methodology that they would have used with Irrfan. The parallel cinema or the 'other' cinema methodologies with Irrfan and the rest, crept into popular cinema. So if you see Imtiaz's work, to some extent Ashutosh's work, the work of Farhan [Akhtar] and Zoya [Akhtar] and all these people, you will see the influence of this other kind of cinema. Zoya makes her first film with Konkona [Sen Sharma] in the main lead! I mean, she's Javed Akhtar's daughter, she could get whoever she wanted. And this is because of people like Irrfan. There's a kind of cross-pollination that happened. So overall, I think Indian cinema became healthier. Even popular cinema became somewhat less of a loafer's point of view; a certain kind of sensibility crept in.

SG: And that, you think, is down to the way Irrfan acted and presented himself.

SM: Somebody to look up to. You could be proud. You could go abroad, you could say, 'Irrfan!' And people knew. He gave a certain credibility to another kind of cinema. Because of that, there was another kind of actor. He was a wonderful ambassador for Indian cinema.

SG: That's a lovely way of putting it. So after *Yeh Saali Zindagi*, did you think of him for your other films?

SM: I wanted to work with him, before he passed away. I had written an idea. With Irrfan, like I said, you couldn't guarantee that he would like an idea. I was working on my cast. He passed away and then I stopped. He had said, '*Mere saath banao.*' [Do a film with me.] And then …

SG: What was it like to be on set with him?

SM: Great fun. But sometimes when he was in a bad mood, he could be very difficult. But it was not personal at all and it was okay the next day and we were working again. I mean, when one is working on a film as a director, you are so caught up that all the background action only the assistants and some other people know. We learn of things later. When he worked with Saurabh [Shukla] – the grace he had, the way they interacted. I mean, Irrfan was very jealous sometimes, you know, if you paid attention to a lady. He was unafraid to rib you. People paint a very boring picture; he was not boring at all! He was always on the set – inquisitive, thinking, listening to music, talking, looking at the location, the history of the place. And acting, he just did. He was so well prepared from before; he had read the script fifty times. Then he was very open to the moment; he was not like an actor prepared, obsessed, like, 'Don't talk to me; I'm in a part.' He was there, you know. It was quite amazing, fascinating to see him. Very alive to everybody – to all the assistants. Everybody will remember him very fondly. If you're not up to speed, he would speak his mind also. You remember the times he also said uncomfortable things to you. He was not always cute and admiring, you know. He would not say, 'Sir, I love your work and I grew up watching your work.' He would speak his mind, and if you didn't like it, too bad. That was what was very refreshing about him.

SG: Sutapa told me that towards the end, in between, things had started to look a little hopeful – he was still reading scripts. And he was so excited about getting so much work. As you said, this would have been his time.

SM: This would have been his time. Not all mainstream actors are capable of, or want to, or have an affinity for a certain kind of film. You could do a slightly more ambitious film with Irrfan. So a lot of films will now not get made, or they will get made in different ways. And Irrfan would have been wonderful in most of them. I mean, he was at the top of his game. When I saw him in *Gormint*, I was floored.

SG: Many people I have spoken to have said that he was a huge star. Other people have said that he wanted to be a big star, but because of the Bollywood hang-up with numbers, he was never treated as one. What do you think?

SM: Well, he was treated with huge respect and, in most people's eyes, he was very big. But when you talk to the pure number guys, you were confronted with the fact that you couldn't make a very big film with him in the lead, till *Hindi Medium*. So that was something that he was quite aware of. But anybody who met him, met him like a star, because he had that ... specially towards the last five–six years. Young people met him with a lot of reverence. He was like the last word in acting. Irrfan Khan was like a metaphor for ...

SG: Metaphor for?

SM: For quality, experimenting, for taking chances, excellence.

SG: So why did he drop the 'Khan' from his name?

SM: I think he was looking for experience and change. Maybe Sutapa can talk about this.

SG: Naseeruddin Shah told me that maybe it was some numerology thing.

SM: It could also be a numerology thing, maybe. Because Irrfan might have thought, '*Chalo, yeh bhi kar lete hain; kisi ne bola isse chal jayega.*' [Let's try this too; somebody said it could work.] Why did he drop the 'Khan', I don't know. He once said, '*Yaar*, all this Bakri Eid and all the sacrifice – why? It's not necessary.'

He was not a practising guy, no, but he was Muslim. I think so. I have never seen him pray. But I think he wasn't rejecting where he came from. Not at all. He knew who his family was, who his father was. He had evolved, reached a certain place where he could look at them objectively – with affection but not necessarily in agreement. And he could see the flaws. Again with affection. Maybe, I don't know, he didn't want to be seen as another Khan.

SG: Talking about being Muslim, do you think the India of today would have actually looked at him as a great actor, or as someone with a surname like Khan? Right now, people are being targeted for their surname …

SM: I think, mercifully, [the situation was not] vicious, but it had started to happen and that was disturbing him. He was so politically aware that even the Western view of this Islamophobia used to affect him, and I've had conversations with him on that. So he had evolved somewhere, and not in ways that were necessarily comfortable for everybody. I guess when he went to the West, he was not enamoured of America. That's what he was – complex. He was, in a sense, practical. If he gave you his body, he didn't give you his mind. If he gave you his physical presence as an actor in exchange for whatever – money, fame – he was not necessarily giving you his mind. He never gave his mind to anyone. He remained slightly amused, detached.

SG: And one last thing before you go – when you think of Irrfan, what is the one thing that comes to your mind?

SM: I think of a guy soaking in experience – like an experience junkie.

'A spirit trying to understand life'

ANUP SINGH

Anup Singh, director and screenwriter, fell in love with the movies on a ship which transported him from his beloved Dar es Salaam to Bombay with a screening of *Sahib Bibi aur Ghulam*. He directed Irrfan in *Qissa: The Tale of a Lonely Ghost* and *The Song of Scorpions*. Singh speaks of their abiding friendship, and the very special experience of working on *Qissa*, a film that can be counted amongst Irrfan's best.

***

SHUBHRA GUPTA: Whenever I revisit *Qissa*, it's such a gift. How did you think of *Qissa* as a film? And was Irrfan the only person that you thought of as the lead?

ANUP SINGH: These are all good memories. Before he passed away, we were in fact working towards our third film together and I'd already written quite a lot of it. We were very amused by how the script was developing. He had always been teasing me, saying, 'You want to cast me in your films, but your films are all about women. When will you do a film with me?' That was a kind of running joke between us. Finally, I went to him and said, 'Irrfan, I have written something that is just for you, as a man. As the actor that you are. However, this character in the film likes to dress up as a woman.' We had a great laugh about that, but he was very, very challenged and excited about the role.

When I go back to India, it will be such an absence. Because one of the first things I would do as soon as I would land is call him, you know.*

I come from a Sikh family, and the main reason that I think we finally landed in Tanzania – in Dar es Salaam – is that my grandfather lived through Partition in a very brutal and really quite a strange way. As you might know, violence had started in the country much before Partition. There was already talk of asking for a separate nation. There were many occasions where a village was attacked by a different community. From what I heard while growing up, my grandfather's village was attacked. He was an orphan, but he had a sister. He lived with his maternal uncle. This family used to have these huge wheat grain storage pots. He [Singh's grandfather] must have been four–five years old. They put him in that pot and his younger sister in another pot. Later, when the children came out, the whole village was massacred, and his family had disappeared. They had just left the kids and run away. So here were these two very young people roaming around in this burnt-out village. They were found by some distant relatives who now had to decide what to do with them. Another maternal uncle had emigrated to Tanzania many years ago. They got in touch with him and he said, 'Send the children to me.' That's how my grandfather came to Tanzania. That's where my father was born, where I was born.

These stories have been in the family since. I had the story within me; I never knew what I would do with it. My mother

---

* Anup Singh lives in Geneva.

had stories from her side of the family, but it was nebulous, like a feeling more than anything else. And then, as I was slowly putting things together, my grandfather passed away, and that is when I really started writing down memories of things he had told me. I was speaking to a much older relative – by this time we were in Bombay – and he said to me, 'You know, Anup, you had a cousin.' 'Yeah? I have many cousins,' I said. 'You have a cousin, my daughter.' I never knew he had a daughter. So I said, 'Where is she? I've never seen her.' He said, 'Just like your grandfather's village was attacked, ours was also. And as it used to happen during those times, the women would jump into wells.'

It's been more than fifty years and, every night, he dreams of his daughter in the well looking up at the sky, waiting for her father to come and get her. He said that's the dream he has had all this time. For me, that is where *Qissa* began, really; that was the one image that started my whole process of putting a narrative together. Everything that was fragments, a dialogue, a gesture, suddenly started coming together through that image.

I was thinking to myself that my uncle, even after more than fifty years, can speak to me about what happened to his daughter. But what about those women, you know? Where is their voice? I wanted this girl to speak to me, and that is what I tried in *Qissa*: to tell *her* story.

After I had written the first draft, I really felt I needed someone to bounce things off, so I collaborated with Madhuja Mukherjee, who knew the Bengali side of Partition. So that's how *Qissa* came about, as a film that we would finally want to make.

SG: Was Irrfan your first choice for the lead character?
AS: When I was writing *Qissa,* I had Balraj Sahni in mind. There is a sense of self that he carries. There is a fearlessness about him.

He's not the sort of actor who looks away and tries to show you that he's thinking. It's like he's already lived life, and therefore, he will look at you straight and his gestures are very precise. At the same time, he is a very compassionate man who has a great sense of his own dignity, and of what it means to be a human being in relationship to others.

If there was anyone who could come closest to that kind of gentleness, to that kind of inner fire, that quality of dignity, that understanding of the body, it was Irrfan. A voice that reaches out to you almost like a touch, you know. I thought: Irrfan. Irrfan would be the person to play it.

SG: Did you know him well when you reached out to him for *Qissa*?

AS: I didn't know him well at all. We had done one thing for television together. This was for Star TV, one of their [*Star*] *Bestsellers* episodes, and his name had been suggested by Mita Vashisht, his classmate from NSD.

I remember I was setting up a shot for this *Bestseller*. It was a very small crew; the actors were around. And I was in front with the cameraman, looking through the lens, and I was sort of choreographing the action. Many a times while doing so, I tend to hum something, just to [comprehend the] rhythm of the material. So I was humming something, unaware, and then suddenly, behind me, I heard someone singing what I was humming – a lyric from a *qawwali* sung by Nusrat Fateh Ali Khan. It was Irrfan. He had been listening. And from that moment, I think we really sort of bonded. Not only in terms of Nusrat saab, who was very, very important to our work, but also this whole idea of rhythm, that we both, in our own ways, seemed to have found important for us in our work.

These things for television you do very quickly, so we didn't have much time to interact. This was our one moment of interaction, us singing together. And when we did the shot, we enjoyed it immensely, because suddenly the rhythm was there. I could see Irrfan bring a quality that actors nowadays just don't have. So I had him in my mind, and I had a very affectionate sort of feeling for him from then on.

When I finally decided that I would like to cast Irrfan in *Qissa*, I called him and he said, 'Ah, I've been waiting all these years for you to call me.' There must have been a gap of ten years between the *Bestseller* and *Qissa,* and we had never met or spoken in between. But we carried each other in our spirit. I read him the script and I could see he was quite taken by it. He said, '*Anup saab, yeh toh mujhe haunt karti rahegi.*' I still remember those words: '*Yeh toh mujhe haunt karti rahegi, lekin main nahi karoonga yeh film.*' [It is going to keep haunting me, but I will not do this film.] I was completely taken aback. I said, '*Nahi?*' He said, '*Itni dark film hai.* Just think of it from my point of view. I have to live with this for at least six months – how am I going to live with this kind of darkness? I can't do it, I'm sorry. *Aap kuchh romantic likhiye na mere liye, jaise woh* Bestseller *ki thi humne.*' [Why don't you write something romantic for me, like that *Bestseller* we had done together.] I was superbly disappointed and left.

This is when he was still living on Madh Island. I took a rickshaw to the ferry. It was late in the evening. Really, I didn't know who else to cast. I didn't know whether it would be possible to make this film. As the rickshaw drove towards the ferry, I suddenly calmed down and thought about it – I realized that Irrfan had actually got the film completely wrong. And perhaps the fault was mine; maybe I wasn't able to narrate what was at the core of the film. So I rang him. I said, 'Irrfan saab …' – I still called him saab at the time; later I started calling him *janaab* – that worked very well between us. It carries, for me, all the respect I have for him. He always called me Anup saab; he never called me Anup. I always called him *janaab*. That little distance it created, a little formality, was very important because what we were doing was very fragile and intimate. That formality was important to balance the intimacy that we were trying to work out in our film. So I said, 'Irrfan saab, I think I haven't been able to say what I really wanted to say. Can you give me ten–fifteen minutes – let me just come back.' He said, '*Haan, aa jaiye.*' I'd left the script of *Qissa* with him and he was in the room upstairs. Sutapa [Sikdar], his wife, brought me in. She was a little sorry because I think she really wanted Irrfan to do the film and she liked the script very much. Irrfan came down the stairs with the script and pushed it across the table to me, which I understood to be '*Aap apni script le jaiye. Main padhne wala nahi hoon kabhi.*' [Take your script with you. I am never going to read it.] I said, 'I remember that you like the music of Nusrat saab very much.' He said, 'Yeah, of course.' I said, 'You know, when Nusrat saab sings, his whole face distorts. And sometimes that face can look really violent and monstrous. But the voice that comes out is the most beautiful voice that we have heard. That, to me, is this film.' He thought about it for a moment. Then he said, '*Achha, chaliye, upar chalte hain – thoda Nusrat sunte hain.*' [Let us go upstairs and listen to Nusrat.] 'I have some things of his that you might have never heard.' He took me upstairs and set up the music. Then he turned to me and said, '*Haan, main karta hoon na film, main karta hoon* – yes, I'll do it.' And that is how he agreed to do the film. Then that whole evening we sat, late into the night, just listening to Nusrat.

SG: This is such a lovely *qissa* about *Qissa*. So, once you had Irrfan on board, how did you get the rest of the cast? And once you had them all, what was the shoot like? It must have been really intense.

AS: I was very lucky in terms of casting. Pushpendra Singh [the filmmaker] was assisting me, and I gave him the responsibility of doing the auditions. He knew the script very well. Even when I did my shot breakdown, I made sure he was always with me, because I really wanted him to be a part of the film very deeply.

But there was something else. I felt that if I died – this was just a thought – there must be someone to finish the film. I trusted Pushpendra to finish it. So he was the one who gathered actors to come and do auditions. We had found someone who could possibly play Rasika's [Dugal] role – Neeli. I remember Pushpendra was not very happy but I thought this young woman would be good.

And then during auditions – strange … even to this day, Tillotama [Shome] and I laugh about it – we are not sure what happened. There was a room in some apartment. When Tillotama came to the doorway, she probably tripped and she came rolling into the room. There was a kind of *dhurrie* which rolled her up. She had to extract herself from the dhurrie. It was something magical. I thought you can't make a better entrance than that. I spoke to her for a few moments and then we asked her to do a scene. As soon as she started, I turned to Pushpendra and we knew that she was absolutely the person that we wanted to play the role of Kunwar. That is how we found Tillotama, by pure chance. I am so happy that she tripped and rolled into the room.

Pushpendra knew Rasika quite well because they are from FTII. I knew Rasika also because I had gone there to teach and she was around. But I was working with the direction students, so I didn't have much to do with the actors. Pushpendra said, 'Why don't you see a diploma film that she's done?' He showed me the film and I thought that she had the kind of restraint that you feel in the *alaap* of *Dhrupad*. That you just hold back, you hold back; you don't give. And yet things are slowly coming into being. She was amazing in that film. Her role in *Qissa* was completely the opposite. She had to play a young woman who comes from a family of performers. Banjaras. Pushpendra said to me, 'Why don't you meet her?' I met her and this was a totally different young woman. She's just giggling all the time, no matter what you say to her. Her movements are really eclectic, you know? She's never steady. She's constantly bouncing. She has this tremendous energy. And I told Rasika that I already have someone cast for the role; do you know *toona* [black magic]? If you do some black magic and that other woman disappears, then I'll cast you. She said yes, very seriously: 'I know *toona*, I can do *toona*.' She must have done some *toona* and we finally cast Rasika.

SG: When the film opens, Umber [Irrfan's character] says: 'Neeli, open your eyes. Tell me: what am I? Who am I? What curse have I brought upon myself?' Something so prophetic about these lines, now that I know this hilarious story of the '*toona*'.

There's so much of Irrfan that you see in that film that I'd never seen anywhere else. How did he, for example, speak that Punjabi? It's not something he knew from before, did he?

AS: Not at all. Despite the fact that he had been in Delhi for quite a while during his NSD days. But at that time, he was very much within the Hindi theatrical tradition. Well, there is a story there too. As you can imagine, with Irrfan, there are many *qissas*.

We had a Punjabi tutor who would work with the actors on

their diction and accent. Tillotama, Rasika and Tisca [Chopra, who plays Umber's wife] picked it up magnificently. Irrfan was having trouble. And he kept saying to me, throughout the shoot and even later, '*Yeh kaunsa toona aapne mere par daal diya hai, Anup saab?* [What kind of black magic have you done on me?] I should have never said yes to this film.' Every time he had difficulties with the dialogue, he would say that to me. After two–three days of the shoot, we were in the *haveli* where Kunwar [Tillotama's character] grows up. I had just finished shooting something inside with Tisca and Tillotama when I came out for a breath of air. It was evening – dusk. And I saw Irrfan in the garden – there was a grove of trees – and there was something strange in the way he was walking. So I stopped at the threshold of the door, just to watch him. He was walking through this grove; then suddenly he would stop and his hand would rise, and his other hand would go the other way. Something in his body would turn. And then, I heard him speaking. And humming. After a while, I realized he was speaking and humming the dialogues of the film. I watched him for a while and then asked, 'What is it that you are singing?' He said that he was singing the dialogues of the film.

During the rehearsal process in Bombay and then when we started shooting the film – from the very first day – an immense trust had built up between us. I also think that both of us felt we could push each other to go much farther than we might be ready to go. At the same time, we knew that we were safe with each other. Usually, I don't think Irrfan would speak about what he was doing. But by that time, I think we had formed this very deep trust. Of course, we had spoken a lot about acting, etc., etc. But he said, 'There is something … not in the words. I know the words. But that is not Umber. There is something in the way Umber speaks that I want to find.' And I said, '*Sunaaiye* – what are you doing?' So he sang a phrase. And I was quite struck by it. I said, 'There is something here.' Because, instead of speaking the words, he was just using one sound. Like an *aakaar*. He was creating a kind of rhythm with the words. Up and down, and stretch; up, stretch, down, up. I suddenly had a feeling that by not using words, he was in a sense not doing *sa re ga ma pa*. Where you have everything in order, in sequence. But by choosing to sing the words in *aakaar*, he was going between them. And thereby entering what were not established tones. He was somewhere in between. Therefore, he touched feelings and emotions which, if he had just tried to memorize the dialogue and speak the lines, he never would have. We would never have got that quality of Umber in *Qissa*. That was our breakthrough in the film.

From that, even I learnt a lot, in terms of how to move the camera, how to choreograph a little more finely the quality of light, how the light falls and how the shadow falls. It was all from these small exchanges that he brought to the film; he helped me see the film in a much larger way. In his playing of Umber, he is not doing the *sargam*, you know, but he is doing the *aakaar*, as in an *alaap* in *Dhrupad*.

When he does a gesture, it is always in process. In the sense that it finishes, but there is no agenda to the gesture. Usually when you look at an actor's performances, especially within Bollywood, when they turn, or they do a gesture, or they say something, everything has a fixed meaning to it. Now I am sad; now I am angry; now look at this glamorous me. The emotions are recognizable. The beats – you know them. With Irrfan, because he's working with rhythm, the beats keep on shifting. Sometimes they come to an end and you feel that the emotion is growing because that rhythm is still growing; the rhythm has not come to a stop. The rhythm from his body, his hands, his look, has entered into the tree, has gone into the sky. So that's what he was doing; he was bringing those qualities to the frame, to the composition, and therefore, to the film.

I think he was very conscious and keen always to search for himself. He never felt that he had *become*, you know; that he was now a complete human being or a complete actor, a complete husband, a complete father. He always felt that there is something more. What could I also be? What are my possibilities? He always thought in terms of possibilities. The search is what helped him then find techniques like singing the dialogue or letting the gesture be pure rhythm. What gives these techniques that solidity, that powerful emotion is a spirit trying to understand life.

This is my feeling about Irrfan's best performances: when an audience sees a performance like this, they are no longer seeing it from the outside. That quality of search enters them, that rhythm enters them. And therefore, his search becomes their search; they begin to find within themselves emotions, feelings, fragilities that they didn't know were there. I think that is why they love him so much. That love goes beyond being fans; that love is a very personal, intimate, deep affection that you have for something that is very fragile inside you. And that is Irrfan. Irrfan is the fragility of what it means to be a human being that we all carry inside us.

SG: That's so beautifully said. I think that's why when we heard about his passing, we all felt it so deeply. Did you keep in touch with him all through his illness?

AS: We were constantly in touch. We spoke every three or four days. If we didn't speak, we would text each other. After *Qissa*, we were together all the time. Even when he was in London, we were in each other's thoughts. I think a tremendous and deep friendship had developed between us. We were no longer just director and actor but we were really friends. But friends who never gossiped – I think that helped our friendship. We had no time for unnecessary things; we spoke about our work, what were our possibilities, where were we going together.

I was in Geneva when he called one day and told me about his illness. I just held myself back because I wanted to be pragmatic. I wanted to find a way out. I didn't want to believe that this was the end. These were early days. Even before he had gone to London. He asked me to find out in Switzerland about cures and what the doctors thought. And he sent me his Indian doctor's report ... Sutapa actually sent that to me. And I was very, very careful not to let him know how scared I was. Whenever we met or spoke, I always spoke about the next film we were going to do. He said, '*Saab, main toh nabbe saal ka ho jaoonga hum jab tak yeh films khatam karenge.*' [I will be ninety years old by the time we finish making these films.] I said, 'Yeah, yeah, we'll continue even after that.'

In London, I spent a lot of time with him in the hospital, at his apartment; took him and Sutapa to the Kew Gardens. Oh, we went to restaurants, we went to cafes. My wife came with me quite a few times because there was great affection between her and Irrfan; they teased each other a lot. They were much more informal than me and him. I saw the steady disintegration – which is a horrible word. One of the worst was much, much later – I think that's the last time I saw him – he was at the Lilavati Hospital. I had arrived in Mumbai and I said, 'I'm coming to see you.' It was afternoon. There was this strong sunlight streaming into the room from a large window; his bed was on one side of the room, covered in shadow. He was sprawled across the bed, like a broken puppet. I'd never seen his body like that. He was asleep, so I went and sat down on a chair. He must have heard me, because he lifted his head. Suddenly there was a transformation. He was in great pain, but he lifted himself and rested his back on the pillow and said, 'Ah, I wish I'd had this experience before the death scene in *Qissa* – I would have done it much better.'

SG: Oh my goodness.

AS: I said, '*Koi baat nahi*. I have another film where you also die, so you do it better there.' We just sat and joked about things, and it was wonderful because there was this certainty about him that he would overcome. And we would soon be working together. There was so much that he wanted to do; his search had not ended. There were dark times also, but I'd rather not talk about them.

SG: What does the world without Irrfan mean to you as a filmmaker and someone who knew him well? What does it mean to have a world without an artist of his calibre, and a human being of his – to use your word – fragility?

AS: I think there are two aspects to this. One, as a man. Without him, as a presence in my life, there is a sense of being lost. I don't know if I'll do all these films that I spoke about. Even the script that I've finally written, which was this third film we were supposed to do together, I have no idea whom to cast in it. My producers have seen the script; my friends have. And they have no idea who could play it; they all see Irrfan in it. That's one level.

The other is, as a friend. There is a small story I could tell you about our friendship. *Qissa* was a hard film to do because I had a horrible producer – very arrogant and aggressive. One particular day, I was in despair. However, we had to shoot the film, and so I had to keep up a front. We shot during the day, and then at night, I was in my room. It must have been around 1:30 a.m. We had to wake up around 4–4:30 for the next day's shoot. There was this knock on my door and Irrfan came into the room with his music system. He said, '*Ah, toh neend nahi aa rahi aapko? Mujhe bhi nahi aa rahi – chalo, kuchh music sunte hain.*' [You are unable to sleep? Me too – let's listen to some music.] So he switched on the music, and Nusrat started playing. And he knows that the actor who is very, very important to me, other than him, is Dilip Kumar saab, who means a lot to him also. So he said, 'Before we start, let's look at this thing from *Ram Aur Shyam**. So we watched the first sequence of *Ram Aur Shyam* on the laptop and we are laughing away; it's really a joyous sequence. He just sat with me all night. I think it was around 4 a.m., just before everyone started waking up, when he finally left. I tried to send him away many times because we had to sleep; we were shooting in the morning. '*Nahi, sunte hain, aur ek sunte hain.*' I realized that one of the production people had told him about my fight with the producer and that I was in bad shape, so he just came to be with me and give me strength. So, you know, not only as an actor was he reaching out always, but even as a friend. I've forgotten now what your question was.

SG: What is it like to live in a world without Irrfan, as a human, as an actor?

AS: I'll miss listening to music with him. On the other hand, as an actor, he has created something, given us something, that just lives; it's with us all the time. I don't even have to watch his films; I just have to think about one of his films and, even if I don't see a particular gesture or hear a certain tone, there's a feeling

---

* A 1967 Tapi Chanakya film

I get of his presence. And that presence is something that all of us have, or need, within us; it is our humanity. Our being open to the world, being able to observe the smallest things and enjoy them, our not having an agenda, not judging people – most of the characters that he plays have that quality, even when he plays really murderous characters. There is something about that questioning that he always carries. That is a gift he has left with us, of becoming more than what we believe we are. And not to allow our prejudices, our society, our ideologies to stop us, but always find a way – like in an *alaap* – to go between the tones and find something that lets you communicate in a much more sensuous and complete way with the world.

'I want the kind of journey Irrfan had'

RASIKA DUGAL

Rasika Dugal's impressive CV is dotted with a clutch of fine performances in films (*Tu Hai Mera Sunday* and *Manto*) and web series (*Mirzapur, Delhi Crime*: seasons one and two). One of her finest performances is undoubtedly that of the 'Banjaran' girl Neeli in *Qissa*. She speaks of what it was like to be on set, how she went about fulfilling the demands of her difficult role and sharing the same space as Irrfan.

———

SHUBHRA GUPTA: Tell me about *Qissa* and sharing a set with Irrfan.

RASIKA DUGAL: *Qissa* was such a long-drawn process. Between the shooting, the release and the festival circuits, it was over three years. So I met him reasonably often in those years, but not so much after 2015. Of course, my association with him during *Qissa* was very, very special because the combination of Anup [Singh] and Irrfan introduced me to the possibilities of performance. I didn't know that magic could happen in the time between action and cut. When you experience something like that with somebody, they become a very important part of your life, even if you might not have met them as often as you may have liked. A part of you almost doesn't want to meet them as often later. Because what you shared in that moment was so special, you know that life cannot match up to that. I wanted to preserve the beauty of what we shared in the time between action and cut. The first time I had that experience was on *Qissa* with Irrfan.

There's a point in which the film gets into a magical-realism space, which audiences and critics had many different things to say about. I always wonder what I would have felt about the film if I was viewing it as the audience. Would I have been enthralled when the film suddenly entered a space I didn't expect it to? Or not thought of it as two different parts?

I didn't have work for the longest time before *Qissa* came. To do a film with Irrfan, Tisca [Chopra] *and* Tillotama [Shome] was hugely exciting to me. I had worked with Tisca briefly before, but to be working with Irrfan was one of the thrills of the project. I remember reading this particular magical realism part in the script and thinking *ki* how am I going to execute this? I was familiar with Anup's work; I had met Anup often during my time at the Film [and Television] Institute, so I was nervous about how he would pull it off. I told myself: I'm sure he has a plan because he's that kind of director; he knows what he's doing. But how am I going to help him execute what he wants to? And these were also the final scenes of the film. Therefore very important, because that's what you leave the audience with. So it needed to be special. Especially the scene right before Neeli, the character I play in *Qissa*, she kind of falls off – or jumps off – the terrace. There's this moment where she's sitting and there's an interaction between Neeli and Umber – the character Irrfan plays – where he articulates his feelings around the loss of his land and his home. He talks about what it means to be a refugee. At that point in the film, he is a ghost, and she's interacting with him. How do you prepare for such a scene, right? And just before that, there was another scene in which Neeli sees this ghost-like creature for the first time and there's something about him which is like Kunwar, the person whom she loves, who is played by Tillotama. There's something about him which is like ... Umber. So she's trying to negotiate this very strange space between the love she feels for Kunwar and the fear that she feels for Umber, who had tried to rape her.

We were nearing the end of the film's shooting schedule. So far, everything we had shot had been, in my opinion, very, very special. I knew when I was living it that it was special, magical. That the experience I was having could not be traded for anything else, you know? It was so beautiful to live with that kind of joy for those two months, where you're not constantly questioning or second-guessing or trying to adapt. And so far, the shoot had gone so beautifully – I wanted every scene to therefore have that magic. And that's kind of unfair to expect out of every moment in a film. But as this was one of the final scenes, it had to work. I had to make it work. But nothing we were doing was really working. It was functional, it was efficient, but it didn't have the energy of the scenes that we had done before. Anup was dealing with a lot in terms of production, like many directors do while trying to make a film on a not-too-great budget. They have scenes to move on to; you can't get stuck on one thing. If you don't shoot the scene today, you're going to have to scrap it from your film. Anup had to move to the next scene. So I thought it was unfair to take my insecurities to him.

We were shooting in a village close to Chandigarh on a winter morning. I remember Irrfan was sitting on this terrace, rolling a cigarette. I went and sat next to him but didn't say anything because I'm also a little shy. I just looked at him in extreme desperation, as if to say, 'Please help me, you know better than me, you have so much more experience.' Irrfan just turned around, looked at me and said, 'Hmm.' Which was actually pretty soothing at that point because it told me that he also knows that the scene has not gone well, but he was just saying that it happens and we have to let go. I think he was mildly amused by my desperation to try and make it work, because he's probably been there and knows what an actor feels at that time when you know something is not working and it is the only moment you can try to make it work. So that 'hmm' meant, 'I understand what you're going through. I wish I could help you, but hey, this is life and this is what you have to learn as an actor.' So I was like, even he feels that the scene wasn't done right. At least I'm not wrong.

A couple of days after we had shot this scene, I technically had *chhutti* [leaves] for two–three days because they didn't need me for those days, as per the schedule. I had been out of town for two months when my husband [Mukul Chadda] came to Chandigarh to meet me. We went to watch a film in a theatre. I remember I was coming back from watching that film when I got a call from Anup. He said, 'Hey, I know Mukul's in town and you have the day off tomorrow, but would you mind if we reshoot that scene?' I was like, 'Would I mind? I would drop my life to come and shoot this scene!' A part of me got very stressed. Because if we are reshooting this scene, it means the scene was pathetic and that I have to bring my best game tomorrow; otherwise, it's not going to be worth it. So how do I now bring my best game if I don't know what to do? So I'm like, 'Anup, can I come and meet you right now?' He said, 'Okay, come meet me once you reach the hotel.' I went to his room to eat dinner together, and I said, 'What do you want me to do? Tell me so that I can prepare.' He said, 'Just turn up.'

Anup has this way of working which sometimes is very beautiful and sweet, but sometimes, on a bad day, it can also be a little confusing for an actor. Whenever you ask him a question – 'Anup, what do I have to do?' – he'll say, 'Have you read this poem?' And he'll recite a poem to you. I think the experience of working with him really taught me to let go of logic. It's really something you have to practise because, in life, you're taught so much to do it the other way. So I said, '*Theek hai*,' and I just turned up the next day.

It's an early winter morning. Irrfan is there, Anup is there. We start shooting the scene again. When we'd shot the scene earlier, Irrfan and I are facing each other and he's telling me how he feels about being a refugee. So Anup said, 'Rasika, when he's telling you this, can you just sit down?' I thought, *yeh kya bol rahe hain*. As it is, it was not working when I was looking into his eyes; now I'm supposed to sit down. This is feeling a bit *ajeeb*. But I said, '*Theek hai*,' and I sit down. And Irrfan just held my hand – of his own accord; it wasn't scripted. Then, after that, I pulled my hand away, got up and walked out.

Now, him holding my hand and me pulling my hand away was not directed or scripted; it hadn't happened when we shot the scene before. It was just something he felt like doing, something I responded to. Anup asking me to sit transformed the scene completely. We did eight takes of that scene because, after I get up and walk out, the camera has to track back, and there were technical glitches every time. In every single take, it was special, it was different. And none of those things I experienced at that time is something I can even effectively articulate; it's definitely not something I could have prepared for. There was one moment in that scene where I go and sit down, when there was almost something sexual about it. Which was not intended. And I remember there was this other take where I sit down and feel a fear gripping me because of the way Irrfan looked at me. The kind of fear when you feel somebody's going to … the best thing to compare that to is this fear I used to constantly feel in Delhi, as a college student. I would feel that somebody's going to come and grab me from behind. So it was varied and bizarre. In different takes, it was different. And I thought that, in life, it's very rare to have this experience, where you've been hit by magic. After that shoot, I thought: this happened to me? I was numb almost. I thought these were just things people write in a book or say in an interview.

Qissa was shot in 2012 and the first time I saw it was at the Toronto Film Festival in 2013. I had seen nothing of it before that. We were not allowed to look at the monitor during the shoot. When we had to dub a few bits of the film, Anup would only show me those three seconds. And I would be like, 'Anup, I need to watch the scene to be able to dub this.' He said, 'Trust me. I'm not showing you more; this is it.' And I'd be like, 'Anup, please can you show me – five minutes? And he's like, 'No, this cuteness is not going to work on me.' Anup is the warmest, nicest human being, but he can be a smiling assassin on some days. So I said, '*Achha, aap ne Irrfan ko dikhaya hai kya?*' [Have you shown Irrfan?] He said, '*Nahi, maine Irrfan ko nahi dikhaya.*' '*Aapne Tillotama, Tisca ko dikhaya?*' '*Nahi.*' When we watched it in Toronto, I was *waiting* for this scene. It had been such a special part of my life. But when I watched the scene, it felt like nothing. Then I started questioning myself. Have I built this up too much in my head? Between *Qissa* and *Manto**, I had very little work.

---

* A 2018 Nandita Das film

I thought maybe I have gone mad; I haven't had work for so long that this has become a big deal for me. Maybe it wasn't like that. Subsequently, whenever I watched the film, I would look at that scene again to see if I am missing something. Why doesn't it feel like it did when we shot it?

SG: Did you ever bring it up with Irrfan?

RD: This happened when *Qissa* was releasing, two years later, in 2015. Until then, I had watched the film about twelve times because we'd been to many festivals. Every time you go to a festival, you're expected to sit through your own film. At every screening, I would look out for this scene. After a few screenings, I was like, I'm not even going to look at it because it's just disappointing now.

I think one day before the release, there was a screening in Lightbox – this small, intimate theatre in Santacruz. After the film, Irrfan is standing next to his car, there are a few other people and we're all chatting. I'm standing next to Irrfan, who's saying, '*Tumne bahut achha kaam kiya.*' [You were great.] I thought, wow, after ten–twelve screenings, finally he's saying something to me. And his opinion matters a lot to me because he's so good at what he does. I had heard from somebody else that Irrfan had really praised me, said that I was a great actor. I was very excited, but it wasn't first-hand like this, right? And then he said, '*Woh scene jab hum shoot kar rahe thay, uss din hum dono ke beech kuchh hua tha, na?*' [When we were shooting that scene, something had happened between us, isn't it?] I was stumped because I realized it meant something to him too. Then he said, '*But screen pe bilkul kuchh nazar nahi aaya.*' [But it wasn't apparent at all on screen.] And I thought, wow, he remembered, he noticed, he felt the same way. And so many years later.

SG: Do you remember the first time you met him?

RD: Yes. It was the first day I was there to shoot for *Qissa*. The film was to start shooting the next day. There was a small get-together that the producers had organized in this very sweet hotel called Five Star Hotel, which had no five-star qualities [*laughs*]. It was a small hotel on a highway by Tarn Taran Sahib [a small city in Punjab], because we were shooting in Attari nearby. All of us had rooms there.

At the get-together, I was a little nervous about meeting Irrfan. He saw me and asked Anup, 'What happened to that other girl?' I don't think he was trying to be mean; I think he just became inadvertently tactless for a moment. I felt very bad. You know, as an actor, you sort of wonder … am I not looking the part? Why did he ask about that other girl? So yeah, that is my first memory of him.

There was this other time when we were shooting in that same village – in Attari – and this road needed to be cleared because the car had to pass. Everybody on that unit was making their best efforts to get that road cleared. But in trying to do so, they were messing up big time. It was like a comedy of errors. This German producer stood in the middle of the road and spoke to some twenty Punjabis, trying to communicate that they need to clear the road. And those villagers were like, 'Who are you, coming to our village to shoot?' It was one hilarious situation.

That night when we were having dinner, everybody started recounting the events of the day. I always had giggling fits, but Irrfan had a mega giggling fit. He wouldn't stop. I remember watching him giggle and cry. You know how you have tears when you laugh really hard? That night, I was also laughing very hard. Anup, Irrfan, Tisca, Tillotama and I would always try to have dinner together, and this was one of those nights when we happened to be in my room. Tillotama and I were shooting the next morning, but not Irrfan and Tisca.

I was very particular – I would go to sleep at ten o'clock no matter what happened because I had to wake up at five and sometimes have a bath with cold water in our 'five-star' hotel. And wash my hair at five in the morning. So I said, 'Listen, I'm not letting lack of sleep affect my acting process, no matter what.' But that night, everybody started giggling, nobody moved. You know, with Tillotama and Tisca, I was comfortable enough to be able to say, 'Bye bye, goodnight.' Anup was generally quite aware, so he would excuse himself when he realized the time was up. But I didn't have the ability to tell Irrfan *ki aap jao*. And Anup is giggling at what Irrfan is laughing about. Anup is looking at my face, knowing that I am stressed about tomorrow and want to sleep. Irrfan is in tears by then. In the middle of laughing and through those tears, I remember him saying, '*Anup, sir, aapko unko* [the German producer] *bolna chahiye ki yeh gaonwale yahan shoot ke liye nahi aaye hain; yeh unka gaon hain. Hum unke ghar aaye hain.*' [You should tell the producer that the villagers haven't come here for a shoot; this is their village. We have come to their home.] And he didn't make a meal of it. It wasn't [performative]; it just came out. I thought it was so beautiful – it really stuck in my head.

SG: This sounds like he was intensely aware of his surroundings; he cared about other people. Was it that? How would you describe it?

RD: I think he was acutely aware of things around him. Anup once said that Irrfan finds a way of being one with the universe. That is something you realize about him in the most intimate moments. That he had this quality of being able to connect with many things in a very intimate way. I was always full of admiration for that. He would notice a lot about everybody around him. I've noticed that about a lot of very good actors. I feel Nawaz [Nawazuddin Siddiqui] is like that as well. There's something that they sort of imbibe in a very casual interaction.

Once, I remember, I was going into the make-up van and Irrfan said, 'Who made this wig that you're wearing?' I used to wear a wig for *Qissa*. I was conscious, so I said, '*Kyun, bura lag raha hai? Wig lag raha hai?*' [Does it look bad? Does it look like a wig?] He said, 'No, it's doing something very interesting to the shape of your face.' I remember watching the film later and thinking he was right. It did. He's aware. He was interesting like that; he had a side you couldn't decipher. To me, he was often intimidating, not because he wanted to be, but because he was also much more accomplished than me. At that time, I was fairly new so I was [given to] a lot of adulation anyway.

SG: Were you in touch with him after *Qissa*? Was there any work together after that?

RD: No, we didn't work together, but we used to meet whenever Anup was in town. At that time, Irrfan used to live on Madh Island, where a lot of people would gather. Once I was late to one of those parties because I had a show in town. When I saw him, the first thing he asked me was, 'How was the show?' I felt like this was my colleague from drama school, just another student asking, '*Yaar, tera show kaisa hua?*'

SG: His passing is such a loss. What is it like to be in a world without Irrfan?

RD: I had always hoped and desired that I would get an opportunity to work with him again. I was very curious to see how his practices would have changed. I had learnt so much from *Qissa* and being with him and Anup. But he's left such a beautiful legacy that it makes me think if you're good at what you do, you last forever. It really made me feel the worth of being a performer.

SG: What's that one special thing that comes to your mind when you think of Irrfan?

RD: Poise. He had this very interesting way of being attractive. And it wasn't an acquired one; it was just there. Anytime anybody would ask me what kind of journey I want, I would always say I want the kind of journey Irrfan had. Because it's so spectacular, so rich. I know the beautiful thing about our lives is that every actor's journey is unique. But I think Irrfan's was very, very enviable.

'A gift that keeps giving'

TILLOTAMA SHOME

Tillotama Shome, who made a striking debut in Mira Nair's *Monsoon Wedding*, would have been, in her own words, equally at home with her first love, academics. In *Qissa*, Shome plays Kanwar, a girl raised as a boy, and how that very singular upbringing impacts her father Umber, played magnificently by Irrfan. It is an unusual, challenging role befitting an unusual, challenging film.

Shome's latest work includes sterling performances in *Sir*, an unusual story of love transcending class, and the hard-hitting crime thriller *Delhi Crime 2*.

SHUBHRA GUPTA: Tell me about *Qissa* and about working with Irrfan.

TILLOTAMA SHOME: Actually, we had done a film together before *Qissa*, called *Shadows of Time**. *Haasil* hadn't happened. Irrfan's success hadn't happened. I was, as usual, reading some book between takes and not talking to people on set, and he kept trying to talk to me. He would come into the room and ask, '*Achha, padh rahi ho kitaab*?' [Oh, you're reading a book?] I would say yes and go back to my book, awkward and hoping

---

* A 2004 Florian Gallenberger film

that he wouldn't ask again because I really didn't want to talk to anyone. But he would come back again and again. You know, I was doing my master's. Finally, he said, '*Tumhari kitaabein toh khatam nahi hongi; baat toh kar hi nahi rahi ho. Toh jo mujhe karni thi, woh main kar hi leta hoon, kyunki mujhe nikalna hai. Mera shoot toh khatam hone wala hai kuchh dinon mein.*' [You are going to keep reading books; you are not talking to me at all. So I'll just do what I have to, as I need to leave. My shoot is going to be over in a few days.] So I gave in and he said, 'You just did *Monsoon Wedding* with Mira Nair. I saw it and I liked your work in it.' I thanked him. Then he asked, 'So will you tell Mira to work with me? Because it's been many years. I got such a small part in *Salaam Bombay!* and then she had promised me she will work with me.'

I asked, '*Kitne saal ho gaye?*' [How many years has it been?] 'I don't remember but it has been long.' It was, I think, ten years since he had done *Salaam Bombay!*. I said, '*Yaar*, I don't know what I can do. *Main email deti hoon – yeh hai email.*' [Here is her email address.] Next day he told me that I had given him the wrong email address. I said it must have changed. I think I wrote to Mira later saying I met Irrfan and he really wants to work with you. I can't even believe that it actually happened. I mean, they did *The Namesake* together!

Then I saw *Haasil* while I was shooting for something up north. I was walking, saw a theatre and went in. I didn't know what film was playing. I just wanted the experience of walking into a dark room and not knowing. It could be the worst film … and it was *Haasil*! I was like, this is the man I had met during that German film. And I didn't speak to him! I had such a phenomenal opportunity, but at that time he was on a different trip and I was on a different trip. I wanted to study; I didn't even know why I was doing movies.

And then I left for New York to study, and it so happened that *New York Times* did an interview of *The Namesake* cast – an actual physical interview, at the Lincoln Center. There was Mira, Tabu and Irrfan. So this friend of mine said that he had tickets and I could join him and his wife. So we go there and the interview is going on and I can see the woman who was interviewing them slide in her chair whenever Irrfan would talk. It was as if she was going to fall off the chair! He can be really philosophical and deep, but that time he was being really normal. I could feel the magnetic pull this man had. Then the lights came on for the audience Q&A and he recognized me in that *bheed* [crowd]. He said, 'Tillotama,' into the mic, 'is that you?'

Please remember that we never spoke much at all during *Shadows of Time*; it was that awkward interaction over 'Please can you ask Mira to work with me?' So he said, '*Baal kaat diye tumne?*' [You've cut your hair?] What could I tell him – that I did cut it to save money. I was a student in New York. He said, '*Baad mein na backstage aana; bhaag mat jaana.*' [Meet me backstage later; don't run away.] After I went to meet him backstage, he looked at me and asked, '*Film kaisi lagi?*' I told him when Tabu gets the call about her parent dying, it was such a moment for me. It had a huge impact. Actually, after watching the film, I had gone to my boss. I gave him my resignation and said that I want to go back home, to India. It was not just the film, of course, but it was the last straw. I think my romance with New York was just coming to an end. I knew I didn't want to get a call about my parents and then sit on a sixteen-hour flight.

All those thoughts were in my head and I told him that Tabu just broke my heart in that scene. '*Uska kaam achha laga, mera*

achha nahi laga?' [You liked her work; you didn't like mine?]
'I didn't say that!' *'Koi nahi,'* he said. *'Agar achha nahi laga toh
achha nahi laga. Waise tum kaisi ho?'* [No problem if you didn't
like it. How are you, by the way?] *'Haan, theek hoon.'* 'So your
love affair with New York is over?' he asked. And I just looked
at him and said, 'How do you know this about me? You're not a
close friend, you're not somebody I keep in touch with.' And he
just looked at me.

You know, not too many people from middle-class families
get a chance to study on a full scholarship and do what they want
to do. On the surface, I looked fine, and he just saw through it.
He said, *'Chale aao, wapis aa jao.'* [Come back.] I was very taken
aback by this man's ability. I felt very uncomfortable. How did
he see through this? I thought I'm glad I'm not going to meet
him again.

And then I met him for *Qissa*. I was already feeling so
vulnerable with just being in Bombay, being who I am and, by
then, Irrfan was Irrfan, the great, celebrated actor who everybody
wanted to work with. My part was so tough that in order to also
enjoy playing it, one just had to do so much homework every day.
I also had that incident in New York at the back of my mind. I felt
like he could see through me.

But Anup [Singh] was really like our glue. The reason I got
very close to Irrfan and Rasika [Dugal] was because of the kind
of set-up Anup had created and the workshop that we went
through. I don't know if he told you about our rehearsal process.
I had walked in late, because I was coming from my Kalari
class, or my swimming class – I don't know which one. Irrfan
was waiting, knowing I was in some class. He said, 'I just got so
exhausted listening to how many things you're learning for this
film.' And I was like, 'Yeah, it's really busy. Punjabi, then Kalari,

226

then swimming and then driving.' To which he said, 'What were you doing all your life? You didn't learn anything? How can you put so much pressure on yourself for one film?'

I was so taken aback – what a rude thing to say! I thought he'd say, 'Wow, how sincere,' like other people do. But I felt like he was teasing me. And I thought I had to fight back. So my relationship with him was always very tense and I never thought of him as a friend. I knew we were just colleagues. But I perceived that he was also charming me. And I wanted to fight back and to engage with him because, secretly, I felt he was accessing something which was very aspirational for me – the idea that I have, the notion of an artist, as some kind of conduit between worlds. There was *something*; I can't explain it in words, Shubhra, which is why I find it very difficult to talk about Irrfan. But for me, he was a body, a medium, a vessel, and I felt that there were galaxies that he was communicating with.

In certain films, I felt it didn't work. I remember feeling comfortable telling him, 'I saw this film but I thought you were so distracted in it. I know people are talking very highly because it's a big filmmaker and it's you, but I felt you were a little bored.' I could never have said this to any actor other than Irrfan, unless they were a close friend. He was not a close friend, we didn't fraternize. We never socialized. I have hung out with his wife and had long chats, but not with him; I always kept this distance. Because I didn't want to be close to him; I wanted to just observe him. If I became close, I might have missed out on being able to really watch him from a distance.

I know he has impacted me in a certain way. He and Anup came together at a certain time, and it was like a planetary movement that perhaps happens once in a lifetime, where these two people with two very specific kinds of aspirations and desires meet. I was somewhere on their radar and I really enjoyed watching Irrfan's conversations with the universe.

Someone, I remember, told me how Irrfan always looks away [during a scene]. I only understood much later why he did that. One day Anup showed me a Chinese painting as prep for the next day. I said, 'What is this?' 'In Chinese painting, there is a "dragon stroke", which is the masterstroke,' he told me. 'Every other element in the painting is either at odds with it or in harmony with the dragon stroke. Our film too has a dragon stroke. Each scene can either be in harmony with it or against it.' He said that as an actor in this scene, you have to think about what is around you. It's not just your co-actors, but also this house, this *haveli*. And then if you go out of the *haveli*, the hills, the trees. And what are they? Are they your friends; are they friendly? This environment, is it antagonistic, are you in harmony with it? And that's when my mind exploded. I was only concentrating on co-actors and lines and feelings and context and subtext. Suddenly I realized so much more: this house, the banyan tree which has witnessed the violence that my father and his fathers perpetrated, the hills behind, the field. Do I feel ... does Kanwar feel comfortable, comforted, by this field? Or intimidated? Would Kanwar hide in this place? Suddenly every element became an element to play with, to engage with. Then I started noticing Irrfan trying to converse with every bird, leaf, branch. I think, if anyone had worn a perfume a hundred years ago and walked by, Irrfan's soul, his mind, might have just picked up a waft of that perfume, which is what caused his head to move a certain way in a scene. And you may wonder why he looked away. It's because there's a lot going on around us and he wanted to feel it. Anup helped me understand that Irrfan embodied it in a certain way.

SG: It really helps me understand the process that all of you used to put *Qissa* together. And the effort. The Punjabi that Irrfan spoke was almost flawless. What is it like for you to speak that language? And to interact with Irrfan in the way you did?

TS: I think we went past language. Me being petite, maybe Anup should have taken a taller actor to play Kanwar's part – slightly more masculine. We had spent so much time on the language, we were prepped – that wasn't even a concern on set. It was really a most joyous set. Given the ghosts that were haunting the story, and the spirit of the film being already so heavy, Anup created the most joyous environment to work in. He had also invested so much in knowing each of us individually. He knew what worked for Irrfan would not work for me.

He could make Irrfan listen to a song when he was stuck. I would panic; the lyrics wouldn't go in. He realized that he needed to give me imagery from nature, because that was palpable and physical, [possible] to understand, see and emulate.

I don't think Punjabi was really an issue. We had seven months to work on it, and we made fun of each other if we messed up. Once Irrfan said something and it almost sounded like Tamil. I wasn't there on set; Anup and Rasika were shooting a scene – I think when he buys her jewellery? When they came back that night, Rasika and Irrfan were recounting. Rasika was saying, 'Today Irrfan's Punjabi was exceptional, and Anup said it was extraordinary!' And I was like, 'What? I missed it! Irrfan, why don't you show us what you did?' After he said something, I was like, 'What?! What language is that?' And he said, 'I just got so caught up in the moment that I forgot which language I had to do the film in. It was just a sound that escaped.' But that was his way – he was always making it sound like he wasn't prepared enough. I think in *Qissa*, we were just trying to catch a certain sonar frequency and trying to make sure we were all on the same frequency. Because we had to feel the spirits. Umber is haunted very strongly by certain things, and Kanwar understands his/her father's ghosts. We had so much prep and so many classes – all that was really taken care of. What was really important was knowing that we are on the same *sur*—

SG: *Sur?*

TS: Yeah, Anup's world. Because it's a very specific world. I'll give you another example. We were eating dinner one day, mid-shoot, and we were coming close to shooting the scene at the end of the film – the magical realism bit in which the father and son become one. Rasika and I were saying to each other, 'Did you understand what happens?' When they become one, it's a very common imagery of the father, son and the holy ghost. We understood it intellectually but we thought, let's just ask Irrfan over dinner, very casually and see what he understands of the scene. Very slyly, we said, 'Irrfan, that scene – what do you feel about it?' He just saw through it and asked, '*Kya hua – samajh mein nahi aaya?*' [What happened – you didn't understand?] And Rasika and I were like, *oh shit, he knows! Of course he knows, he knows everything.* Then he said, '*Koi nahi, mujhe bhi samajh nahi aaya.*' [Even I didn't understand.] I said if none of us have understood, and only Anup understands, what is this film's destiny? I told Irrfan we were really worried – would people understand this tale?

He said something so simple, Shubhra. He said, 'Tillotama, just be happy that you are getting to work with someone like Anup so young. You're really lucky, okay? It's really boring to understand everything; it's very rare to be in a situation where you don't understand something. And the understanding may or may not come. Believe me, you will look back on not understanding this scene as one of the biggest treasures of your life.' I was like, okay, this is Irrfan being like Anup, giving some kind of philosophical, rubbish answer to a question, when an actor's really asking him to explain the scene. He will act well and get away with it, whereas we will get stuck. But this is the answer I got.

The day we shot the scene, we realized that what was happening on set was beyond language; the mis-en-scène was so strongly drawn. Not just at the physical level but the colours that we were wearing, the foliage, the contrast – everything intoxicated us. We knew we were just following something – a spirit. And then that scene arrives where he lifts me up and opens his mouth wide. For the shot to work, at some point I have to slide down and fall at his feet. While the camera stays on his mouth. And I have to be at his feet for quite some time. The sand was hot. And this is where he swallows me and becomes this younger Umber.

When I did that scene, I fell at his feet, and Shubhra, I saw his feet. His feet are so beautiful; his nail bed is like a perfect petal, like these lotus feet. I didn't know he had such beautiful feet. I forgot that the sand was hot, I didn't feel the temperature – I was looking at his feet and I felt so much love for them and, somehow, in that moment, that scene made sense to me. That this is probably how Kanwar feels for Umber: it's irrational; it's love. It makes no sense. And I didn't care – anyway we never saw the monitor – but when I saw the film, I remembered what I had felt.

And that's what I felt when I watched the film: for me, I was literally at his feet, through the whole film. Of course, with that one solitary transgression of shooting him in one life, but otherwise, Kanwar was very much in awe and in love. Retrospectively, I realize that I feel that kind of *shraddanjali*, or whatever is the word. I don't look up to him – I see his flaws as a human being. I really love Sutapa. I argue with Irrfan about a lot of things, I feel like he can really be a provocateur; he's provoked me a lot. He would always tell me, 'You're so thin; why have you lost so much weight?' It used to annoy me, because I found it very hard to put on weight and it's something I'm very conscious of. I told him, 'Do you know how thin you are? Have I ever mentioned it?' And I walked off. I stopped short of saying, 'Have some grace. You are sounding like one of my stupid relatives.'

But I think during *Qissa*, I observed him, I learnt that when you are surprised as an actor in a scene, the audience will be surprised. They can't help but not be, because *you* were surprised. And that magic happens.

SG: You said he was not a friend, but he saw you. Was he perceptive in ways that were deeper than other people?

TS: I've not known him for that long and yet, he's been able to see through me. And I don't know if others have had this experience, but this is my experience with him. It has made me uncomfortable but it's also made me, as a result, reach out to him to try and understand everything. I still communicate with him. He'll continue to live in me and Anup and in anything Anup and I do. If there was a trinity, I was lucky to be the third leg.

I'm beginning to understand him more now. When he was there, I was so busy fighting him. I understand when Anup says that it's as if a song is playing in Irrfan's head when he's walking. Like, there's a rhythm, you know? When I started trying that in my work in other films, I realized it can completely change a scene, depending on which song you have chosen to play in your head. It's the same scene, same lines; now just switch the song that's playing in your head, and everything changes. I have got a treasure chest of such things – it's infinite. Irrfan is a gift that keeps giving.

We were shooting for *Angrezi Medium*, to which I said yes because of a scene with Irrfan. He had come back from his treatment and I wanted to meet him, I wanted to be in a room with him. My mum had already been diagnosed with cancer. He looked at me and said, 'Something's changed; you're looking very happy.' 'I *am* very happy, Irrfan. It's so nice seeing you.' Then Homi [Adajania] came and talked about the scene. And again Irrfan asked, '*Tell na, why? Kuchh toh badla hai since we met.*' I told him, 'I am getting gigs – maybe it's that.' He said, '*Arre*, that's very nice but I don't think this is *kaam-wala* happiness.' Then *baat-baat mein*, I said that Mumma has cancer. Then he was like, '*Achha*, no wonder.' And we both started laughing. We didn't have to say anything. I never talked about his disease but we just looked at each other and laughed a lot, and he said, 'Everything's changed, *na*?'

'Yeah, everything's changed. I don't feel anything when I don't get a job or when I walk away from a job. Everything's changed.'

In that moment I felt, perhaps, like an equal, where I had a glimpse of what it feels like to have your brush with mortality and to dialogue with it that close. To then laugh and feel free of this industry and its standards of success and failure. How immaterial it all felt, ever since my mum was diagnosed. I could understand him in a way that I would perhaps have not been able to before.

SG: You used the word 'fighting' – you kept 'fighting'. What did you mean?

TS: See, in retrospect, you are very, very wise, but at that time, I felt hard done by the industry. I was bristling with a sense of tragedy. I would say: 'Why am I not getting work? I want to work hard, Irrfan; you don't understand what I'm feeling.' He said, 'I understand; I've been there. Don't be a Meena Kumari. What book are you reading?' Always deflecting the topic. I would think he's deflecting but he was actually asking me to go back to the love of reading, which was my steady companion way before acting came into my life.

Then I realized that he's just telling me that's where I was naturally going; why have I taken a U-turn and now complaining about not getting work? What happened to all that astral contemplation? But at that moment, when I didn't have the kind of work that would make me feel secure, his success was so aspirational. Because I had access to him, I felt like he wasn't being helpful. 'You're not mentoring me,' I said. 'There's nothing to mentor; you'll have to go through this.' I thought it was so cold, so matter-of-fact; Anup was far more sympathetic. I don't want to use the word 'fighting' as if we were fighting as equals or had some misunderstanding. The little bits that we have exchanged is absolutely the path that I am happy walking. He was just telling me that I was wasting my time trying to fit in. Because I was so hungry to be accepted, and he was like, 'You're so lucky that you're not. Do you know how boring it is?'

SG: He used the word 'boring'?

TS: He used the word, yeah. He was often bored with the things he did. I didn't see that; I looked at it as just volume of work. Which is why he would tell me, 'Do you know how lucky you are? Just relish it for as long as you can. Let *Qissa* open in your life.' I get it now, since my mum's illness, that one doesn't have to reach a great experience immediately, you know? One can let time pass, let that experience have its time to grow.

I think that's perhaps what Irrfan was trying to say, trying to ask me to enjoy the gaps and the silences without the noise of a set or people. And it really worked for me, being able to walk away and then come back to a set after a year and [experience] the kind of joy you feel in giving yourself, because you're so replenished.

I remember during *Angrezi Medium*, the director said, 'When you come on set, we'll discuss all this with Irrfan also.' I said, 'No, no, we'll just try it. If I start talking to him about what to do, he'll get bored. It's better to *do* it. I'm a hundred per cent sure.'

And Irrfan did say, 'I'm very bored.' I was like, 'That's not good at all because I have only two days of shoot, and you have the whole film.' I thought, *oh shit, man, he's bored; I chose the wrong day to come on set. Whatever – I'll just try.* So I tried something and we finished, and he was just laughing. He was like, '*Yaar, itna mazza aaya*; that was great!'

During the next take, I did something that was written and safe. He came up to me and said, 'What happened to you? Why did you stop having fun?' I said, 'I just thought maybe I pushed it too much and one should just do what is safe.' He said, 'Please, *please*, Tillotama; I've been dying to have fun.' So I was like, 'Okay, then. You want to have fun?' I don't know if you remember the scene where I say this is how much it's going to cost you – *ek crore, ek crore* – and we just went at it. I swear, after that I realized we could have found a hundred different ways in which '*ek crore*' could have been said. By the end of it, we were just dying with laughter inside.

I realized that he's so secure as an actor that he is up for you to change things around. He doesn't say 'Why didn't you discuss with me?' before trying something – I was caught unawares by it. For someone who has worked as much as he has, is so well regarded in the industry and can be pretty intimidating [by way of being] elusive, I have to say he really allowed me that space.

SG: When you think of Irrfan, what is the one thing that comes to your mind?

TS: I think of a kite. There's a thread that holds a kite between the sky and the earth. I've seen Irrfan fly a kite. I feel like they're one and the same. Seeing Irrfan on a *chhat*, the kite fluttering, his *lungi* fluttering, you just feel like you're part of something. When he's there, there's something so expansive and light.

'He would have been the king of good cinema today'

NIKKHIL ADVANI

Nikkhil Advani directed *Kal Ho Naa Ho*, one of the most enduring, endearing Bollywood romcoms. He also made the gritty action thriller *D-Day*, in which Irrfan plays an Indian undercover agent. The film gave Irrfan a strong footing in mainstream, starry Bollywood: his co-stars were Rishi Kapoor and Arjun Rampal.

Advani has since expanded his corpus with films like *Airlift* and *Bell Bottom* and web shows like *Mumbai Diaries* and *Rocket Boys*.

SHUBHRA GUPTA: *D-Day* took Irrfan into a zone which was not his. He wanted to do the bigger films – films that would take him to an audience which was not niche. I think *D-Day*, like *Life in a… Metro,* took him to a much more mainstream platform.

NIKKHIL ADVANI: I did *D-Day* after the failure of all my so-called 'highly commercial' films: *Chandni Chowk to China, Patiala House*. I really had been written off in the industry. I remember Anurag [Kashyap] meeting me and saying that I have to go back to the *Is Raat Ki Subah Nahin* days, the Sudhir Mishra days – return to that zone.

Even when I took the idea to Irrfan, it was Anurag who convinced him that he is not the director of *Kal Ho Naa Ho*, he is the writer of *Is Raat Ki Subah Nahin*; he will do the film that he's promising you he's going to make; you will not have to spread your arms out in Karachi. Trust him. Irrfan and I met in Anurag's office. We had gone to see the trailer of *Gangs of Wasseypur* and Irrfan, in his typical fashion, was rolling his cigarette, and his whole issue was that it is a good script. 'I love the script, I love this space, I love this genre, I want to do it; I don't know whether he [Nikkhil Advani] will be able to do it.' So Anurag had to convince him.

But I think that he definitely wanted to do bigger films with the so-called 'more mainstream' directors. He had done so many films he was so proud of that had not seen the light of day. He had done *Paan Singh Tomar* and that hadn't released yet. I promised him that when *D-Day* is made, it will have scale, and that it won't be just another film which nobody was going to get to watch.

SG: Let me take you back to your beginning. You did *Kal Ho Naa Ho*, which makes every romcom list. The films that followed were in the same zone. How did *D-Day* happen?
NA: At that time I was writing a film which, later on, I'm glad I didn't make. It was very much in the same fluffy, bubblegum-y zone. And *D-Day* came to me because I stopped fooling myself that I needed to stick to those films as a big-time filmmaker. Instead of basically just telling a story. The idea of *D-Day* came about from the extraction of Osama bin Laden in May 2011. I didn't have any money. To make *D-Day*, I sold my house in Alibag.

In forty days, we sat down and wrote the script. And it excited me, it excited everyone who was hearing the idea, whether it was

Rishi Kapoor or Arjun Rampal. It just happened that I was on the set of Sudhir Mishra's film, *Inkaar*. Arjun was between shots. We were chatting. I told him about *D-Day* and boom, next thing you know, he was in the film. And it's a good thing because, if I had taken somebody like a John Abraham or an Ajay Devgn, Irrfan would not have done the film. Because Irrfan really understood the film. He used to tell me that the hero of the film is Rishi Kapoor. He said that he's a king; everything is about him. We are serving the process of what is going to happen to him; he's the one who has the great entry, the great interval point. He said, 'I don't know why I'm doing this film, because all the beats lie with him. But I just love this genre, I love this space; I've never done this before. And you have to promise me that you will do it like this.' Then I showed him a BBC documentary called *Secret Pakistan*, in terms of how I wanted to treat the film. And he said, 'Are you sure you're going to do it this way?' I said, 'Hundred per cent.'

On the first day of the shoot, I landed up with my piece of paper with fifty shots all broken down. '*Irrfan bhai, main aise shoot karoonga, phir next shot aise karenge, phir idhar se,' wagerah wagerah.* [I will shoot in this way, then the next shot will be done in this other way, then from here, etc., etc.] He looked at me and he said, '*Yaar*, Tushar is the cameraman. *Tushar shoot karega; tu mazze le na?*' [Tushar will shoot; why don't you relax?] 'Don't do anything else; just observe. *Masti karo; agar tujhe lag raha hai ki kuchh mil nahi raha hai na, tab tu mujhe bol.'* [Have fun; if you feel you are unable to find anything then tell me.]

So, honestly speaking, what Irrfan did for lots of us filmmakers was that he allowed us to become honest. He told us *ki* just do it; you don't have to start manipulating everything. When you're doing a *Kal Ho Naa Ho*, you're only thinking of how to manipulate this huge audience to cry at this point, to laugh at this point.

You're not allowing them to follow that story. And Irrfan just said, 'Don't do anything. You've written a good script, everything is working, the cast is there. Let's just enjoy ourselves.' Irrfan allowed me to become a little more spontaneous in everything that I did after that. So yeah, he was phenomenal in that sense.

First of all, he makes everything so effortless. He just comes over there and he's on. You think, wow, when did we do this? When did we prep for this? Everything that I had inside my head, he's actually doing it over there and doing it better. And then you realize that maybe it was just one conversation we had some time over chai; he observed, he figured it out.

Irrfan became this mega star, but unfortunately, it happened by the time he went. But he gave the answer to the question that the industry had: can Irrfan open a film? He proved he could. He proved that with *Hindi Medium*, with *Qarib Qarib Singlle*. And then he went. So what it allowed people like Anurag [Kashyap], Vikram [Vikramaditya Motwane], the filmmakers struggling with this whole notion of how to capture that Friday. Irrfan was there for you, to help you make the films you wanted to make, and still capture the Friday.

SG: That's a good summation of the Bollywood that used to be and the Bollywood that it was starting to be. What I'm hearing you say is that Irrfan was able to do the part as well as help the filmmaker in getting where he needed to be. Like, get the performance in there and get the story in there. And get the producers to fund it. I mean, would getting funding be an issue with an Irrfan film?

NA: Your observation is bang on. But also what happened was that in the early 2000s, when Irrfan started out, Hrithik Roshan was breaking out. Hrithik wanted to be the star like Aamir Khan and Shah Rukh Khan, right? Same with us directors. In 2003–2004, when you are a debut director and you are making your first film, you don't think beyond Shah Rukh, Salman and Aamir. We used to just think about these three. And it was filmmakers like Tishu [Tigmanshu Dhulia] who were working with Irrfan around the same time. *Haasil* came out in the same year as *Kal Ho Naa Ho*, you know?

But for the next generation of actors, after Hrithik, Abhishek [Bachchan], Akshaye Khanna, all these guys, for the next lot of actors, the person to emulate was Irrfan Khan. Ranbir [Kapoor] used to talk about Irrfan's performances. Ranveer Singh would talk about Irrfan's performances. It was no longer about Shah Rukh. I think Aamir was clever, because he straddled both worlds. He would do both commercial and the more offbeat.

For a Ranbir or a Ranveer, it was Irrfan. So somewhere or the other, Irrfan started being accepted by a larger section of the industry. If he was doing the film, more money started getting pushed so that the film became bigger. And at the end of the day, the thing is that you cannot shoot *Paan Singh Tomar* any differently than the way Tishu shot it. The problem lies in the way it gets released, right? I mean, it does not get released in a fraction of the way as a *Dangal** or a *Chak De! [India]*† – both films about sports – get released. What happened is that more and more studios and directors and producers started believing that Irrfan Khan can bring the money. The minute that happened, people did not want him to just do the offbeat films; they wanted to take a larger punt on his films, but for larger returns.

---

* A 2016 Nitesh Tiwari film
† A 2007 Shimit Amin film

SG: But I did not actually get the sense that there were so many people lining outside his door and saying, 'We want to work with you.' Because his audience base was still not the masses, as it is with the three Khans or Akshay Kumar or Ajay Devgn. So I'm intrigued when you say that his films started to go bigger. When do you think that happened?

NA: I think *Life in a ... Metro*? Although it was an ensemble, people noticed Irrfan Khan. I remember it being a massive hit. And I think *D-Day* too.

D-Day took me by surprise. I had no idea that it was going to become the kind of talking point that it became. The interesting thing about *D-Day* for me is that people forgot I made *Kal Ho Naa Ho*. So for me, that is a lovely thing.

SG: I was going to ask you, was that a boon or a bane, that people forgot you made that film? Your debut.

NA: This is my analysis. Because of *D-Day*, people finally gave me credit for *Kal Ho Naa Ho*.

Because everything that happened post *Kal Ho Naa Ho* with my relationship with Karan [Johar]. I was in Dharma Productions and I was part of *Kuch Kuch Hota Hai** and *Kabhi Khushi Kabhie Gham*†. And then comes *Kal Ho Naa Ho*. Then I leave Dharma Productions. All the films I did afterwards, including *Salaam-e-Ishq* ... People didn't believe I could make one love story, so I chose to make six love stories [*Salaam-e-Ishq* has six love stories]. I was arrogant, I was angry: why are you not believing that I could make one love story? I'll make six, and I'll do it better than anybody else. And it didn't happen. Every time, I was only trying to prove, prove, prove.

---

* A 1998 Karan Johar film
† A 2001 Karan Johar film

D-Day set me free. Irrfan Khan set me free. He told me, 'You don't need to prove anything to anybody. I'm telling you, if you make another *Kal Ho Naa Ho*, I'll walk out of the set. You just do what we have discussed in the readings, the research, what we have discussed when you narrated the script to me.'

The first person who saw *D-Day* was also Karan. I called Karan and said, '*Yaar*, I want you to see it; I've finished it.' I had a screening for him in the afternoon. He said, 'You know, this is what you were supposed to do. I don't know what the fuck you were doing all this while.' And I said, 'I was trying to beat you!' Because I never got my due. Everybody felt *Kal Ho Naa Ho* was directed by Karan, not Nikkhil.

After *D-Day*, I read a review, Shubhra, which said the maker of *Kal Ho Naa Ho* has done a 180-degree reverse, and I actually got tears in my eyes. For the first time, they said 'the maker of *Kal Ho Naa Ho*'. Today when I talk to ADs [assistant directors] and young filmmakers and say, 'So you want to talk about *Kal Ho Naa Ho*,' they say, 'No, sir, we want to talk about *D-Day* and we want to talk about Irrfan.' I don't think Irrfan expected the kind of reception that *D-Day* got; I don't think any of us expected that.

SG: It's such a coincidence that *Kal Ho Naa Ho* came out the same year as *Haasil*. Obviously, someone like Irrfan would never have occurred to you when you were casting for *Kal Ho Naa Ho*? Because you needed a certain kind of look, and Irrfan was tall, rangy, lanky; he had a very striking face and I think he was sexy as well. But he did not fit into the chocolate-box hero mould. Do you think the way he looked sort of worked against him?

NA: Yeah, like I told you, Shubhra, we would not think beyond Shah Rukh Khan or Salman Khan or Aamir Khan. As young debut directors in that so-called milieu that we were all working within

– whether it was Yash Raj [Films] or Dharma [Productions], whether it was Excel [Entertainment]. Even a Farhan [Akhtar] needed a *Dil Chahta Hai*, you know?

Irrfan Khan would always be either the villain or the inspector who turns out to be the murderer in the end. The notion of Irrfan romancing Preity Zinta and dancing to '*Maahi ve*' in *Kal Ho Naa Ho* is completely unbelievable. And then you see a *Life in a... Metro* and what Anurag [Basu] is doing with these actors – Irrfan Khan, Sharman Joshi, Dharmendra – and you're saying, 'Wow, I can make an ensemble romcom in which there is no Shah Rukh or Salman.' And it works, man. Irrfan's playing Monty, and this is the same guy who was in *Haasil*, in *Maqbool*. So yeah, given the opportunity, Irrfan would surprise you totally.

SG: Do you think Irrfan was a disruptor? And do you think he came at the right time?

NA: Yeah, he was definitely a disruptor. And I think that he also empowered several other disruptors. Whether it was Vishal [Bhardwaj], [Anurag] Kashyap, Tigmanshu [Dhulia], and [Anurag] Basu himself. I mean, if you look at *Haider*, you have Shahid [Kapoor] for two hours of the film, and Irrfan lands only at the interval, but you come back thinking of Roohdaar, in those cool John Lennon glasses. And he would empower you; he empowered me. He basically said, 'Don't think about the money; think about the story. *Money aa jayega.*'

It's funny, because when I was shooting *D-Day*, we actually came upon the opportunity to produce *Airlift* with Raja [Krishna Menon, the director]. And Raja's first choice was Irrfan.

SG: Oh, not Akshay Kumar?

NA: No. I had been telling Irrfan, 'Look at this script; it's fantastic, written by the same guy who wrote *D-Day*.' So he hears the script and then says, 'It's fantastic. And I might regret this but I cannot do this film because you need a bigger star to do this.' I remember exactly what he said: 'My shoulders are not broad enough to carry this film. Because you need a budget and I can't give you that budget.'

SG: So he had a very clear perception of his own worth.

NA: Yeah, yeah. It does not happen with most actors. Most actors have no clarity and do not know what they can bring in, what their value is. And I think that is something that Irrfan actually got by working in the West. Where, if you're working with Tom Hanks, he treats you as if you deserve to be there. Nobody's doing you a favour. His approach was always that: he made you feel very comfortable, he made you feel that you are everything at that point. He made me work very hard to get him on my set. But once he was there, he was just superb. I'm thinking about the films that he did with Kashyap ... He never did a film with Kashyap, did he?

SG: No, he didn't.

NA: It's so funny, *na*? Even somebody like me, who's a friend of Kashyap's and has followed his career, I cannot imagine that they have not done a film together. Because, in a sense, he enabled Kashyap to think like Kashyap. And whether they did films with him or not, everybody was writing for him at one point. I wrote *D-Day* thinking only of Irrfan Khan; there was no question. For me, Wali Khan *was* Irrfan.

SG: Everyone I've spoken to has said that this would have been his time. What do you think?

NA: I totally agree. The people that he empowered and the people that he enabled, they have become extremely powerful in the industry. And those same people are in a position today, thanks to the advent of Amazon and Netflix, etc., etc., where they are calling the shots in terms of what stories to tell. I know Irrfan was doing *Gormint* with Amazon, which will never see the light of day.

See, indie cinema was always edgy; it was always pushing boundaries, rewriting the formulas, trying to tell stories in a different way. But you cannot talk about mainstream cinema being edgy without talking about Irrfan Khan. Whether he was part of the film or not. He would have been ruling today because every director worth their salt today would want to pick up the phone to talk to Irrfan before anyone else.

Honestly, I don't know if I'm making sense, but Akshay, or some films that Akshay does, fall into that category. When he agreed to do *Airlift*, Raja asked: 'Will he be as good as Irrfan?' I said, 'I don't know. *You* make him as good as Irrfan.' We had actually gone to Akshay with a different script and he said, 'Why are you not giving me *Airlift*?' To which I said, 'Because the director doesn't want you; the director wants Irrfan Khan.' So Akshay replied, 'I will do whatever Irrfan is doing; I will do the readings, I will do the workshops with the director, I will do whatever you want me to – just let me do this film.'

Like, I'm so happy for Manoj Bajpayee. He is working with Kabir Khan on a film, with Raj [Nidimoru] and [Krishna] D. K. on [*The*] *Family Man 3* now; we are talking about doing a film together. Manoj has reached a stage where he can say, 'I don't have to only *think* about working with directors; I can pick up the phone and say, "I heard a script – would you like to direct it?"' And he can set up the film. Which I think Irrfan would have also been doing today.

When Irrfan passed away, I called up Tabu and we spoke about that lovely shot in *The Namesake*, where he turns around and he's looking at her in the airport. And on his face, there is this thing: will I ever see this woman again? There's no dialogue and he just does it beautifully. I told her that there's a scene in *D-Day* where he's saying bye to his wife and his child at the airport – a similar scene – and he does something over there which I could not have directed; he did it. So yeah, he would have been the king of good cinema in this country today.

SG: What is the one thing that comes to your mind when you think of Irrfan?

NA: Effortlessness. Everything was effortless with him. There was no tension at all; there was no stress. He was quite Sufi in that sense. I remember my costume person coming to me, aghast, saying, 'I cannot believe the conversation I've had with Irrfan – he's upset with me that Arjun Rampal is looking broader on screen than he is. And can we give him shoulder pads?' I said, 'Are you kidding me?' So it was not as if Irrfan Khan did not have insecurities. But it did not show at all on the screen. Once he had decided what he wanted to do, it was effortless.

PART III
2013-2020

'He was always looking for something meaningful to do'

RITESH BATRA

Irrfan got into the global eye with Asif Kapadia's *The Warrior*. Mira Nair's *The Namesake* deepened and broadened that awareness. But it was **Ritesh Batra**'s debut feature *The Lunchbox*, which got Irrfan not only film festival acclaim but also international box office rewards in non-traditional Bollywood territories.

Batra has gone on to do *The Sense of an Ending*, *Our Souls at Night* and *Photograph*, successfully straddling Hollywood and Bollywood.

SHUBHRA GUPTA: When you were writing *The Lunchbox*, did you always have Irrfan in mind for the role?

RITESH BATRA: Yeah, I did. I mean, after I finished writing, I did, absolutely. And I had written significant portions with him in mind, so if he didn't do it, I would have to rewrite it. Luckily, he did it. One of the executive producers of the movie had sent him the script, because she had worked with him on *The Namesake*. And he loved it; he could see himself in it.

SG: When you reached out to him, how did that go?

RB: We met in his office the first time. He and his wife Sutapa were there; they had both read the script and loved it. He was telling me how rare it is to come across material like that. And he was very kind. He asked me how I planned to shoot it and, at the end of the meeting, we just shook hands. A few weeks after that, I met him at his house for dinner and also to go through the script – he had a lot of thoughts. That's when I asked him clearly if he was doing it and he said, 'Of course I'm doing it.' So it was kind of a very pure thing. There wasn't much back and forth or thinking.

After that we started meeting regularly. When I got into pre-production, he was shooting another movie. And he would just call me if he was on another set. You know, in Bombay, the two-hour drive home, the traffic – we would just take advantage of that. I would get in the car with him and we would go through the script. We would meet at his place. And every time we spoke, I rewrote a little bit and he appreciated that. Each time I would give him a new draft. He was trying to get into the script and I was trying to get the script closer to him. Since then, I've always worked like that and it's helped me a lot.

SG: Irrfan has played people older than his age many times over. He got the body language of Saajan Fernandes so beautifully. So I was wondering whether a lot of that character was in your head, or was it something that you both created together?

RB: The thing was very clear in the script and also when Irrfan and I spoke: I never asked him to walk like an old man and he never did. He actually didn't have the body language of an old man in that movie. Like, we were very static in the movie. In most of his scenes, usually he's sitting on the desk. When he walks out of the office, it's pretty fast, because he's trying to get away from people. But it wasn't the story of an old man. It was the story of somebody who feels old, you know? Somebody who's just done engaging with the world.

Once, I remember, the casting director was on set and the three of us were talking and he asked us, 'Why didn't you cast Naseer [Naseeruddin Shah] in this movie?' I think he knew the answer also; that it was never the story of an old man; it was the story of somebody who feels old. Irrfan was very smart; he read into all that. He was a person who drew things from inside himself. If it was a story of somebody in their sixties and he didn't have that well to draw from, he wouldn't do it; he was too smart for that.

SG: I actually didn't mean old in the 'old' sense; I meant older than him at that point. He was not as old as Saajan Fernandes would have been.

RB: Sure, but I think my answer answers your question, right?

SG: Absolutely, yeah. But I really thought that he just *got* the character. He wore it like a second skin.

RB: Yeah, he was really good at what he did.

The thing with him was that he was very open. For him, it was like a journey. It was not like we were there to cover a script. Even though he and I loved the script, it was like a journey that we were going on together. And it was very pure. We spoke a lot, and sometimes he would be like, 'Oh, this costume is not right and we should not shoot unless we get it right.' And I would say, 'Yeah, absolutely.' And then we would change our plans. He was very protective of the details but he was also open. So it was really very pure, working with him. I think everybody was just in a zone of creativity.

SG: Right. So let me take you back a little bit: when was the first time you became aware of Irrfan, the actor? Had you been following his work?

RB: Yeah, I had seen him in the TV shows – in *Banegi Apni Baat* and stuff – when I was growing up. And he made a real impression. But I've always been aware of him. Then when all his other movies came out, when he became very successful, with *The Namesake* and *Paan Singh Tomar* and all that, I always followed his career. I had finished writing this script, I was ready to shoot for a year or two, maybe three, before we actually shot, so all that time I really wanted him in it. One day we had to stop shooting early – there was some problem – and he told me he had once decided not to act anymore. Then he did *The Warrior*. I think he and I got close through *The Lunchbox*. And we took it around the world, all the releases – it became a real friendship. He used to talk to me a lot about Asif [Kapadia] as well, so I got in touch with Asif towards the end and when Irrfan passed away. It seemed that Irrfan built his creative community with people he trusted over time and then we were always looking for something to do with him again, but it didn't happen.

SG: I was just going to ask you whether you were planning on doing something together after *The Lunchbox*.

RB: Yeah, we were planning to do something together; we were just waiting for him to get better. So it's still sitting here. I would say the last three–four years of his life, we were talking about it, a lot.

SG: It's quite amazing how well he came to be known, and not just in India.

RB: He's super well regarded and everybody I meet or talk to or work with always mentions him. And a lot of people really took it as a big personal loss, you know, across the world. He was in demand. People who can watch a performance and see how complex it is – they want him in their movies. Once I was watching *Hamlet* in London and Danny Boyle was sitting in front of me, so I just tapped him on the shoulder and said 'hi' and introduced myself. And then right away, he knew. He was like, 'Oh, you worked with Irrfan; I worked with Irrfan too.' I mean, he was definitely regarded as one of the best actors in the world. Not just someone really good who came from India.

And also for *Lunchbox*, we both had a conviction that it was going to work outside. He was really pleased that we could tell an Indian story to the whole world.

SG: How hard is it for an Indian actor to find work in the West?
RB: I think for anybody who's not from a system, it's really hard to get any work or to get anything done. It's a very, very difficult business. For directors and writers, it's difficult in a different way because we've spent years developing something and we're hoping for a green light. But for actors it's even harder because they don't have any control. They are not at the inception of the thing, so for something to come their way and for somebody to have the imagination to say, 'Oh no, this person should do it' – you're really depending on other people's judgement. But I don't think he was waiting around for anybody; he was just doing one thing after another. I mean, he was a stalwart. I would have been so excited to see more of his work in world cinema; it would have really been something. He would have really furthered the goalpost for all of us. It was just the beginning.

I don't think he ever looked at any project like a ... great Western project or Eastern project; I think he would try his best to do something if it was really interesting and if he felt that the people who were doing it were capable of executing it. That was very important to him. Sometimes some things came his way and he would be like, 'Oh, this is really good but the people who are making it don't seem capable of executing it.' Then that's pointless; that's not going to translate from the page onto the screen. He was very astute about that, and he was just interested in putting out good work. That's a really humble way to be. I learnt a lot from him about that. Because I think, you can't spend time broadcasting your intentions and you can't say, 'I'm going to do this, I'm going to do that.' You have to *do* it first, you know? And then it'll become whatever it'll become. He was pretty much in that mode of thinking. He could have moved to LA if he wanted to and he would have got a lot of work. But he was interested in just … finding good work, anywhere it existed. If it was a good part for him and if it was a good movie, he would do it.

SG: Yes. The pairing with Nawazuddin Siddiqui in *The Lunchbox* led to some of the best parts of the film. How did you think of casting Nawaz, or did you already have him in mind?

RB: No, I didn't have him in mind because Nawaz hadn't done a lot by then. But I had seen him in *Peepli Live** and I thought he was really soulful. Then I met him and we spoke about it. He and Irrfan had a prior relationship; they had worked together before. So that made it easier. It was really great. We would rehearse, always together – he [Irrfan], I and him [Siddiqui] – those scenes that we did. And then leave it, you know. Those were some of my most fun things to shoot also. I wish they could have worked together more after that; I would have loved to do something with them.

---

* A 2010 Anushka Rizvi film

SG: Did you have some special ways in which you vibed to get what you did in the movie?

RB: No, we just talked. It was easy because it was very specific. We were both invested in the script and we had talked so much before and I had rewritten so many things. So we had some things that we really came together on. But on that point, I think I noticed on the set that he was reading a lot of books, because by the first week, he had figured out the pace. The pace of the film is very special, you know? It takes its own time; the tone of the movie is very specific.

He was reading all these Murakami books on set. He was reading *Norwegian Wood* at one point, and books of the same tone and pace, and I thought that was really interesting because, to help me get into the shoot, I had also read some Murakami books. What the tone of the film is going to be, what speed it's going to move at – that's a very hard thing to get a handle on. And the sooner you get a handle on it, the better it is for the movie. I never spoke to him in those clear terms because I didn't want to make it intentional. But he picked up on it. I know he was always watching and listening. In so many ways, we were on the same page.

SG: What is that one thing you thought made him this great actor? What was that thing about him that drew people to him? That drew the eye to him?

RB: He was just an amazing presence on screen. It is a gift that he had as much as it was a craft that he had honed, you know – it was both things. But he had a very 'star' presence. Not everybody has that. Aside from that, I think he was a person who worked from the inside out. And in the short experience I have had, I've worked with only maybe three actors – including Irrfan –

who have that … the ability and desire and to go deep and to invest so deeply in something. I don't want to tell you anything cliché but he was always looking for something meaningful to say, something that would stay with people. He wouldn't just do any work.

I don't know about the past, but since I met him to even a month and a half before he passed, when we spoke on the phone, he was always looking for something really meaningful to do through his work. That's the side of him I know. There was no settling for anything less. There's something interesting he said in an interview once. We were in India and somebody said, 'What do you think now that your movie has made …' *The Lunchbox* apparently made ₹140 crores outside India; I don't remember, but it was definitely more than a hundred crores. So Irrfan said that the movie's not a piggybank, to go around the world and collect money. It's not a begging bowl. There are deeper reasons to make a movie. I've met random people in some small town here or there who've said, 'My favourite movie is *Lunchbox*.' That movie really travelled deep into the heartland of the US. Even in France, everywhere in the world. If he had something to say, he would say it through his work.

So I don't know how to answer your question about what made him a great actor because his skill and his craft were just perfect. He had a really great knowledge of the medium too. So I think he would have been a great director as well.

He was always playing to the camera but very subtly. And, you know, I have studied these things and I've worked with actors who have decades of experience over him but much less awareness of the camera. In the end, that's the instrument through which you're telling the story. He had this great skill with the dance between the actor and the camera. That's not something everybody has:

you have to be very observant; you also have to be invested in what you're doing.

SG: Do you miss him? Do you miss him as someone who is not there to make all these great movies? I've been asking this question to everybody: what is it like to live in a world without Irrfan?

RB: When it happened last year, I had some notice but honestly, for me, it's been really hard – I can't lie about it. I haven't felt a bigger loss in my life. For a lot of people, it was like losing a family member. There are very few people in the world who are unabashedly themselves. And they give you the wherewithal to be yourself too. When somebody like that passes away, it's a big loss for everyone. Just knowing he was there on the phone even; I could just WhatsApp him, send him a song or something that I'd watched. Recommend a show, send him books – we were both big readers – a package of books that I know he would like and vice versa. You know, that connection, I really miss that; I miss talking to him. It's a hole, where he was.

'Almost like an oracle'

SHOOJIT SIRCAR

Shoojit Sircar, director of successful films such as *Vicky Donor*, *October* and *Sardar Udham*, gave Irrfan what no one else in Bollywood had: a chance to play a regular guy next door, without any discernible quirks, in *Piku*. Not a cop. Not a villain. Not a complex, conflicted lover. Rana is just an everyday guy trying to navigate the tangled skeins around a quirky father–daughter duo, making us believe that the gorgeous Deepika Padukone – Piku – will fall for him.

SHUBHRA GUPTA: I think Rana Chaudhary was a fabulous character. So I wanted to know, when you were looking to cast *Piku*, was Irrfan the only one who came to your mind?

SHOOJIT SIRCAR: Yes, we started off writing Rana thinking only about Irrfan and nobody else. When we were conceptualizing the character and the film too, we instantly knew that Rana was Irrfan. We told him, 'We're writing something like this and we'll come to you.' He was anyway quite excited because he liked me, my work, but most importantly, he liked Juhi's [Chaturvedi, the screenwriter] style of writing and approaching a story. So he wanted to work with us. We knew if it wasn't Irrfan, we may have to scrap Rana's character completely and think of something else because it was one of the most dull characters, a character who has got nothing, who is just sitting there, observing this Bengali family. So you need some really high-calibre actor – or an artist, I would say, not just an actor. There are many things that Irrfan brings in. So he was always in our mind and we couldn't think of anybody else.

SG: In your journey as a filmmaker, you must have been aware of Irrfan much before you did *Piku*, right? What was the first time you actually saw something that he was in?
SS: It was Tishu's [Tigmanshu Dhulia] film – Tishu and Jimmy Sheirgill … what's the name of the film? The one in UP?

SG: *Haasil*?
SS: *Haasil*. That was the film which had a very strong impact because of Irrfan. Then I went back to see *Ek Doctor Ki Maut**. He just disappears into his character in the film. And any actor who disappears, I consider one of the finest actors. I think *The Namesake* had already come by that time. That was another one which evoked a very beautiful feeling. See, we knew that he's an actor with much artistic skill, which is different from a lot of method actors that I have seen and worked with, being from theatre. As a person, he was very evolved. Whenever we met him, we just spent many hours sitting there, drinking chai, eating *jhaalmuri* in the office, and we'd just talk. There are moments when you come to know a person, when you're not talking about cinema but about many other things. Of course, cinema, acting, we keep discussing in this industry. But we also talked about

---

* A 1990 Tapan Sinha film

various other topics, from places to philosophy to astronomy to astrophysics. All that was quite beautiful, which made us bond with each other. We enjoyed our sit-downs.

SG: Do you remember the first time you met him?
SS: He had called me and said, '*Maine tumhari film* Vicky Donor *dekhi.* I just want to come to your office and have chai with you.' So he just came in and started talking about Juhi, asking how she wrote the script. Then he started asking about my interests. He came to know that I love football. Then he said, 'My elder son Babil loves football – *usko bhi leke jao khelne ke liye. Woh kya karega mujhe maloom nahi. Woh mere jaisa hi hai.*' [Take Babil with you to play football. I don't know what he is going to do – he is just like me.] And we got him some Bengali *jhaalmuri* and he said, '*Yeh yahan milta hai?*' [This is available here?] I said, 'Yeah, of course, *sab kuchh milega.*' [Everything is available.] So that was the first interaction and he really liked it. First day, he came to the office just to tell us, 'I like you guys, so whenever you want, give me a shout and we can collaborate.' And then we kept meeting. I organized a very special showing of *Madras Cafe* for him. He came out and told me, '*Mujhe kyun nahi liya usme?*' [Why didn't you cast me in it?] Straightaway.

SG: *Achha*, he wanted John Abraham's* role?
SS: Yes. Of course he said it half-jokingly, but there was something serious about that joke. So I said, '*Irrfan, ab toh film bann chuki hai.*' [The film has already been made.] Because he was alone, he gave me a ride and then we spoke – that's it. Then, of course, finally *Piku* happened with Irrfan.

---

* John Abraham plays an intelligence officer in the 2013 film.

SG: Now that Irrfan isn't with us, who else can you think of for your films?

SS: Who else now? He's no more and I feel that void. Whenever I think about it, I wonder: where do I go? I have no one to cast. I have nobody. It's a pure compromise I'm doing at this moment. Because these two–three film subjects which were running in my head were with him in mind. Irrfan is the biggest loss. His particular way of looking at the character, the mannerisms or the method that he brought into a character, was way above ... he was almost like an oracle who is fulfilling a prophecy.

I remember one scene in *Piku*, from the first day that he came in. I had never seen him in front of a camera. I'm watching the monitor; he's there doing nothing, just hanging around, but I just felt that oracle there. Oh my god, you know ... He was just *telling* me something. He brought that mystic quality with him, which you rarely see in actors. In rare films you could feel that mysticism; why and how, it's very difficult to explain.

In *Piku*, of course the character was written, but I wanted to see more of him, his pure performance. As a director, I craved that somehow he could be there in some more scenes and for some more time. That's why he is so beautiful. He was a solace not only for the director, but also for the film. His presence was so, so deep. For example, when I would tell Irrfan that this is what we are doing for tomorrow's scenes, he would say, '*Aap sab ko brief kar ke aa jao mere paas.*' [Come to me after you have briefed everyone else.] So I'd brief everyone and go to him. And he would roll his cigarettes. And he would keep listening. At some point, I would get exhausted talking about the character. So he would say, '*Nahi, nahi*, you keep talking; *mujhe bolte raho.*' He had some hard disc in his head, which he filled and filled and filled. So when a scene happened, you wouldn't know what he'd do. I'd given complete freedom to all the actors, *ki* you don't worry about your restrictions; you do whatever. Sometimes he'd turn back, sometimes he would just come in front of the camera. Sometimes he would not *look* at the camera for some of the important scenes; he would just look away and do something else. But everything was so organic. Such a dull and dry character could be beautiful – only Irrfan could do that.

SG: Yes, 'organic', the word you used – which is to say that he literally grew out of the scene. It was as if you could not imagine that scene without him.

SS: Yes. And also, his emphasis on certain words would make a difference. Normally you have to push the actors to the last moment and you have to extract. For him, it was a free flow, you know? I could enjoy sitting behind the screen and watching him. Once I had finished my briefing and he'd taken it all in, he was just on his own. It's like theatre: he's on a stage and he's on his own. In *Piku*, the advantage was also that I shot very, very long scenes. The camera would roll for ten–eleven minutes. It's almost like a small act on stage. He was so happy that we were not calling 'cut' and just letting them do whatever. Of course I had lived with the script for two years, churning out, detailing everything. But when you see things playing out in that frame, it's beyond my control at some point. And what Irrfan does is like an enlightenment.

SG: Was it fun to be on set with him? How did he react to Amitabh Bachchan's presence? Were they very intense actors disappearing in their different little corners and then returning for a scene before going away again? Or did you all hang out?

SS: That takes a couple of days, for them to acclimatize with the environment of the set. It was all pretty normal. There were days when Irrfan and Deepika [Padukone] would just go off the set and prepare. So I would ask, 'Are you ready to shoot?' They would say, 'Ready.' That surely happened between them.

With Mr Bachchan, I think everyone working with him for the first time is very aware that they are working with him. I had seen that Irrfan would sit on the side and observe Mr Bachchan. Not just his acting, also how he was preparing. And whenever I was sitting with him in his van, he would say *ki*, '*Yeh aise hi prepare karte hain har film mein tumhare saath?*' [Is this how he prepares in every film he does with you?] And slowly, within a few days, he was completely free of the legend of Big B.

Before we took the script to Irrfan, he thought it was a romantic film. After the first reading, he said, '*Mujhe toh laga yeh romantic film hai.*' So I said, '*Nahi, Irrfan, yeh kuchh ajeeb sa hi hai but aisa hi hai.*' [It is something strange, but it is what it is.] He was expecting some love story because it had Deepika. So we kept talking and talking, and he was thinking. Then it took us a few days of reading and sitting and having chai before he understood our groove. When he got into our groove, he was absolutely what you see.

I wanted to tell you about the first time I bonded with him. My first – not meeting – conversation with him was on a phone call. I was about to go shoot this film called *Shoebite* [unreleased]. And one lady calls and says, 'Irrfan wants to speak to you; can he call you?' I said, 'Whenever he wants to.' He called me in the evening. I never expected this call – Irrfan calling was a big thing for me. He called and said, '*Shoojit, maine padha aaj news mein – tum* Shoebite *kar rahe ho?*' [I read in the news that you are doing *Shoebite*.] This is all before I met him for *Vicky Donor*. I said, '*Haan, Irrfan.*' He almost sighed and said, '*Nahi, yaar*, Shoojit, don't. *Main bhi toh same subject pe kaam kar raha hoon. Tum mat karo, yaar.'* [I am also working on the same subject. You don't do it.] I said, *'Yaar,* I am going to the shoot.' So he told me, *'Haan, I know tum shoot pe jaa rahe ho* – I read in the paper. *Main teen saal se iss pe kaam kar raha hoon.'* [I have been working on it for three years.] I thought, oh shit, I've committed a crime! I said, 'Irrfan, I am feeling very bad. I didn't know you were working ...' 'No, no, of course you don't know but ... *nahi, yaar, tum jao shoot karo.* [You do your shoot.] *Suno, agar tum by chance yeh film chhod dete ho, nahi karte ho, mujhe bata dena, yaar. Aur agar koi nahi karta, main kar loonga tumhare saath. Collaborate kar lete hain. Tumhare paas apna script hai; main apna script deta hoon.'* [Listen, if, by chance, you quit this film, let me know. And if no one else does it, I'll collaborate with you. You have your script; I'll give you mine.] I remember this was our first conversation. It was a crazy one.

SG: So did he actually have a script?
SS: Yes. He was working on exactly the same idea.

SG: Such a coincidence. Why did he have to look outside India? Was he interested in going international because he wasn't getting his due in Bollywood? Or was he just getting offers he could not refuse? Artistic fulfilment? Money?
SS: No, I think he was offered and chased because of the kind of actor he was. Whether Iranian filmmakers or Bangladeshi filmmakers or, of course, Hollywood and Europe – the way he was going, he was just starting up, I'm sure. As an artist, that hunger is always there, to perform, to tell stories. As I said, he was really interested in astrophysics and astronomy. So he would

always talk about magical feelings. And when he was diagnosed, he would speak more about this. Every day when we spoke, he would say, 'I'm feeling more magical.' Then he would go into the micro details of philosophy and Sufism and I don't know what else. And he wanted to be with those people; he didn't want cinema at all. It was purely about Darwin, about black holes, the galaxies; I don't know where he was going. I think that he must have felt that magical thing.

He got a taste of Hollywood through *The Warrior* and everything, but in the Mira Nair film [*The Namesake*] he really got completely intoxicated with the performance. He used to get lost when he was performing. He just wanted that *nasha*, that intoxication. There is no doubt that the international scripts and the films that he was getting, they were steering and stimulating him as an actor. And this must be the reason he was not getting the kind of fulfilment he wanted from here. But for *Piku*, he left a very important Hollywood film. He said, '*Dada, main yeh aap ke liye chhod raha hoon.*' [I am leaving it for you.]

SG: Amazing.

SS: Yeah, because they were shooting at the same time. See, it was Mr Lee [Ang Lee] who wanted to work with Irrfan on *Life of Pi*. Of course the character called for it, you know. When it came to *Slumdog Millionaire*, they wanted to work with him; there was no other actor they thought of. So I think this must be the reason that he was getting his due. And international films have the kind of exposure and money; those would have been other considerations. But I am sure he would first try and experiment. And he would surely bring in some depth in the character, whether the script had it or not.

SG: Even if he did get these big films, his roles were all very small. Except for *Life of Pi* …

SS: I was once discussing *Life of Pi* with him. He said, '*I wish mera jo pehla performance tha, ussi ko rakhta.*' [I wish they had used my first performance in it.] He said this after the film released and he saw the climax.

SG: I think he did his best work with people in India, his own people, in his own language, his own ethos. And that ethos did not really give him his due till he did *Hindi Medium*. Until then, he had always been somebody who was doing interesting work but not being a very traditional Bollywood hero. Because he didn't look like one.

SS: You are absolutely right that in the Mumbai film industry there are many taboos and many, many issues. An actor feels that insecurity: how will he be accepted? I remember when I told him that he was working in *Piku* with Mr Bachchan, he was excited. He didn't know, at that time, who was playing the girl's character. I told him Deepika was playing Piku's character. I think this increased Irrfan's acceptance in the mainstream. Before *Piku*, she [Deepika Padukone] had done mainly mainstream films, box office-driven. That was a big moment for him – that an A-grade actress had agreed to work with him. That helped them bond, because Deepika was scared that she was going to work with Irrfan. With Mr Bachchan, she had already done a couple of scenes. But Irrfan was known as an artist, so she was scared of that in the beginning. On the other hand, Irrfan was not scared of working with her; he was more excited that he would work with a popular mainstream actress.

SG: They were so good together, especially in that lovely badminton scene.* You just leave it there ...

SS: I suggested that we finish the story with badminton. In some friendships, you don't know what they're going to do with their life later. Some people in your life, they are never quite defined.

SG: So many of the people, including you, have said that now they don't know whom to turn to, without Irrfan. While Naseeruddin Shah and Om Puri created space for someone like Irrfan, Irrfan was bigger because he had a broader base, and he made space for people like Rajkummar Rao, even Ayushmann Khurrana. Do you agree with that?

SS: No, not completely. I think that space was already there. I can think of some of the finest actors from the golden period of the sixties and seventies, even up to the nineties, from Soumitra Chatterjee to Dhritiman [Chatterjee] in Bengal, from Utpal Dutt to Pankaj Kapur to Amol Palekar, and Naseer saab [Naseeruddin Shah] and Om Puri.

What Irrfan brought was the acceptance of an actor like him in mainstream movies, not just in offbeat films. There was something mesmerizing about him that ordinary people wanted to see. It was not only the cinema intellectuals and lovers, but normal people. For example, in *Paan Singh Tomar* and *Haasil*, he made everything special by being real, organic. Just by being human. Irrfan Khan was not just an actor. I knew him very personally. He was much more than just a method actor who's come from an acting school and is just going to do a film. You have to have that something more ...

---

* The film ends with a scene in which Irrfan and Deepika's characters, Piku and Rana, play badminton.

SG: What was that something more?

SS: I think that's why I said when I saw that first frame of his in *Piku*, I thought it's an oracle. I thought this man is telling me something; something is happening here. He's *talking* to me. He's bringing such a spirituality into the film, you know? Just seeing his performance, I did not have the audacity to cut. After *Piku*, many people said they felt that it was a very spiritual experience for them. And I gave that credit to Irrfan. He brought that purely by just being there.

SG: I think you were in touch with him through his illness. A part of this spirituality that you spoke about, Sutapa Sikdar said that it really helped him navigate that tough journey. That must have been hard, for both you and him, when you were in touch in those days. I know that from everyone who's spoken to me, including Sutapa, that whenever he had some time, he would reach out to people that he valued.

SS: I came to know of the disease through the news. So of course I was in complete shock and felt devastated. I was just thinking: how will I face him now? What do I tell him now? Then I got some courage and I called him: 'Is it okay if I come?' He said, '*Haan*. We are just planning what to do next, whether to go abroad or stay in Mumbai, do alternative therapy, etc.' So I went there and sat with him. After a point we started talking about it. I had a lot of experience in terms of cancer, so I wondered when I would see him next so easily. I didn't know about his mental condition. Of course it had disoriented him completely, shocked him, because he didn't expect this. So I gave him whatever I could. And when I was leaving, I said, 'Irrfan, will you come with me inside the room?' I took him inside and just showed him a couple of breathing techniques. I said, 'Irrfan, don't stop this. Chemo and everything will happen, but don't stop this.' *'Haan, dada*, I'm going to.' Next day he said, 'I did it in the morning and enjoyed it.' And then every alternate day I went there and just sat with him. I have my own breathing exercises which I have invented myself; I just show them to whoever I think can understand. So I showed them to him. And then I took him some books. Third day, I took the big books of Vivekananda, Ramakrishna Paramahamsa. I said, 'Irrfan, I don't know if you will have time or not; just read a line here and there. He said, *'Dada, yahin rakhna* – I'll take them.' And then he went to London. I told him on video call that I could not go to London. I think some other friends went. Because he knew my interest in spirituality, astrophysics and everything, he said, *'Dada*, I have kept so many things for you. You must come to London.' The words 'magic' and 'magical' and spirituality don't come to someone suddenly. It was there in him; it was always there. It bloomed in him maybe because of his diagnosis. He was alone, he could assess, he could think about himself.

SG: What is the one thing that comes to your mind when you think of Irrfan?

SS: The other day I dreamt of Irrfan. I was holding him and I had tears; I don't know where it was. I just see him smiling. If I get him again, I will just run and hug and clutch him.

SG: Never let him go.

SS: I'm going to clutch him, yeah.

'We do not have another Irrfan'

SANJAY GUPTA

Sanjay Gupta, maker of trendsetting action-packed movies, several of which were inspired by South Korean hits, gave Irrfan the kind of part in kidnap-caper *Jazbaa* which is usually written for Salman Khan. Irrfan jumped right into the whole leather-jacket-dark-glasses-one-liners act, shooting off a sardonic line here, blasting a kick there, playing second fiddle to the real hero of the film, Aishwarya Rai Bachchan. As usual, he elevated the material.

Gupta is best known for *Kaante*, *Zinda*, *Shootout at Lokhandwala* and his latest, *Mumbai Saga*.

SHUBHRA GUPTA: As someone who has been firmly in the commercial–mainstream zone, how did Irrfan get on your radar?

SANJAY GUPTA: I have known Irrfan for a really long time, because we were all aware of his work. And he had also worked in one of my films called *Acid Factory*, which was way back in 2009. He was the main antagonist in that film and yeah, I was always looking for an opportunity to work with him again. At that time, I was contemplating either *Jazbaa* or *Mumbai Saga*, which just came out [2021]. I first narrated *Jazbaa* to him. And he said, 'Fine, it sounds great and an opportunity to work with Ash [Aishwarya Rai Bachchan].' That was also a big clincher.

SG: It was?

S: Yeah, because around then, he was coming into his own more as a commercial hero, so he was doing a film with the bigger heroines like Deepika Padukone. At the same time, I also narrated *Mumbai Saga* to him for the cop's role [which eventually went to Emraan Hashmi]. And he was very, very keen to do that. He said, 'I want to do a nice commercial film in that space, but not over the top, you know, mass-y.' But the timing didn't work.

For *Jazbaa*, I really couldn't think of anybody else to play that role. And I wanted an actor who would bring gravitas as well as some commercial viability, of which he was the perfect combination at that point.

SG: When did mainstream Bollywood actually figure out that here's someone that we can actually use? Was it *Life in a... Metro*, Anurag Basu's film?

S: Yes, post *Life in a... Metro*. Then there was *Paan Singh Tomar*. These are the films that actually gave him the credentials of a saleable hero, that yes, you could take him and mount a film. In any case, he didn't charge the earth and the moon, and you could make his films on a relatively tighter budget. That's when he became commercially acceptable to the directors or producers who were not from the periphery.

SG: So why did it take him so long to get to the centre of mainstream Bollywood?

S: I don't think he wanted to be at the centre of it. One of the reasons he dropped Khan from his name was that he did not want to be in that category. Because we knew that there were three Khans who were ruling for over two decades. He just wanted his own identity and that's why he removed the Khan from his name and just stuck to Irrfan. And he was very well aware of himself, of his shortcomings as well as his strengths. He knew that he was not this conventional hero material. That's why he did not even try to do that, or be that. I'm the only one who actually tried to push him in that space. Because when he agreed to do *Jazbaa*, he told me, '*Yaar*, this is Aishwarya's film. She's the hero of the film. *But do cheezein mere liye kar dena.*' [Do a couple of things for me.] I said, '*Kya hai?*' '*Yaar, tera yeh jo hero ka presentation hai na*, do that with me. I want to be presented like that. And just give me at least some cool one-liners.' So it was an afterthought in *Jazbaa*, where I actually sat down and reworked the script and added a punchline in literally every scene that he's in. Which was at some point criticized. I said that was my intention with the character. That was also my promise to him, that every time you're on screen, you will do something fab.

SG: '*Toh kya main Singham banke ghumoon?*' Yes, I remember that line. Suddenly here are these Salman Khan-type dialogues coming from an Irrfan Khan, and he looked as if he was loving saying them.

S: Of course! He has thoroughly enjoyed *all* those moments in *Jazbaa*. He would always say, 'I don't care what people are saying; *mereko toh mazza aa raha hai.*' [I am having fun.] And I could see that. Even Ash would tell me that this guy is having a blast. The other thing about him is that he is so bloody effortless. Because he had the eyes which did half the job, you know. He would express everything just through his eyes – you can't take that away.

SG: Do you remember your first meeting with him?

S: I think I met him at a party thrown by Ronnie Screwvala [the UTV producer at the time], to celebrate the success of *Metro*. And it was at his house – a dinner – quite a few industry people were invited and that's where I met him for the first time. He was with his wife, Sutapa [Sikdar], and he introduced himself and I was like, 'Yeah, yeah, of course I know you.' He told me he was an admirer of my work and so it would be fantastic if someday we could work together. I said, 'Certainly, why not?' And that is how *Acid Factory* came about. *Acid Factory* at that point had Fardeen Khan, Manoj Bajpayee, Aftab Shivdasani, Danny Denzongpa and Dino Morea. And Irrfan. I know that in that particular phase of his career, he was the highest-ranked amongst them. Or rather the highest paid among that cast. Fardeen Khan was a regular commercial hero, but Irrfan had, by then, broken out and kind of made that space for himself.

SG: For that kind of space, wasn't thinking of Irrfan counterintuitive? Only a few 'commercial' directors reached out to him: you, Pooja Bhatt, Anurag Basu … In *Jazbaa*, he was pretty much doing everything that a Salman Khan or any other action hero does. Because he's fighting, chasing, he's doing the one-liners.

S: Absolutely. But that was always the intention! Even the way he's dressed: the boots and the jeans and the leather jacket and those glasses.

SG: It took him a long time to get to the mainstream, right?

S: Yeah. But then, see, he wasn't chasing that. For all those years, when you say it took him a long time, he wasn't chasing to be a mass hero. He was happy in his space; he was happy in the kind of work that was coming his way. He knew that people would not go to him with trivial, meaningless characters. So that is a space – a niche – he had created for himself, which was his forte.

SG: Seems like the film industry was looking for someone like Irrfan and he turned up when he did. But he also turned towards the international arena to look for roles. I was curious about that. Other actors like Naseeruddin Shah and Om Puri had done it. But Irrfan went and did the big-ticket, tent-pole Hollywood things like *The Amazing Spider-Man*, etc. Was he not getting roles here, or did he really want to broaden his horizon?

S: He wanted to broaden his horizons. This is my reading: I don't think he wanted to be a conventional Hindi film hero. There was a space, and I suppose it was correct timing. For example, when *The Namesake* happened, that did more for him internationally than in India; they suddenly sat up and took note of him. Steven Spielberg talked to him for *Jurassic World* and things like that. And Ang Lee's *Life of Pi* ... the projects came to him at an opportune time.

SG: So he didn't go chasing those roles; they came to him?
S: That's my belief, yes.

SG: Because at one point of time, it felt like Bollywood had forgotten about him. Around 2009, after he had done *Life in a... Metro*, he should have got the roles, but it wasn't as if there was a line outside his door. He did many films in the mainstream space, some truly terrible ones too, but it was a long haul till *Hindi Medium* in 2017. As an actor, what do you think he brought to the table that his contemporaries did not?
S: His unique style of acting, his unique personality. His performances were extremely effortless; you never felt that he is

acting. He was himself. And yet, he would become a part of that character. I would call him a chameleon of an actor.

SG: Why didn't he get the lover boy sort of role? He wasn't chocolate-box-looking but he did have a very strong appeal.
S: No, he was also too old by then to be doing the lover boy roles. He saw stardom at forty-plus! So he was way beyond that age of running around trees or for the conventional love story, as we put it.

SG: But you did give him this interesting little edge with Aishwarya in *Jazbaa*. He really likes her. She's not very sure. But he's very clear, and there's a nice interplay between the two of them. You'd done it deliberately, right?
S: Yeah, that was on purpose. We did not want to commit to it. And that is why the last dialogue of the film is also one of the best: 'You let her go?' And he says, '*Mohabbat ke liye toh jaane diya; zidd hoti toh baahon mein hoti.*' [I let her go out of love; had I been stubborn she would have still been in my arms.] With an ordinary actor, this line would have just been a corny dialogue. But it's the way he delivered the line. You felt it; you knew that he's being honest.

SG: So which are some of your favourite performances of his – that are not from your film.
S: *Metro* definitely was one. And *Maqbool* was the other. There's very little not to like him in, but he did some films which he really shouldn't have because they did nothing for him! I remember he did a film with Sanjay Dutt*, which was a remake of a Hollywood film, where Irrfan's character is in a phone booth throughout. It's a handful of films where I felt that was no need, but I guess … each to their own.

---

* *Knock Out*, a 2010 Mani Shankar film

SG: Also, the actor's CV means that you need to have all kinds of movies in it, right?

S: Yeah. But then, with Irrfan Khan, you're clearly not following the ... beaten path.

SG: When he did *Hindi Medium*, that movie broke into the '100-crore club' right? It was his first solo-hero film which made that kind of money. And this was just before his sickness. At that point, was the industry looking at him in a different way, in a way that they would write movies around him? Not just cop roles?

S: Absolutely. He had become a bankable hero, especially after that film. One could safely say that he pulls in the audience; do a good film with him, it does the numbers. So yes, the timing of the illness was very, very unfortunate. Because he had just broken out: independently, solo.

SG: Do you think that post-pandemic, when OTTs are ruling and we are forced, in a manner of speaking, to create movies inside our own homes, is the time when he would have done more, or done exactly the same things? What do you think would have happened to his trajectory?

S: You see, what happened is, OTT has given a fresh lease of life to, say, a Manoj Bajpayee's career, right? Now OTT also is unconventional stuff from a traditional point of view; it's non-commercial, non-formula. But the thing is that Irrfan was already doing that in the commercial space! He was doing non-formula in the formula space. He had come with a *Hindi Medium*, which goes on to do a hundred crores and it is not your *Singham** or *Dabangg*. In that sense, he had created his own space and he would have only, I guess, bettered it. He would have consolidated it.

---

* A 2011 Rohit Shetty film

SG: Would you like to share anything special from your time of working with him?

S: It was always pleasant and conversations with him were always very interesting because we would be discussing Rumi and Charles Bukowski to a Guru Dutt film and Abrar Alvi's dialogues. It was a varied spectrum of conversations and never about that film having done so many crores or what is this guy doing next. He had a life beyond films.

SG: What is the first thing that comes to your mind when you think of Irrfan?

S: A really chilled-out actor, completely comfortable in his skin. There's no insecurity, no looking over his shoulder, nothing of that sort.

SG: Did you actually get to know him beyond the sets at all?

S: No, no. He would drop by occasionally; we'd have a drink or two, chat, he would come over for dinner. In that sense, of course there was a bond.

SG: What is it like, being in an industry which is now Irrfan-less?

S: There is a void. We would probably be having this conversation even if he were alive. Because he is somebody worth writing about, talking about, emulating. He is somebody who's made something out of his career; he's chosen, or rather, shown a path that you can take as an actor, where you don't need to be insecure. And those are his life choices ...

We do not have another Irrfan and I don't think we ever will.

'I don't think we made the most of him'

MEGHNA GULZAR

A dinner-table conversation led **Meghna Gulzar** – director of films like *Raazi* and *Chhapaak* – to reach out to Irrfan for the film that brought her back into the reckoning as a filmmaker. That film was *Talvar*, based on the 2008 Aarushi Talwar murder case, in which Irrfan plays a senior cop investigating the shocking real-life murder of a fourteen-year-old girl, with her parents as the chief suspects. It is a hard role to pull off without taking sides, but Irrfan does so with aplomb.

———

SHUBHRA GUPTA: How would you like to describe yourself as a filmmaker?

MEGHNA GULZAR: Right now, I'm the kind of filmmaker who tells true life stories. I want to tell stories that are inspiring, I don't want to be forgotten the moment the popcorn is over.

We're speaking because you want to look at films that have formed a part of Irrfan's journey. I'll flip that on its head and say that *Talvar* formed my journey. I was blessed that he was a part of that film, and it was a rebirth for me as a filmmaker. He was pivotal to my journey.

SG: Let's talk about *Talvar*. How did you think of doing this very disturbing story as a film?

MG: Two things. One, I was tracking the case; not from the point of view of making the film. It had grabbed my attention like it had grabbed everybody else's. And I tracked it up to the point where the reporting on the case stopped. Then the second team came to investigate and there was an embargo by the Supreme Court on the reporting of the case – till then, I was following it. But then it kind of fell off the radar of news coverage and I had my son and, for the next three to four years, I shut shop because I wanted to be with him in the formative years of his life. My son was about three and Vishal [Bhardwaj] sir was at home for dinner. He asked me *ki*, 'What are you planning to do next?' I said, 'I really haven't thought about it.' He said, 'How long are you going to hide behind your son?' And he can talk to me like that because he's always been like an elder brother. I know that my father [Gulzar, Vishal Bhardwaj's mentor, whom he is very close to] and he had probably colluded in this conversation. And so he said, '*Chalo*, let's make a movie together. What about something like this or the Aarushi Talwar case?' He just blurted it out and I said that's what I want to make.

I thank my stars that I didn't blink for even a fraction of a second to make that decision. And it was completely removed from anything that I had made before, right? I was stepping into a whole new world. And even technology, Shubhra, apart from the scripting and the genre of the film; even my last film was shot on film, you know? Our music was still being recorded on two-inch tapes. The technology has changed; everything is digital. You can do stuff on VFX that I had never imagined. So for me, it was like starting from scratch as a filmmaker.

Once we decided that, I spent a year and a half researching the case, pulling out news articles. Then Avirook's [Sen] book* came out. By that time, we had finished a draft of our script. It came out in July and the film released in October. So it was not like his book was my material, but he was covering the trial and he had a column in *Mumbai Mirror* which I used to archive, along with anything that came out on the case. The good thing was that the case was in trial, so all the stories that we had heard eight years ago without any kind of vetting process were now getting vetted and filtered in a court of law. That made the work easier and then we worked out a timeline between Vishal sir and me, after which he took it away and made a dialogue draft.

SG: Did you collaborate while he was writing the movie?
MG: Not while he was writing. We just made a structure: this is how the narrative will be; what do we want to do with Irrfan sir's character; do we want to give him a failing marriage; do we want to give him a daughter. Just broad strokes like that. My job was to verify the facts and just give him [Bhardwaj] everything as it happened and work out a timeline, and then he turned it into a screenplay with dialogues and so on.

SG: Was it always going to be Irrfan when you thought of the character?
MG: Always. I don't think anybody else popped in our heads.

SG: And when you reached out to him, what did he say?
MG: Vishal sir did that. He already had an equation and it actually happened while Vishal sir was putting *Haider* together. He had

---

* Avirook Sen, *Aarushi*, New Delhi: Penguin Random House India, 2015.

promised me that he would give me a draft before he went off to shoot *Haider*. And then he finished shooting *Haider* and came back and the entire team of *Haider* came on to *Talvar*. He had already spoken to Irrfan sir, who asked to meet me. That's when I went and met him.

SG: Tell me a little bit about that meeting.

MG: It was … it's difficult to talk about it. I am surprised at myself … at how his demise catches me off guard from time to time. I went to meet him at his residence in Madh Island. The thing with Irrfan sir and his craft … he is extremely prepared; he does his homework. But he'll never show that the work has been done. It doesn't even show in his performance. His performance is so nonchalant, but you know he has thought the smallest thing through.

So even for this meeting, he had read the script, he had read up on the case. But he wanted to know how much *I* knew, what I believed, which side was I on, was I leaning in one direction? Because we were very sure that the script needs to have both perspectives represented evenly … Because there was no conclusion to the case, there's no way we could have given it one. So his whole thing was to kind of measure me. But I didn't even realize that at that time; I realized it years later. At the time, they seemed like very innocent questions. '*Achha*, then how did this happen? Then what happened when they found the golf club [the suspected murder weapon]? Then that thing about the report and the typographical error, how did that happen?' I sat with him for about two hours, I think, we were just discussing the case and then he said, 'Yeah, it's very intriguing and, as actors, you really look forward to doing things like this.' But he didn't say if he's doing it, not doing it, nothing. He said, '*Haan, theek hai, main baat karta hoon,* and I left from there and I was driving back not knowing whether it went well, if I met his expectations, did he think I would be responsible enough to handle this? Then I got an SMS from Vishal sir saying Irrfan called, he is on. So that's him, you know? Nonchalance is a word that I use for him.

SG: Did you know him before the film? Obviously, you must have met with him, bumped into him …

MG: Yes, briefly, off and on. Vishal sir's office or a screening or something. He would always ask, what are you doing, when are you making your next film, etc. I had seen him in *Kirdaar* [1993–94], which was Papa's [Gulzar] serial in which he had done one of the short stories. I can't say I knew him. I can't even say that I got to know him through the process of *Talvar*, because there was too much reverence. Shubhra, I would still refer to him as Irrfan sir on set. We would discuss the role or the scene, but I would never question his process, I would never ask him what he thinks. When we had our cast and crew reading, I was reading his lines; he was not reading them. He said, 'I'm not going to read; you read.' Again, that was his way of understanding how I'm seeing this character without coming right out and asking me. Because that's just such a pat way of doing it, and nothing Irrfan sir ever did was pat. There was always a subtlety, an illusion, a suggestion to everything and it showed in his performances. And he's not a conventionally good-looking man, right? We all know that and he also knew that. But he weaponized that. Let me not say he used it as a strength; he *weaponized* it. The way he used his eyes, the way he used his – I will say this again – nonchalance. The way he interpreted the character.

He was aware of the tiniest things. We were shooting the sequence where they were finding the trail of blood on the stairs.

It was forty-nine degrees. And so he asked for a *rumaal*. Then he wiped himself and continued. The supervisor was like, 'Ma'am, the handkerchief – take it away; it's not supposed to show.' And thank god for the reverence, because I didn't go up to him and say, 'Irrfan sir, I need to take that handkerchief away.' He rolled it and tied it around his palm. How a normal human would wipe themselves, Irrfan Khan has tied the *rumaal* like that. He's thought it through, you know? It is such a small thing but that's how much he's thinking about the character.

SG: I always thought of him as a thinking actor, as an actor prepared. Was Tabu your first choice for the estranged wife?
MG: Yeah, yeah. I was fortunate that everybody we wanted were all our first options for the film. There are many actors who prepare, more so now than ten years ago, but Irrfan sir, he's a man of *dehaat*. And he remained one. I mean, he's worked in Hollywood and come back. Totally simple and raw at the core. So he would think of the small things. Along with the broad strokes, which I think was his added forte. For example, we knew we wanted Ashwin [his character in *Talvar*] to have glasses. He agreed to the glasses and then he said, 'I want my glasses tinted. I don't want clear glasses.' I said, 'Why, sir?' He said, 'I want a little bit of secrecy; I don't want anyone to ever look at my eyes and know what I'm thinking.' Then a key scene where he is supposed to cry, he didn't want to. He said, '*No, yaar, bada ghisa pita; har film mein hota hai.*' [Too hackneyed; it happens in every film.] It was not like he was psyching me. He was pushing me to constantly up the game – by throwing those questions at me and asking for the answers and finding the solutions along the way, in a genre that I had never made before.

SG: How does it feel having an actor like that on set? He's read the script, he's had a conversation, he's done a rehearsal and yet he manages to surprise you. I find so many actors calling attention to their craft. There was never, ever any sign of that in his performances for me. How does that, as a director, make you feel?

MG: It's a huge security. I can't say it in the present anymore, that, having him, I know I will not have to worry. It's extremely unfortunate that I never got that privilege again. But having Irrfan sir on your set, you knew that even if your execution was flawed, he would make up for it. If a scene or a script had a weak element, it's not possible that he wouldn't have pointed it out. But if you had reached that point where it's gone through and it has been pointed out, somehow he would cover up for it. I could be completely biased feeling this way but that's how I feel. Shubhra, till the end of the film, I didn't know which narrative he believed [in *Talvar*]. He knew the part that he was playing, and so he was executing one narrative. But I didn't know which one he believed.

Even while we were filming, doing really tricky scenes where he's interrogating Aarushi's father or he's come to search the house or he gets to know about the golf club. And he would throw a question at me: *but what if it actually happened like that?* Where he's playing the devil's advocate and saying: *but what if the theory was true and what if we are going completely wrong?* So I would always tell him this: 'Sir, there's enough material to support both narratives and, from what I have read very, very closely, the narrative of the parents being innocent is far more compelling, particularly in terms of the material evidence as well.' '*Accha? Chalo, karte hain.*' [Let's do it.] He would not commit to believing in a narrative, at least in front of me. And we never reached that point where, you know, we hung out after a shoot or had a meal or a drink together. So I don't know, when he was offline and he was not being the actor on set, what he actually thought. But on set, till today, I don't know which narrative he believed.

SG: He was an actor ahead of his time. Why did it take Bollywood/ Hindi cinema so much time to zero in on someone like Irrfan?

MG: I don't think we zeroed in on him as much as we should have, even till his passing. I don't think we made the most of him. For two reasons. One, I think, in our heads, we kind of slotted him into cerebral, realistic, artistic cinema. There were a few offshoots, like *Qarib Qarib Singlle* and *Karwaan* and *Angrezi Medium*, but too little too late, right? You see him in a film like *D-Day* – he will bring credibility to the most so-called 'commercial films'. And I don't mean this in a denigrating way, but you would not imagine him in a hardcore, commercial, star-studded film like *D-Day*. But he blended right in and brought credibility to the film, as an actor who was a chameleon.

And he has still carried his non-acting-*wala* acting in all those movies. But my point is that I don't think we utilized it as much as we should have. At that time also, realism in our films was very late coming in.

SG: Is that why he kept going to the West? Was Hollywood the last refuge for him?

MG: No, I think he kind of straddled both boats. I don't think he ever went away, as such. But he was also a very restless spirit. He was like the child who wants the *saamne wala* child's toy all the time. He'll be doing a Mira Nair film but he wants to do a Rohit Shetty, then when he does a Rohit Shetty, he wants to do an Ang Lee. When he's done an Ang Lee, he wants to come back to Tigmanshu Dhulia. You know what I'm saying? Because as an actor, he was just always hungry. He was never satiated. And it's like he's painted with all the colours. He's done every kind of movie there is. And it's not because he was not being accepted in a particular genre, or not accepted in a particular industry, or didn't succeed in commercial films so he did art films, or didn't succeed in art films or didn't get enough money and so he wanted commercial success. That was not it at all. I think it was just the actor in him constantly wanting to satiate himself in new and different ways all the time.

'A consummate actor'

SAKET CHAUDHARY

Saket Chaudhary has delivered films like *Pyaar Ke Side Effects* and *Shaadi Ke Side Effects*, that turned out to be sleeper hits, and that is also what happened with *Hindi Medium*. It did not just give Irrfan a chance to demonstrate, with great flair, how to drape a sari as the owner of a garments shop in Chandni Chowk trying to entice a sticky customer; its huge box office success finally catapulted him into becoming a saleable star, who could 'open' a film on his own. It made Bollywood sit up and take notice.

———

SHUBHRA GUPTA: What got you interested in *Hindi Medium*? Was it your own story?
SAKET CHAUDHARY: The idea came from the writer on *Shaadi Ke Side Effects*, Zeenat Lakhani. We were researching couples and families, etc., and Zeenat had come across this article about this father, a businessman who wanted to get his daughter admission, and the school refused because they wanted only children of parents who were professionals, and he was just a graduate. So he enrolled himself in an MBA programme so that he could be considered a professional and his daughter would get admission.

We felt that was a very interesting premise to build a story on. So that's how we started researching. Initially, it was supposed to be part of *Shaadi Ke Side Effects*, but we realized the scope of it was much bigger. Then we researched it and turned it into *Hindi Medium*.

SG: Was Irrfan your first choice to play that role?

SC: Among the first choices. See, from the writing to making the film was about a two–three-year process. I think what fundamentally happened was *Piku*. We'd seen Irrfan in several things and his work is exceptional. For me, the most exceptional piece of work was his track in *In Treatment*. So the fact that he was an incredible actor who had already become this international star was already there. But the one thing that we didn't know was whether he could be a comic hero. Because, before that, before *Piku*, I don't remember him in any comedy.

SG: *Life in a… Metro*?

SC: Yeah, *Life in a… Metro*, but I still saw him playing a more serious character where the situation was funny. But with *Piku*, maybe because it was more along the lines of our film, time-wise, he can be a comic-romantic hero. And more than that, there was this opening scene. We'd written most of the script but we didn't have the opening scene of the film – how to introduce our character. We wrote the character as someone who's this really smart salesman, manipulative but charming. At that time, we were absolutely one hundred per cent sure that this was Irrfan. Then we couldn't think of anyone else but Irrfan. Fortunately, we took it to him and he immediately agreed to do it after the first narration.

SG: Was that your first meeting with him?

SC: I'd never met him before that. The first time I met him was for the first narration of the script.

SG: What do you remember of that narration?

SC: I'm trying to recall. Unfortunately, when you're narrating, you keep rehearsing for two days, so it's like a performance that you've got to put up, as a director. Because both Zeenat and I did the narration together, it's like a performance that we have to put up together. And I've never acted, so it's incredibly stress-inducing. You've got to say the dialogues in a certain way and there is a pause. Zeenat would do a bit of the screenplay reading and I would do the dialogues, and then I would do the screenplay reading and she would do the dialogues, and we would have to remember these cues. It's a very stressful process. And because Irrfan is such a consummate actor, he knows that his reaction to a narration is very important. He enjoyed it but he also constantly gave you feedback that he was enjoying it. That sort of encourages you more and you knew this was going well.

SG: So that is also a performance, what he was doing.

SC: As an actor, he understands that people need your reaction when they're narrating to you. So that was very important; we started getting a sense of where this is going and this is possibly something that could happen.

SG: But it was *your* film that actually got him into the so-called '100-crore club', suddenly bringing him into a different kind of focus. Were you aware that this had happened? He was always this fantastic actor, but do you think that your film actually elevated him into a certain kind of star, who was more saleable than he used to be before?

SC: See, *Pyaar Ke Side Effects* was a sleeper hit but a small sleeper hit. And *Shaadi Ke Side Effects* had done moderately okay. So it's not like I had a great sense of what a big Bollywood film is. That time, what I would be considered is a small/medium director. So the expectations from *Hindi Medium* were broadly this. We believed it was a small film, you know. And as much as *Piku* was a hit, it also had Deepika and Amitabh Bachchan. So you assumed that [they contributed to] the scale of the success. So we felt *ki haan, humari picture agar bahut achhi bhi niklegi, toh pachchis–tees crore wali picture hogi.* [If our film does well, it will earn about twenty-five–thirty crores.] And that would be the most optimistic scenario because *Madaari* had released just around the time he had said yes to our film. So the phenomenal success that followed was as much a pleasant surprise to us as it was to everybody else. Some people liked the film, some people gave us very positive feedback. Nobody ever told us, '*Arre yaar, yeh toh blockbuster hai*.' We never got that feedback even after the screenings. So the success came as a surprise. I think the scale of the success came from Irrfan, actually. There was a success party and, as we were heading back home, Irrfan stopped us and said, 'Thank you for giving me this film. If you had taken it to Aamir, this would have been three hundred crores.' So I think he, more than us, realized that this had sort of elevated him into that category of a saleable star. I mean, for us, Irrfan was the actor we wanted in the film; we had never imagined other actors. So I think he sort of picked up on what the success of the film meant to him before we did.

SG: What did it do for you?

SC: When we started *Hindi Medium*, a lot of people asked us, 'Why would you want to make a film like this? Why would the audience be interested in watching a middle-class couple trying to get their child into school?' I think it gives you more confidence that the idea that you've taken up has merit. So you can counter those doubts and criticism a lot better because you know that you've picked up an idea and turned it into a script that turned into a successful film.

SG: What was the experience like of working with him?

SC: I've never believed that I'm a director who can tell actors what to do. My understanding of direction is to give a clear brief of what the scene is about and what you expect the outcome or the performance to be. I've always felt that actors know about acting, I know about directing. And Irrfan is such an accomplished actor, you're not really going to tell him how to play a part. You sort of lay out the material and then you let somebody like him interpret how he wants to play it. Because Irrfan is such a great actor, you think that it would be this whole organized process – these script readings, and everybody will sit around a table and there will be great discussions on the character, etc. But none of that happened. Because we realized that he likes his process to be more internal. He's not going to tell you what he's going to do, he's not going to have great discussions over it. He'll constantly keep making you read the material to him as he is sort of processing it. There are actors who will constantly tell you what they are going to do. But with Irrfan, it was never like that. He doesn't create a myth about his performance. And then, when the camera starts, when you say 'action' and he starts doing it, you start realizing what he's really going to bring to the performance: the timing, how he's internalized the accent, his idea of what that Delhi businessman is like. You're discovering it all once you've said 'action' and not before. So it can be scary with another actor, but it was extremely reassuring here because, suddenly, you felt there was this new life that was being brought into your material.

SG: It's some kind of an alchemy, isn't it? A kind of magic that happens.

SC: You know, from the outside it would seem like magic, but you would see him rehearsing with himself before the take. So you know that there is a method; it's just that he doesn't feel that I have to tell people my method or share my method. But that method does exist. It's spectacular for a director. You constantly feel: are you just going to get exhausted by the material? Especially when you're doing a comedy, you feel, when I say 'action', will it be funny? Because you've already read it and heard it so many times. So when he does it, it's exceptional, because suddenly your material has come alive and it's become fresh to you. But because there has not been this constant rehearsal process, the other actor can be suddenly taken aback. I think the reason Deepak [Dobriyal]* and Irrfan had such great chemistry was that they would not be taken aback. But every time they were surprised, they would add something more to it. That was a very interesting process.

SG: That brings me to my next question. The leading lady [Pakistani actor Saba Qamar] was also a very interesting choice. How did you zero in on her?

SC: My mom was a big fan of Pakistani plays. At that time, Zee had just started this channel where they were playing Pakistani television shows, and I had seen a series called *Maat*. It was about these two sisters. And you know, Pakistani television shows

---

* Deepak Dobriyal co-stars with Irrfan in *Hindi Medium*.

have better melodrama than our melodrama. But it is essentially melodrama. There she [Saba] played this younger sister who was extremely self-centred – it's a very striking performance. There are two reasons. One is, we needed somebody who can come across as that slightly upwardly mobile Punjabi; that woman who has that aspiration *ki* even though I'm from Chandni Chowk, I can make it in south Delhi. So we needed that slightly funny yet very motivated and very determined character ... with this desire for sophistication.

SG: Chanel handbag, LV, Prada ...

SC: Yeah, yeah. We wanted somebody who could carry that. And Saba carries that quality exceptionally well. And the second thing was that we had faced the challenge of finding good actresses who were willing to play a mother. A lot of actresses consider that to be the kiss of death to their careers. But Saba had no such apprehensions; she just saw the role, the character and she wanted to do it.

SG: When Irrfan and Saba first came together, what was it like? Did you know at once that it was a lock?

SC: I don't know whether this happened because Irrfan had also started turning producer, but he is constantly very aware of all the talent that is around him. The person who wrote the dialogues, Amitosh Nagpal, was also a name that he recommended. So he was aware of Saba. He had also said, 'If you're not getting an actress here, why don't you look across the border? At that time, it was possible to do that. So he was very much on board. I think the first time they met was at their press shoot, and they were good. You knew they were a fit right from then onwards.

We did the press shoot to see how they're going to look together. As an actress, we already knew we liked her. We'd done readings for her for two days; she kept telling us, 'I'm a very big actress in Pakistan; I don't do auditions and I'm doing it for you.' We were like, 'Thank you so much.' But I think the moment they did the press shoot together, we knew this was a good match, this is good casting.

SG: Was the film all shot in Delhi? Was it on location, or on set?
SC: It was all in Delhi. There was a little patchwork stuff that we did in Mumbai, but it was straight forty-three days in Delhi.

SG: And when you were shooting outside, was there recognition of Irrfan? Did a crowd ever become a problem?
SC: Yeah, they recognized him; he was already a star. But not to that extent. I had worked with Shah Rukh; when Shah Rukh came out to the road, you could not shoot. When we were doing *Asoka**, we had to find locations where we thought people would have no idea. And then a full crowd would gather and people would tumble over each other. So it wasn't of that level but people would come and gather and I think people were extremely respectful. They also saw Irrfan as this thinking actor, so their reaction was also extremely dignified and civilized and they would come to him in a very respectful manner and take selfies, etc.

SG: You know, I just flashbacked to that sari scene! Did Irrfan actually learn how to tie a sari for that scene? Or did he wing it?
SC: He learnt it at the location; he was extremely reluctant to do it. He kept asking me, 'Are you sure you need this?' Honestly, it was Zeenat – our writer – who convinced him. Once he got convinced, we had one of those salesmen who do these things on

---

* A 2001 Santosh Sivan film

standby to show it to him, but then he picked it up immediately. And he did it right there. But he refused to rehearse it; it was a bit of a struggle to get him to do the scene.

SG: Anything else that you would remember?

SC: One incident that I do remember, and this speaks volumes about him as an actor and how self-aware he was: We had the climax, which had this speech. And it was a struggle because speeches are always a struggle; you don't know if it's going to work and we had been struggling to write it. We'd had multiple people come in, write it, change it around and, in the end, we'd completely given up and requested Mr Vishal Bhardwaj to write the speech. And that's when the speech came alive. That was two–three days before the shoot. Which was a big shoot, because we had all these junior artists. And then he came and the hall was filled with four–five hundred junior artists. He did the speech and there was loud applause. You know, you don't expect junior artists to start clapping. So you felt that this has worked; the most scary, most doubtful part of the film has suddenly worked because you got an immediate reaction from the quasi-audience that was sitting there. And then we went back to the edit table, and there we realized it hadn't worked. We called in Irrfan because we felt we might have to reshoot it and Irrfan wanted to know why we wanted to reshoot this. He saw the edit and said, 'Yeah, you're right, it hasn't worked.' You know, it's a big step to tell an actor that the climax speech – an actor's monologue – has not worked. But Irrfan immediately agreed, and he said, 'I think the reason that this has not worked is that I did not perform for the camera; I performed for the audience. I was looking for a reaction from the people sitting there but you need a performance to be far more subtle, far more personal with the camera, and that's what I've done wrong.' And that's what he corrected in the reshoot. We didn't have that insight at all, so that, I think, spoke volumes about how much that man knew about his performance.

I remember him talking about material and scripts – especially in the mainstream space – talking about performance. He really did believe that the camera was a collaborator for an actor, you know? His understanding of camera movements and what it could do for every shot that he delivered was exceptional. Because you are looking for momentum from the camera. What is a camera going to do for you? What is the frame, the lighting going to do for you? How is it going to impact your performance? I haven't made that many films, but in my interaction with actors, I've never found somebody who was so aware of his craft like Irrfan was.

SG: Yes, that's what Naseeruddin Shah also said when I was speaking to him about *Maqbool*. He knew exactly what he was doing, even though he did not let it show. And that, I think, is an amazing thing because, if you start letting the effort show, then you're telling everyone, 'I'm such a great actor: look, look.' Which is why I was so struck by this character. He's sitting in that rickshaw, and they are leaving, and he's looking as if he's always sat in that rickshaw ... What is the first thing that comes to your mind when you think of Irrfan?

SC: I think his eyes, how they were constantly absorbing everything. And the cigarette that never leaves his hand. I could go back and look at *Hindi Medium* and I am looking at the mid-shots and thinking, all the time he would always have a cigarette hidden somewhere in those mid-shots.

SG: Did you keep in touch with him; were you planning to make something else?

SC: When a lot of the material that you write is about ordinary people, sometimes middle-aged, you realize … with Irrfan not there, it's so difficult to cast that material. That quality which Irrfan could [evoke], of something exceptional in the ordinary, you don't find that among stars. Once you work with Irrfan, you keep thinking, 'Oh, Irrfan would have been so good for this material.' And then you think, 'But he's not there, so who's there to do this instead of him?' The sad thing is that he went when, commercially, he was at his peak. He was now the star who could be the base on which films could get made, but unfortunately that journey got cut short.

'He was my Guru Dronacharya'

PANKAJ TRIPATHI

As a struggling actor, the very fact of Irrfan's success gave **Pankaj Tripathi**, and so many others like him, hope. If Irrfan could, so could they. The two worked together for only a day in *Angrezi Medium*, but Tripathi's deep study of Irrfan and his 'philosophy' inspired the former greatly. He is now one of Hindi cinema's most popular actors, best known for films like *Bareilly Ki Barfi*, *83*, *Gunjan Sharma*, *Ludo* and his bravura performance in the web series *Mirzapur*.

———

SHUBHRA GUPTA: *Aapki Irrfan se sabse pehli mulaqaat kab hui?*

PANKAJ TRIPATHI: *Mujhe lagta hai ki meri unse sabse pehli mulaqaat cinema ke parde pe hui.* Haasil *film dekh raha tha. Aur* Haasil *ke pehle* Maqbool *aayi thi na? Ya* Maqbool *baad mein aayi thi?* [I think my first meeting with him happened on the movie screen. I was watching the film *Haasil*. And *Maqbool* came before *Haasil*? Or did *Maqbool* come later?]

SG: Yes, *Maqbool* came a little later.

PT: So yes, first meeting was *Haasil*. I think at Liberty, the movie theatre in Delhi. We had run off from drama school to watch the film, two–three of us best friends. The director of *Haasil* [Tigmanshu Dhulia] is from NSD, the actor [Irrfan] is from NSD – a lot of the actors in the movie were from NSD. The excuse was that it's our seniors' film, so let's go. So my first meeting was on the screen, and the amazing thing is that my in-person meeting with him has been close to nil.

Sach muchh toh pehli dhang ki mulaqaat, hum dono ki physical mulaqaat, woh sirf aur sirf Angrezi Medium *ki ek din ki shooting pe hui.* [But truly our first proper meeting – our physical meeting – that happened on the one day of shooting *Angrezi Medium.*] But he too used to meet me on the screen – I came to know about this much later. *Toh badi hi adbhut aur adhyatmik humari mulaqaat thi unse.* [So my meeting with him was wondrous and spiritual.]

I remember the first time I met Irrfan after *Haasil* … I find it troubling to say Irrfan; I'll say Irrfan sir. So there was a play at Rajendra Gupta's [the actor] home in Aram Nagar. We were performing in the play – I was doing a small part. The play ended; he had reached late. He'd got stuck in traffic – Mumbai traffic – so he could not reach on time. [That's the day I] saw him in person for the first time. I thought he was looking taller than he does on screen – slim and tall. After that I saw him at an awards show, where he bagged Best Actor. He was coming out and there was a big crowd around him; I was also standing there. I smiled and said 'hello'; he smiled at me and left.

The most interesting thing that happened was when I got to know that he knew about me. I had no idea that Irrfan knew there's an actor named Pankaj, who is from the drama school, his junior. One day I was sitting in a flight from Goa to Mumbai and was about to put my phone on flight mode when I received an SMS. I opened the message. It was from the director Anup

Singh, who has made *Qissa* and *The* Song *of Scorpions*. He told me that he was in London and the day before he was sitting with Irrfan and—

pauses

The problem is that I get emotional thinking of him. So the SMS said that he had a talk with Irrfan at the hospital a few days back and Irrfan was talking about me. He was saying that I am an incredible actor. He was talking about me with a lot of love – with warmth and regards. The way I got so emotional talking about this just now – it was a similar situation on the flight; I went quiet and started crying. I thought, *Yaar*, he knows me?

I think six–eight months after that, he came to India and found out that *Angrezi Medium* is being made. Dinu [Dinesh Vijayan] – the producer – offered me a very big role in it. I did not have dates; I was doing *83** and *Ludo*†. So I said, '*Yaar*, I'm already committed; I'll have to leave one of those films.' Shooting for *Ludo* had begun; for *83* there were big preparations [to be done] and we were going out to shoot in May. 'But do one thing,' I told Dinesh, 'give me any role – two days, four days *ka*. I want to share the screen with Irrfan; want to be in one frame. Dinu said, 'Okay, done.' Then I got a call from Homi Adajania that they will only need one day from me – there is a *khoobsurat* cameo. So I said, 'Done, I am now ready to manage it all.' We settled on a date, we went for shooting that day, and that was our proper interaction – our first meeting. And that, in fact, was also our last *mulaqaat*. With a lot of warmth he hugged me and spoke to

---

* A 2021 Kabir Khan film
† A 2020 Anurag Basu film

me and ... even while doing that scene I somehow did not know what to do. I reached the set and told Homi that this character is from Delhi but lives in Dubai, so I'll make his Hindi slightly *galat*: *Aati hai, jaati hai; jaanke bolta hai kuchh bhi*. Changed feminine to masculine. So without any logic, any preparation, I, Irrfan sir and Deepak [Dobriyal] did that. And there was one moment in that scene when all three of us started laughing and shooting stopped for almost ten–fifteen minutes. The camera director is sitting and the three of us are going on laughing. Then, I think, Irrfan sir was in some pain, so he had a hot-water bag which he used for compression. In my acting career of fifteen–sixteen years, since I came to Bombay, this was a special assignment for me, an incredible day. Because that day I finally got to know the person *jinki pehli teen filmein dekh kar hi main unka mureed ho gaya tha*. [His first three films turned me into his admirer.] It made me think that he is doing a different kind of performance – something new. The impact is great but the effort is seamless; it looks effortless. So I watched those three films and thought this is how one should do acting; this is the acting I want to do. In fact, after that, in one or two scenes I was trying to imitate him – at the time I was in NSD. Then I realized he is already a very big actor –why am I doing it like him? I should learn and take inspiration from him and find my own way; then I can be something different. So I used to dig up his interviews to read – video, audio, write-ups – for his *phalsafa* [philosophy]. That is what makes me emotional – our relationship was one of Eklavya and Dronacharya. And it's not just me, a lot of actors in my generation saw Irrfan sir and realized that there can be a different way of acting, without too much pressure, too much stress, without bringing in too much modulation, you can say the same thing as strongly.

SG: To you, what was the most important thing in Irrfan's acting?

PT: The *asar* [effect] that he created, the impact he brought through performance, while telling a story. So when you get influenced by someone – when a new actor gets influenced – then he starts mimicking him, copying him. I too in the beginning – never in cinema, but in theatre – started copying him. Then after two–three such instances I thought: why am I copying him? I want to bring that *asar* without copying him.

In a sense he was my Guru Dronacharya – not that I ever took an acting class, nor did he ever conduct a class. But to learn another actor's approach, an actor watches all his work, how he brings unpredictability in his performance. The way in which he would break that *dhharra*, that thing called modulation. The norms of the craft, the graphs – that this is how he has to make his movement from here to there; what is the motivation behind it? Irrfan used to break that motivation; he used to bring a new motivation, something unthought of. He was a guru in that sense. I looked at his interviews alongside his films. Whatever I could find to learn about his preparation, I would read. What was his approach, his philosophy? Even in life. I have collected things from here and there by reading about his entire journey of life right from his birth. Many times I read Sutapa-ji's [Sikdar] interviews to understand him; I read different sources to know about him.

His point of view on life, on society, on religion was just wonderful. Ma'am, acting is a job which includes a lot of other arts. It has painting, *sur–taal*, dance. All *kalayein* [the performing arts] – they are included in acting in some form or shape. I am saying all this because I was thinking about him.

Just half an hour ago, while doing yoga I was thinking: what will I talk about, what will I say? Because my *vaasta* [connection] with him was a very distant one – an Eklavya–Dronacharya connection. Maybe he didn't know; I never even said it to him so he wouldn't even have known how much I loved him. When I found out that he knows me and likes me, that was an *adbhut* moment for me – while sitting on that flight.

I have not seen a more lovely person on screen than Irrfan Khan.

Main jab parde pe Irrfan ko dekhta tha, main unhe premika ki tarah dekhta tha. [I would watch Irrfan on the screen like a lover.] We are very quick to label – that this is a hero, this is a character. People still call me a character actor. Everyone is doing a character; in a film, the hero is playing a character. I mean, he was such a big actor, but Hindi cinema – especially mainstream Hindi cinema – took too long to get it.

SG: Why?

PT: I don't know. Maybe because it takes too long for our understanding of a real hero to form. The mindset is such. Maybe the Hindi cinema industry lives in their self-formed clichés that this is what a hero should be.

SG: Had Irrfan still been around, would he be doing his best work now? What do you think?

PT: He made our path easier. He inspired innumerable actors like me. I have come to Bombay; many might be in Patna, in Delhi, in Jabalpur. Irrfan has inspired many boys in the theatre fraternity. I came from drama school in 2004; not even in my wildest dreams did I imagine the number of people that know me by name today. But I used to see that *Haasil* was being talked about, *Paan Singh Tomar* became a hit, despite that film not releasing for over two and a half years. So Irrfan sir has laid down a field – and it's a beautiful field – so that small players like us can come from far and wide and play around. We're playing in it, but he's the one who enabled that. It's him and Manoj Bajpayee. His contribution to cinema, his contribution to acting, is extremely wonderful, and it's huge.

SG: Of all his films you've watched, which of his roles are your favourite?

PT: I could never be critical of him. When you are in love, you are not critical – you are just in love. But yes, for me, *Paan Singh Tomar*, *Maqbool*, *Haasil* … a lot of his work on TV.

My wife really likes *The Lunchbox*; she keeps watching it, so I also go sit with her. So it was a personal loss, his going away. It felt like a family member went away. Whenever we watch his film clippings, we are *anayas* [very easily] brought to tears. To have such a *judaav* [connection] with an actor – it doesn't normally happen. His connection with crores of spectators like me was wonderful.

My connect was more spiritual than direct. I didn't meet him, nor did I directly speak with him; I never asked him questions about acting. But anytime I had doubts or questions in my mind regarding acting, I would pick a film of his and, while watching it, somewhere in the middle of it, I would find the answer. That's why I said that he was spiritual. While acting he is not just performing a scene; it feels like you're watching a masterclass. The person is teaching; you may pick something if you choose to learn. And then whatever you pick, implement it according to yourself, try to understand it. So our questions – for new, upcoming actors like us – related to acting, found answers in his performance. And in his interviews, I found answers to questions relating to life. That's why I say that ours was an *adhyatmik* [spiritual] connection. Neither did I ask, nor did he answer. But a lot of my questions got answered.

And the one day that we spent together … it would have been fun if I had the chance to do something proper and serious with him. But it was a funny scene and we just sat and laughed. Vinod Pradhan was the DOP [Director of Photography]. He said, 'You guys do it, *yaar*; we won't do anything. We will sit and watch.' Homi kept on saying, 'I wish I get these three actors for a complete film. I will not do anything; I'll place a camera and keep a map saying that this is a map, the journey is yours.' So I feel quite sad about the fact that I had not got the chance to do something better and serious with him. It would have been a lot of fun; I would have learnt a lot. His passing is *dukkhad* [tragic]. But however much he has done will inspire actors for generations to come. If tomorrow my child or any other young actor comes and asks a question about acting, then even twenty years from now my comment will be, 'Go and watch one of Irrfan sir's films.' They will be showcased in some film school, taught in acting classes – and this is an actor's biggest achievement. For generations, acting classes in Hindustan will talk about Irrfan. And this is the only kind of *uplabdhi* [achievement] worth celebrating.

SG: Just one last thing. If you think about Irrfan with your eyes closed, what is that one thing that comes to your mind?
PT: His very beautiful *muskurahat*. When he smiled, it wasn't just his lips doing the work; he put his entire soul, his entire *aatma* into it. That smile came from somewhere within.

'Bollywood woke up late to his talent'

TANUJA CHANDRA

Tanuja Chandra wrote and directed several films that released in the late nineties and early 2000s (*Dushman*, *Sangharsh* and *Sur: The Melody of Life*). Her power-packed comeback of sorts, *Qarib Qarib Singlle*, gave Irrfan a chance to play a man looking for love. Yogi, his character, has found versions of it a few times before, but never the forever-after kind that only a few luck into, until he comes upon Jaya, played by the terrific Parvathy. The romance is tender and amusing, and that rare thing in Bollywood – a pair of grown-ups testing the waters and seeing where it will take them.

———

SHUBHRA GUPTA: Anurag Basu told me something interesting. He said that Irrfan was difficult to convince about Monty, the character he had written for him in *Life in a … Metro*. When finally he agreed, he liked it so much that he wanted to do another Monty kind of character. And Irrfan told Anurag that *Qarib Qarib Singlle* [QQS] was that film. As a filmmaker who's been in the business for a while, it took you some time to reach Irrfan for QQS, right?

TANUJA CHANDRA: Yes. I always had this longing to do either a comedy or a fun film. Not exactly a romcom though; I've always been a little sceptical of whether romcoms really have the depth that I like to try and explore in movies. I had always wanted to do a funny film, but I knew that a funny film is far more difficult to do than a dramatic one, for me, personally. It's easier to just get into the meat of high drama where somebody's getting killed, there's a murderer, a chase, there are thrills, all that stuff. Somewhere, I suppose, in its thrill value, it's a little less like life in many ways. Whereas a softer, gentler film – comedy is not exactly the right term but for the lack of a better term – just a more life-like film is more difficult to do. So I knew that I would want to do one when I was a more mature director.

When I was starting out, my passion and my longing was, and still is, to do a female-led film and one that had a lot of drama and spoke for the struggle that a woman goes through in any situation – whether it's rape, or a job dominated by men, like in *Sangharsh*. And Irrfan I had approached, right from the start, between many intervals. For some reason, it never worked out. Once when, really early on, he wanted to do one of my films, I was the one who said no. I actually became aware of his brilliance after seeing *Haasil*. I still remember that one scene where he's tied to a chair. I was like, 'Oh my god, first of all this is a great scene, and this is a great actor.'

SG: Can I break in for a second? What about him being in that chair has stayed with you?

TC: His unpredictability. They had to tie him because they didn't know how he would have reacted. They had no other way to control him but to tie him down. To me, it's also him as an actor, which is that there's such an explosive nature inside, but it was always expressed in this controlled manner. It was never loud. In fact, in *Qarib Qarib Singlle*, I had so often wanted him to go a little louder, to be someone who speaks a lot. He does speak a lot in any case, but even then it was less than what I had wanted. I had wanted him to be more of a manic person. But I think that is his idea of good acting – that you feel a lot and you show as little, as we all often do.

I did meet him a couple of times. Once when I think he was shooting for *Slumdog Millionaire*. He said that he had really liked the script I had shown him. Of course that film never got made; he'd liked it but he was busy. He said, 'We'll meet again.' So every two–three years, I approached him. This one [*QQS*], for me and Gazal [Dhaliwal, the screenwriter], was written clearly with Irrfan in mind. He was going to be the first person I spoke to. At the time, he was shooting for the film about the Talwar case – what was that movie called?

SG: *Talvar.*

TC: Yes. He was shooting, so it was very difficult for me to get through, but he did call back and said, 'This is a tough role I'm doing, but why don't you send me a synopsis?' I did. He called me back and said, 'I like it; sounds interesting. I'm going to have to ask Sutapa to connect with you because I'm too busy; let her read the script.' And then she brought Shailja Kejriwal on board. This went on for a year. So I completely understand when Anurag says that he's difficult to convince. He thought about it for a year because he was not sure at that point about a solo romantic role. He did see some similarity between this and Anurag's film but he also did not want to make it like that, you know? He wanted it to be different from that. And he said, 'The day I completely connect with even one part of this guy and fall in love with Yogi – which I already halfway am – I'll say yes.'

During that time, Gazal and I were working on the screenplay so it wasn't time wasted as such, but I had to wait a long time and eventually I did say, 'If you're in two minds about it, pass on this one and maybe we'll work on another one at another point.' He did not say no either; kept me on hold for some time. Till one day, suddenly, he said that there was just one part of Yogi that he immediately related to, which was the fact that Yogi loved his domestic help, his driver, so much. And that to him, the driver was his friend; he wasn't just an employee. Irrfan liked that about him very much. He said that's the thing that turned it around for him, and finally he did say yes. I was thankful and grateful because I would have made the film with somebody else, but it just wouldn't have been the same, of course.

Let me tell you, it's not just convincing him about the screenplay, or to just say yes to the film; the convincing is every step of the way. 'Is this looking stupid?' 'Am I sounding like a fool because Yogi is foolish?' It was a very interesting contradiction, to me, that he would do the foolishness with great conviction; he never felt self-conscious about being utterly silly, which was the charming part about Yogi, but at the same time, he would also have his doubts, and questions all the time.

I supposed it was the need to be innovative every step of the way. So it's not that he has to be the most unusual character that one has never met in one's life; he should be unusual but also make you think of a lot of people that you know in real life. That was the interesting thing about the way Irrfan thought creatively, where he would bring his own experience of meeting people of all kinds from all over the world – but especially Indians, from villages, from cities, including drivers and make-up people and spot boys. He would really sit and engage with them. So that there should be an everyman, a sort of relatable quality in the character, while also an unusualness.

I think all really good actors seek that they'll be memorable and you'll remember them long after you finish seeing the film.

You say that it is hard to point a single finger at films where he is bad as an actor – I discovered this when I was editing *Qarib Qarib Singlle*. While he's shooting, it's nice, you get engaged, it feels good. But it doesn't have its full impact on you as a viewer until you actually see it as a story. And so, while I was editing – and I must have seen that same shot hundreds of times – but each time, that shot grew. There was something dynamic in it, something that was different from the last time. There's something he brought to it which you would always notice in increments later on and then again and again, so you never really tired of it. To me, it's such a fulfilling and beautiful thing that every second or third day, I'll get a message from somebody on Instagram or Facebook, that I love this part of *Qarib Qarib Singlle*. Somebody just sent me that song '*Bade Achhe Lagte Hain*' with the message: 'Thank you for this scene; Irrfan is just so beautiful in it.' By the way, in that scene, he was having the toughest time lip-syncing. If there's one thing he's bad at, it's lip-syncing. To him it was an unnatural thing. If he had to sing on his own, like we do in life, that would probably be fine. Of course he wasn't a singer or anything. So he would just constantly keep losing the sync; it would just go off. And we'd have to shoot again. I wanted him to actually sing out loud so that he would follow my cue, but then I thought that would interfere with his process as an actor so I didn't do it … I think that people continue to enjoy his work and get so much pleasure from it and continue to discover that his performance grows constantly.

SG: Why did it take Bollywood so long to discover this man?
TC: Honestly, it wasn't as if producers would jump in with a whole lot of money and funding if you had Irrfan on board. They would be interested because they had at least recognized

that he was a wonderful actor. But whether he was a star was still something people would question. So there would be a budgetary constraint. I think producers are extremely traditional. So their idea of what a hero is supposed to look like is connected to North Indian, Punjabi good looks. Irrfan doesn't fall into that bracket. On top of that, his acting was unconventional. I mean, even when we were dubbing for *Qarib Qarib Singlle*, there would be dialogues that even he wouldn't understand because so many things he'd just mumble. Of course, he had such command over the language that he could do it. Sometimes he would invert the dialogue, turn it upside down, add something in the end, do something with it. Or sometimes just make songs, because they felt right to him. That kind of acting was considered, I would imagine, niche and ...

SG: Arty.

TC: Yeah, arty is now such an abused word that it has come to mean nothing. But they would think that it's not what the large audiences that actually bring big money to the theatrical viewing of movies would like. And because movie-making started to change, Irrfan started to become more and more popular. He, of course, also had successes, which helps. If you have a successful film, producers are interested in you. They don't really love you yet but they want to sign you because you brought in money in your last film, so there must be something good about you, right? I think that's what happened, but only in a small way. I still think that, by and large, Bollywood is still quite traditional. But new voices started to tell stories in which he fit well. And I truly believe that audiences even in the nineties or the early 2000s would have loved him as much as they do now. It's just that people who are behind movie-making are very slow to take risks. Especially in Bollywood, there's so much risk aversion that you're just not sure; you'd rather go with the safe bet, you know? So it took longer than it should have. But more and more young filmmakers, unusual filmmakers from different parts of the country, started to make movies. The pool of directors and writers has become much bigger, now, especially.

Had Irrfan not passed away so tragically, I think there would have been a huge treasure trove of movies for him to still discover – performances and characters for the next ten years, safely – he would have had no shortage of work. It's sad that there is so much that we could have seen him do that we won't ever be able to. He is so unique that it will be difficult to have somebody replace him. But because of him, we will have more of that kind of actor, who brings his own syntax to the craft of acting and his own politics to his roles, actors who are politically alive and aware. After all, if you like that a character is very close to his driver and treats him like a friend, that is a political sentiment. He liked that Yogi was a feminist. Obviously all that stuff would have only increased had he lived. Too bad that Bollywood woke up late to his talent …

SG: Do you think he went to Hollywood because he didn't have enough big roles in Bollywood?

TC: I'm not sure, but definitely the work in Hollywood would have been a wonderful experience, that he, as an actor, would really treasure. I do remember after we finished shooting and when we were editing, he went to shoot that Hollywood film [*Puzzle*]. When he came back from that shoot, he said that it was the most beautiful experience in terms of the making and what he felt as a performer. He was obsessive about improvising. After two takes, it just necessarily had to change. Something had to change in the shot, something had to be improvised between the actors; they would have to play off against each other for him to actually feel that this was really exciting and fun and the thing that he always wanted to do. Which, I think, is less of a tradition here – not enough improvisation happens. There's a script and then you kind of say your dialogues. Once the dialogue is over and if they know how long it's supposed to last, in their head, actors will cut the shot even before the director has said 'cut'. But you're actually supposed to go on. You're not supposed to stop. But with him, he would want to keep playing. I think he got that experience there and, of course, the chance to work with some great Hollywood directors.

It used to actually give him joy to see Parvathy [his co-star in QQS] do a beautiful shot, you know? For him, half the fun of improvisation was also to see the actor that he's playing off of to excel. He really loved that. I'm not even saying that it's evolved or spiritually amazing; I'm saying that it's such good practical sense. That the scene becomes better if both of us are good. It is no good if I'm the one chewing up the scenery and everybody else is like minions or decorative ornaments – how does that help the story? I think that comes from this feeling of living democratically. To him that was a genuine life value, that we are all equals and we must work with each other and all of us must grow together.

So even with the smaller characters, like the taxi driver that he comes across – he would want him to be beautiful in the scene. He would want Neha Dhupia [his co-star in QQS] to be really wonderful; he would want everyone to be really good. Why? So that the entire film works. If Parvathy comes across as beautiful, Yogi is more appealing. Because she is falling in love with this guy. It shouldn't just be he who shines, and that was a really wonderful quality. He'd constantly be needling her: try this, do that, what do you think, what are you feeling?

SG: How did you think of Parvathy?

TC: We were lucky that our producers, Zee, had this pan-Indian presence, where they like to work with actors from the south, Punjab, Bengal. She was recommended to me by Gazal, who asked if I know this actor named Parvathy. I said, 'I actually know who she is but I haven't seen her films.' And then I saw some bits and suggested her name.

I thought that they would be really interesting together, because not only are these two different in terms of their personalities but they also come from completely different parts of the country. So their difference is only heightened. Also because she's not your conventional fair, skinny, tall heroine, you know? And so, that was a wonderful pairing with Irrfan because, to me, she was as real, as sensuous, as beautiful a person and heroine as all your other stars.

SG: And what did Irrfan say?

TC: When he met her, he found her an extremely intelligent woman with this natural ability for comedy – and she's genuinely funny. She could be funny even though her character was a serious one. The fact that he could be like, '*Arre yaar, Jaya-ji, aap ko har cheez pe gussa aa jaata hai.*' [You get annoyed about everything.] She was really perfect for that. He enjoyed that very much, where she could look at him quizzically [as if to ask] what is his problem, what is this guy? And yet she'd be drawn to him because, of course, it's Irrfan. On screen, you're just just drawn to him. In our film, he's annoying and chatty and talkative and strange but he's also somebody you get drawn to. And because he has gentle moments, there's a tenderness that he speaks with at the same time. So I think their chemistry worked really well.

SG: Taking off from what you said about actors who are political: Irrfan *was* a political actor. And you can be political without being overtly so. Did he have a strong sense of faith, of being Muslim, and did that ever come in the way of his being accepted as one of the best actors that we had?

TC: He did speak up a lot about Hindutva and prejudice in this country whenever it raised its ugly head. Very often he would have to even retract or maybe Sutapa would tell him not to say too much because he would get into trouble. He was a public figure. He had clear opinions; he was modern, liberal, egalitarian, against prejudice of any kind. But I don't think he ever felt that because I am Muslim, I am not being given the great roles. He would have thought that definitely because of his unconventional looks, his unconventional acting. So he would think, 'These people don't recognize the actor and the brilliance in me because I am not, by their standards, handsome. And mine is not the typical Punjabi Bollywood way of speaking. Therefore, they don't think I can have something of value to contribute to a film.' He would have definitely felt a great amount of anger about that. I would like to think that he would have poured that into his work; he would have put that feeling of disgruntlement and anger and unfairness into expressing. Certainly as an actor, he had this explosive quality despite his extremely quiet outward expression. When he says the lines, you cannot even hear them and my sound recordists used to have nightmares. They used to say, 'Irrfan sir, please can you dub a little louder?' And he'd say, '*Kyun, sunai nahi de raha hai kya?*' [Can't you hear me?] 'I can but I need some volume because I'll have to bring up the ambient sounds if you don't speak up.' He just wouldn't! That amazing dual nature of his performance would have been a constant churning mind and heart that thought about these things, about politics. As is Sutapa – they have very clear views and strong opinions on what is happening in this country. So I think a lot of that would have gone into his performance.

SG: When you think of Irrfan, what is the one thing that comes to your mind?

TC: The one thing that comes to my mind is absolute dedication to that fictional reality, completely submitting to it. Which is why, if there was too much external noise or somebody would be saying something, it would take him out of that fictional bubble and disturb him a lot. That kind of dedication is so pleasurable, such a treat to watch in an actor, where they're just giving themselves completely to that moment and not being self-conscious in the least. There would be self-consciousness before the shot and after. Both times there would be a great amount of doubt. 'Is it too much?' 'Is it stupid?' 'Am I looking like an idiot?' 'Should I do it like this?' He'd do the shot and then once the shot was over, he'd say, 'You think it's okay?' 'You think it works?' 'Keep telling me whatever you're thinking.' Because he wouldn't translate it in the obvious manner into the performance, but he would absorb, he wouldn't necessarily act it out, you know? But he'd always imbibe it.

I think that was a very interesting process, where there is self-doubt, which I think is a key component of any artist's life. Even during the edit, there would be immense amounts of doubt. At the release too. I remember, when he and Parvathy had gone to Fun Republic to watch the film with the audience, the audience didn't know that he was there – he was standing right at the back.

And when he offers her that bottle of water to drink [a crucial moment in the film], everybody in the hall just spontaneously started clapping. It just made his day; he didn't expect it at all. None of us did.

As filmmakers, we are always nervous: did we do a crappy job or did we do an okay job? So he was just thrilled. He looked at Parvathy and almost had tears in his eyes. So there was a shroud of doubt all the time but also extreme certainty in terms of giving himself to that moment and then just doing it with absolute conviction and improvising all the time.

That was something beautiful and I seek that in actors, the ability to completely, unselfconsciously become so unaware of what's around them, they don't see the camera, they don't see anything, they just are in that moment. Because no matter how you perform, it's truthful; it's not a lie. It's bound to be truthful because you're actually doing it, you're actually feeling it, you know? I treasure that the most.

He really loved what he did. I think that would also make him, to a certain extent, a difficult person as well. Difficult to please in terms of other people as well as him pleasing himself. He would not be happy with how things were going if they were not according to his way of paying attention to every detail. Even when we were working together, obviously there was some amount of illness already within him, which he was not aware of. Sometimes I would feel that something was bothering him; my answer to myself would always be that he was struggling with the role, how to make it funny, beautiful, charming and real. It's difficult; acting is not an easy thing to do. Now, in retrospect, I do think that there was a physical struggle going on where he couldn't imagine that he was unwell, but he was, I think, fighting it. When we all did find out, it was quite a late stage of the illness.

Which is why they couldn't save him, I guess. So yeah, even then [during the time he was working on the film], something was bothering him, and he used to think audiences shouldn't say at his age he was doing a romantic role, playing a foolish person. And I was like, 'Listen, there's no age for love; anybody can fall in love at any time and Yogi is a guy who's always in a state of love.' So, if I think about all these questions and the extreme self-doubt, it might have been an emotional manifestation of a physical war within.

'He had the eyes of a child and the soul of a mystic'

HOMI ADAJANIA

Homi Adajania, director of *Finding Fanny, Cocktail* and *Being Cyrus,* made *Angrezi Medium,* which released in 2020. It turned out to be Irrfan's last film. During the shoot, Irrfan struggled with his debilitating illness, yo-yo-ing between good and bad days, but the sets were as joyous as they could be. Adajania's deep fondness for the actor shines through as he speaks of the making of the film and the precious time they spent together.

SHUBHRA GUPTA: So tell me about Irrfan.

HOMI ADAJANIA: Okay, let's talk about Irrfan the performer. I think he had a gift which is inexplicable. I remember asking him once, 'Why are you so shit when you do ads? You're just rubbish at them.' He said, 'Homi, it's because I don't believe who this character is.' Even when it came to films, he would say, 'It'll take me a day or two to catch the soul of the character but once I've caught it, there is no way I can give you a false beat, because then I know exactly what the character will not do.' I think that's what also made him so unpredictable, because he didn't have a pattern to it. There wasn't a system to it, or a method. It was something that just flowed within him once he caught that character. When we were working on *Angrezi Medium*, he had not worked for about a year and we had a very unfiltered relationship that was extremely honest ... one second ... very difficult ...

pauses, overwhelmed

He loved the fact that I had absolutely no reservations in talking to him the way I did; he was surrounded by people who would not do that with him. And he was always searching for a truth ... it's too difficult ...

SG: Please, take a minute.
HA: No, no, I'm comfortable, I'm just ...

SG: I had the same experience with Vishal [Bhardwaj] a few days back. He said he could not do this, because his relationship with Irrfan was not just that of director and performer, but something much closer. I think he was still finding it very difficult to speak about him in this objective fashion.

I'm not really after anything other than truth myself. Irrfan mined the truth. Even when the material was terrible, he was the best thing in that film. And you had no idea what he was going to do on screen.
HA: Absolutely. You didn't know what he was going to do when he came on set, when that camera switched on. So he hadn't worked for a year and he came to me, and I told him ... You don't mind if I use profanity, right?

I remember the whole crew was waiting and waiting for Irrfan Khan to walk back on the set. I took him aside and said, 'You fucker, I hope you haven't forgotten how to act.' He laughed and said, 'Maybe I have; I never knew, really, what I used to do.' So I said, 'Maybe you'll know when the camera comes on.' I remember on the first day, before the first shot, I just told him, 'Listen, you're too organic. I mean, I can't predict what you're going to do.' If I tell a guy that he has to walk through the door, Irrfan Khan may not; he won't just walk through the door. I said, 'Irrfan, I can't shoot a fucking movie like this; you come and you block the scene. I can't use my camera and light the whole thing only to have you turn your back on the scene like that.' '*Arre yaar*, you're embarrassing me, *yaar*,' he would say.

But he was much more than an actor for me. We used to both look at life in a very unserious way, and not understand people who took it too seriously. We were always in pursuit of a laugh and, in that pursuit, there were many tears. He was extremely different towards the end, in a very beautiful way. Because ... one second. Oof, this is too tiring, *yaar*. This is more tiring than my shoots, Shubhra ...

SG: Do you want a break?

HA: No, no, I'm okay. He once said, 'If I had to go through this whole experience again, I wouldn't change a thing. I am very selfish towards everyone around me, but this realization I would not have got in ten lifetimes. I was so deluded by the fact that I was Irrfan Khan, the crossover star, the famous actor, the celebrity. I was blinded by the fact that I was Irrfan the label, and we are so not; we just create all these labels and it's just not what your existence is and what your truth is.' By the end of it, he didn't want the attention; he didn't want any sort of adulation. But there was one thing he couldn't let go of. He told me, '*Homi, mujhe mere craft se bahut mohabbat hai.*' [I have great love for my craft.] That was one thing he didn't want to stop; he just *loved* to act. He was actually a very shy guy. He used to tell me, 'Even when I go out in public, I am acting; that's not me. I am playing a role.' He came from a very conservative family, very traditional – extremely patriarchal father. He told me once how he had broken his arm and his father refused to let him put it in a cast. His whole arm had to be reset. He said, 'I don't understand it even today. I've realized that people are different and I don't expect them to understand me.' He said that he was extremely shy; after doing a small course, he had come to Bombay as an AC repairman. He told me, 'I went to the first gig I got, which was to fix one AC and, as soon as I fixed it and left that flat, I thought there is no way I can do this for the rest of my life. That was the beginning and end of that career.'

Luckily the second career worked out well and lasted much longer. But he said, 'Because of my shyness, I realized that an actor can inhabit a character and doesn't have to live with the validation and the approval we seek in our real lives, or the way we want to be portrayed in our real lives. You can play a character that you don't need to justify; you don't care about the judgement. It allows you to be extremely free and extremely fearless. Being an introvert, for me, playing a character who can be anything without my having to explain that to my real self was a joyous discovery. That is what hooked me – I could be anyone.'

A lot of actors you meet will say, 'Oh, we draw from our own experiences and our own trauma.' He never ever did that. His X factor was the ability to inhabit the character and find its voice. And it wasn't that he would find it by doing some major research or educating himself too much about it – he was very averse to being clinical, and that we see in any performance of his. There's absolutely nothing which is premeditated or which looks like an effort or is affected. He had that amazing ability to just ... be. I feel he loved acting for this reason – that he could be things that he couldn't be in his real life.

We shared a commonality with our love for nature. We both had this rootedness in not getting totally swayed by all the crap in the world, especially in this business. When we were shooting *Angrezi Medium*, he finally said, 'Homi, I'm getting out of this hotel, *yaar*.' I said, 'Why? Where are you going to go stay?' He told me, 'I'm going to stay in some homestay-type thing, some farm. I like to sleep outside on the *charpai*, once the bats come in and the sun sets.' That was his trip, you know? Planting trees, going into nature, the smells.

SG: How did *Angrezi Medium* happen? Did Irrfan reach out to you? It's a very different kind of film from the ones that you've made before. And as someone who's both from Bollywood and not of it, I wanted to know from your perspective – did the legacy studios know what to do with an actor like Irrfan?

HA: I feel that you will see Naseer bhai [Naseeruddin Shah], Irrfan, or any of those actors who have immense calibre but, at the end of the day, people have to pay their bills as well, right? You take what you get and you wait for the brilliant stuff. But whatever he'd do, it would be with such integrity that even if it was a crap film, he would come out shining. That was his ability.

As for your question about the studios, I felt Irrfan's time *was* coming. That whole quintessential star, chocolate hero, stereotypical looks which initially he struggled with, I feel all that has changed today. With OTTs and the content that we have access to, today we fall in love with characters. That's why I feel his time would have been now. Finally, it is a commodity which you're selling to a market and it depends on what the demand is and therefore you supply in a certain way. He was well aware of that. I think all these actors, at some point, struggle with the frustration of 'Why am I not getting my due?' And it is a very valid frustration.

But after a while, Irrfan had come to terms with it – that was not a consideration. He was so secure about his ability with the craft that, after a while, he got over that shit. He was doing more work abroad than many actors put together. Because they [the West] knew what his calibre was. And I feel those roles would have also become bigger than just those random slotted [South] Asian parts.

I spent the summer with him before *Angrezi* [*Medium*]. He was doing his chemotherapy, and I had another friend who was doing chemotherapy, so I was basically running between two chemo patients. But I remember we were sitting in a cafe in London and this one guy came up to him and said, 'Oh my god! Irrfan Khan!' And he named two–three of his blockbusters, but before he could even come close to us, Irrfan said, 'Boss, please, *haath jod ke main bol raha hoon* that I am not him; that's an ugly Indian actor who I keep getting mistaken for and it's quite insulting, frankly.' Which was hilarious, because that guy backed off and said, 'Oh, sorry, you looked very familiar.' But yeah, he would take the piss. A lot of foreigners would recognize Irrfan, because of his big Hollywood movies.

SG: Do you remember your first meeting with Irrfan?
HA: We first met during the screening of the *The Namesake* at INOX. We went to a bar after that and proceeded to make it an all-nighter. We always wanted to work together; we kept making plans but then it would fall apart for some reason or the other. We always wanted to make a gritty, edgy film where we could explore him and he could take his craft to … Sadly, that didn't materialize.

So, I absolutely adored *Hindi Medium*. I remember talking

to him about that and I said, 'We have to do something, man.' He used to keep sending me very interesting scripts. It's just that I'm quite a lazy filmmaker. I make a movie and spend the rest of the time living the rest of my life. But in this case, I was in the office, I was actually working on a script on a schizophrenic serial killer. And the producer came in and said, 'Listen, I want you to hear the first half of *Angrezi Medium*.' I said, 'What is that?' So he's like, 'It's a sequel to *Hindi Medium*. But it's got nothing to do with *Hindi Medium*; it's just the same actors.' I remember hearing the first half and I found it hilarious. By then, Irrfan had been diagnosed and this thing was sort of on the shelf, but if it were to happen, it was the next thing he was going to do. And there was no way I'd let it go. So we spoke and he said, 'You're kidding me – you're going to do it? *Bhenchod, Parsi saale, tereko Hindi kidhar aata hai?*' [You Parsi fucker, do you even know any Hindi?] I said, 'That's why it's called *Angrezi Medium*.'

I remember we were thrilled that we were going to work together; not from the point of view of the script, not that we were making a movie, just that we would be able to have a fun experience and laugh at life a bit. There's no other reason, honestly. I didn't feel that *Hindi Medium* needed a sequel; it was a great movie on its own.

SG: In your industry, it's only when you work with people that you hang out with them, isn't it? And then you go your different ways. But you and Irrfan did keep in touch, right?
HA: When I say 'kept in touch', it wasn't like we would call each other and meet; we'd always sort of bump into each other. But when we'd bump into each other, it was like we'd never left, you know? What I'm saying is, I think he enjoyed the freshness, the honesty. There was never any trying, it was never forced; it was just something that clicked. He used to laugh a lot at me, the

bastard. He loved that my humour was not acceptable to the rest of the world. He loved that there was no shyness.

SG: That one all-nighter that you guys pulled, what was it? I mean, you were drinking and having fun, but there must have been something that was the glue. What was that?

HA: No, it was just talking, you know? When you suddenly find a kindred spirit, or someone you've just never known but know everything about, it's like that. You can just talk about everything and there's always a connection. That's what it was. He was very interested in knowing stuff; he was a very curious man. He was always searching, whether it was from a spiritual point of view or just plain knowledge. Like I know he would never go scuba diving or free diving, but he wanted to know things about it. He found my background extremely fascinating.

Maybe I'm overstating what it was, but I think he liked that I was not shy. He enjoyed that slightly brash, out-there person. And also my saying, 'Dude, don't take life so seriously, *yaar*. Laugh at yourself; approach me, laugh at me, I have no issues. If it's making your life happier, go for it.' I think he liked all that.

SG: Can I ask you what you meant when you called him a 'crossover star'?

HA: It was, again, one of the labels he didn't like. He started getting an aversion to labels by the end of his journey. And that was something he had been labelled as – the guy who had successfully 'crossed over'. But the fact is that he *was* that guy, you know? He had crossed over and was straddling Hollywood and Bollywood. I don't know how hard he tried to do that, or if he was just discovered on the merit of his capabilities. I think he did get seen and people realized what his calibre was.

SG: In my opinion, all the Hollywood work he did must have looked good on his CV, but they were not great films. I don't think even Ang Lee [the director of *Life of Pi*] knew what to do with this man.

HA: I'll tell you what: contrary to what you're saying, he was blown away by Ang Lee. He actually found Ang Lee a very interesting director. He used to tell me, '*Tereko Hindi nahi aata.*' [You can't speak Hindi.] So I said, '*Ang Lee koh toh English bhi nahi aata.*' [Ang Lee doesn't even know English.] He said, 'No, boss. For a couple of scenes, I was not sure, but the way that he would talk to you, and the tangential spaces that the man could take you into was fascinating.' So he held Ang Lee in great esteem. He was besotted with Kubrick; Stanley Kubrick, I think, was his all-time hero. In his last year, the year before we shot *Angrezi*, when he was living in London, he had gone quite deep into all of Kubrick's work and was very taken by it, by the man himself and the way his mind worked. So I think he still aspired to do a lot of cinema. Which sadly couldn't get done.

SG: He knew at a point that he may not be able to dial back from his illness. But Mira Nair mentioned that it was amazing how he dealt with knowing that today I am here, tomorrow I may not be. She said something about the grace with which he did that. And Sooni Taraporevala said the shooting for *Angrezi Medium* was a lot of fun. He knew that his time on this planet may be limited, so he knew how to make the most of every moment.

HA: That's exactly what it was. We spoke about this a lot and I remember telling him one day, 'The problem with us all is our dialogue with death is wrong. It's something we fear. Instead of embracing it, we fear it. We should embrace it the same way we embrace birth.' Self-preservation is, obviously, a natural tendency; the fear of the unknown and what happens after.

It's not that he didn't believe that he was going to die, or he had less time left. But he wasn't waiting for that moment. There was no way he was going to live life and take every step towards that moment. He was going to take every step laughing, enjoying his life and being the best way he could possibly be. Sure, there were shit days and bad times but overall, considering what he was going through, he wanted to juice out the maximum he could of the good stuff of what life is actually for. Therefore, every moment on that set was spent looking for a laugh. Because life has good in it. If you want to find it, you can, or you can be a negative person and get stressed by all the trivialities of life.

We were not those people. We actually laughed so much that at some point, he would be like, 'Just stop. I'm not in good shape; my stomach pains, *yaar*.' We really had a great time. And it wasn't just about haha heehee; we also cried a lot. We had a very passionate experience, with Sutapa, him, Babil who was on set, myself, the crew, my wife Anita. There was a lot of compassion, a lot of good energy; there was a fullness. That fullness, in a very ironic way, made me lighter as a person, after he had gone. Made me realize that this is the way to be. If he could be that way, considering what he was going through, I just can't even imagine why we can't. That was a great learning which he left me with.

SG: What is the one thing that comes to mind when you think of Irrfan?

HA: A child. I think of a child with immense talent. The way he could channel a child's curiosity, you know? There's a Bob Marley song called 'Natural Mystic' – that's what he was.

He had the eyes of a child and the soul of a mystic.

PART IV

'You can't generalize Irrfan Khan'

KARAN JOHAR

As a filmmaker who shaped and steered Hindi cinema so definitively in the late nineties, when Irrfan was biding his time in TV and waiting for a break in the movies, **Karan Johar** epitomizes the Bollywood that didn't know quite what to do with this actor. None of the legacy studios did. Johar speaks of being aware of the 'brilliance' of Irrfan but never having a film 'worthy' of him, and of how, as a presenter on *The Lunchbox*, he was proud to finally have an Irrfan film on his roster.

SHUBHRA GUPTA: Why did you never do a film with Irrfan?
KARAN JOHAR: As a filmmaker, when you reach out to the talent in your world, you realize that it's not so much that you've reached a certain position or that you've arrived. Sometimes there are some talents that are way stronger than your own ability. Irrfan Khan was that actor. He was way stronger than anything I could have ever offered him. I never arrived at a screenplay, a film, a thought or an idea that would warrant the presence of the magnitude that Irrfan Khan brought to the table. That's the reason I've never had a film with Irrfan because I've never wanted to be that filmmaker that gave him a substandard mainstream film. I

didn't want to be the blotch in his otherwise beauteous career graph. When I walked out of *Maqbool*, I just looked at Vishal Bhardwaj and said, 'Pardon my French when I say this – Irrfan Khan is a fucking genius.' Because no other actor, I think, has a combination of the various characteristics that Irrfan brought to the table: charisma, cinema intellect, presence, performance, all in equal measure. You can slot many other actors into boxes. You can't generalize Irrfan Khan, you can't put him into a box. It's simply because he was so unique and individualistic.

You know, when I started making movies in the late nineties and early 2000s, we were people who had a certain kind of blocked way of looking at what mainstream cinema was. And we had access to the big movie stars then, we had the privilege to go to them with stories, but we didn't have the ability – at that point of time – to think beyond that box. I don't want to speak for anybody else but, as a filmmaker, I didn't have the ability to think beyond it.

When I was making *Kuch Kuch Hota Hai* and *Kabhi Khushi Kabhie Gham*, it was all about the celebrated movie stars coming together in superb combinations, making these big films, big scales, big songs. I didn't have the chops or the ability, really, to go out of that comfort zone that was created for us – to break that mould and work with an actor like Irrfan Khan. It just didn't strike me and I didn't have the talent at that point of time. So I did what I did as a filmmaker.

So while Irrfan Khan had this trajectory that began properly in 1998, and he had all those movies that were breaking through, I was busy making these big spectacle entertainers; I didn't have the bandwidth or understanding of how to accommodate the magic and magnitude of Irrfan.

I remember when I saw *The Namesake* at the Toronto

Film Festival in 2006, I had a cathartic reaction to that film because, somehow, two years post my father's death, I felt I had internalized all my emotions, and that film made me burst like a dam. I remember going home that night and weeping. It all just came out and I think it had a lot to do with the way Irrfan and Tabu were in that film. Their performances just moved me. The next day at breakfast – we didn't know each other very well – I went and held Irrfan's hand and I said, 'Thank you for giving me closure because what you did last night gave me closure.' And he probably smiled and didn't understand what I meant and I don't think I explained myself. But I really meant it – that was the impact he had. I mean, he went beyond just his projection and portrayal of a character; it kind of touched you in a way you didn't understand.

I'm so glad *The Lunchbox* is part of my roster; I can say very proudly that there's an Irrfan Khan film on my roster even if I'm just a presenter on that film. I feel like I interacted with him on that film and we did our best to make sure that it had a large mainstream audience. I feel that when you walk out of *Lunchbox*, you take back unfulfilled love, which is so many people's story. And when you see unfulfilled love, you think Irrfan Khan in *Lunchbox*. I feel like he really had that connect.

Zoya [Akhtar] and I both agreed that there is no other actor like Irrfan Khan, and there may never be. I don't think it would be fair to compare his journey to Naseer saab [Naseeruddin Shah] because he is a genius in what he is, but I still believe in that combination of charisma, cinema intellect, performance and sex appeal – it's very important to say that women found him sexy; he had tremendous sex appeal. I think we've never really associated sex appeal with an actor who has done work of that calibre. You know, always, it's the actors who do the more cerebral, the more intellectual, the more critic-friendly cinema that you don't associate with sex appeal, somehow. I think Irrfan Khan was very sexy, and it was a huge icing on his terrific talent cake.

SG: I always thought that as a lover, he was quite fantastic. He just stands there and radiates sexiness. Why, I wonder, did it take Bollywood, and you specifically, so long to figure out that here's a man who's ready to move into the mainstream? Was it because he wasn't this templated fair, Punjabi-looking person who had taken over our screens for the last forty years?

KJ: I think, Shubhra, it is also because there is a certain herd mentality that creeps into mainstream Hindi cinema. Where we tend to put people into boxes. The moment a film has too many leaves on it, which means festival-choice films, it scares people who are promoting it. I've heard people saying many times, '*Yaar*, don't put too many leaves on a poster because it looks like it's a festival-type film; it won't draw an audience.' We have weird myths that we tend to live by. So when you say Irrfan Khan, the thinking is, 'Oh, maybe he can't do a song; he can't romance a girl and do a lip-sync song because it's not his domain.' These are all thoughts that are within the industry. I can't speak for anybody else, but I can speak for myself that I tend to do the same thing, fall into the same trap of generalization. It's a huge trap and we all have fallen. Not just with Irrfan; it's happened with so many other people – we all think that certain actors are good for certain things and certain actors are not. But that is not for us to decide because if an actor is a volcano of talent like Irrfan was, he's capable of doing anything. He's capable of romancing, lip-syncing a song, he's probably capable of doing a serious action film as well, which he has done partially – you know what I mean. I think that the fault lies with this slotting, this generalization game that the fraternity plays, which is actually detrimental to so many people who can do so much more.

SG: So when he went away to Hollywood, do you think it was because he got disillusioned by the fact that he didn't get his due? And he looked to the West? Or did the West come looking for him?

KJ: I don't know if he was disillusioned. I didn't know him personally and I can't claim to know what went on in his mind. But I always looked at Irrfan as a kind of cinema voyager; I felt like he travelled from zone to zone, country to country, cinema to cinema. He was a bit like a genius vagabond. I think he went with a certain flow, not because he was disillusioned, perhaps because he wanted to work with everyone, everywhere. He had a completely eclectic perspective and point of view. Yes, there could be a sense of resentment or disillusionment that an industry doesn't recognize your true potential. But in my limited interaction with him, I sensed that he wasn't that man. I believe that he travelled where cinema took him, and he didn't wait in one spot for things to fall into place. He went looking for what would perhaps resonate with him. Some things did, some didn't – he still made that trip. I think that's what actors should do. All actors think: we should work here; we should do this; we shouldn't do this; if we have a small role in an international film, it'll take away from our stardom or it will diminish our stardom in India. Too many myths, too many theories – all wrong, if you ask me. Irrfan Khan broke every stereotype and myth you could think of with the work he did. He knew he could create a magical experience in Hindi cinema as much as he could walk the red carpet in Berlin or Cannes.

SG: When do you think he broke through? Was it *Life in a...
Metro* in 2006, or do you think it happened with *Maqbool* a little
earlier?

KJ: Can I tell you: his real breakthrough moment commercially
was *Hindi Medium*. If you ask me, it was actually as recent as
that. *Hindi Medium* did business of about seventy crores purely
on account of a simple, high-concept, small film, and Irrfan did
it entirely on his own. There was no other star in the film; there
was no other clutch he had. That's when I think everyone woke
up to the fact that Irrfan Khan is a numbers man as well. Up
to the point, everything else – *Life in a... Metro* and everything
that you said – had a great actor, great idea, he worked very well.
But when *Hindi Medium* came out and it did the numbers, that's
when the industry woke up to his commercial possibilities. It was
as late as that, unfortunately.

SG: Naseeruddin Shah and Om Puri actually paved the way for
someone like Irrfan. Who do you think Irrfan paved the way for?

KJ: Irrfan Khan empowered an entire generation of actors. Today,
a Kumud Mishra, a Pankaj Tripathi, a Divyenndu [Sharma], a
Jaideep Ahlawat, a Kay Kay Menon, so many actors are doing
great stuff on digital platforms or even in cinema, so many actors
are prominently placed, because Irrfan Khan paved the way. Not
just for one, he paved the way for at least twenty such actors
today that are doing magical work. That's what Irrfan Khan is
responsible for.

I feel terrible that we lost him when we did. Irrfan could helm
such amazing films today. You'd be surprised, Shubhra, there are
at least five scripts that landed on my table after he passed away
that were screaming Irrfan Khan. I just feel terrible. And you
know why those scripts came to my table now? Because now is the

time that cinema is ready for that material and that material was all Irrfan Khan. Every time I think we don't have a replacement for Irrfan Khan. I keep telling my project development head – Somen Mishra – do you realize we've received so many stories that actually warranted his presence and we have no one to fill that place anymore? Because he really was unique.

SG: Tell me about your experience with *The Lunchbox*. How did you get into the project?

KJ: I watched *Lunchbox* at Cannes and went crazy about it. I think I sometimes give the projection that I'm a certain kind of filmmaker and it's a big standing joke that when people read my name on a poster, they think it cannot be a Karan Johar film because that has to be a different kind of cinema experience; he can't have made something that's not typical.

SG: The song and dance, the big budget and the blingy aesthetic …

KJ: So if and when I do produce the one-off film that has required a lot of critical love, even with those films I feel the critics tend to be a little harsh with me. Like, I always make the joke *ki kaash mera naam Karan Kashyap hota* [I wish my name were Karan Kashyap.] [*laughs*] Sometimes I feel like I am doomed by my own perception, you know? So when I saw *Lunchbox*, no one believed that I was this crazy about the film. Everybody was surprised that I wanted my name on this film. So I rallied Guneet Monga [producer, CEO of Sikhya Films], brought her into a room with Siddharth Roy Kapur [producer, founder and MD of Roy Kapur Films], we decided to put in the publicity and the advertising money, which was high. Because that film was called *Lunchbox*, everyone was like, 'First change its title.' I said, 'No, don't change Ritesh Batra's vision; don't change *Lunchbox*. Let's give it a tag; let's do something like: "How do you fall in love with somebody you've never met?"' That was the tagline I gave the film and it actually resonated in the marketing zone.

After that, we put the film out and we tried to bring as much of an audience for it. I remember at one point, Irrfan told me, '*Yaar, tumne toh bada commercial bana diya film ko.*' [You made the film very commercial.] We had that song from *Saajan** in one of our marketing units. And I think he was very amused because he felt like it was two poles colliding: Dharma Productions coming in to match Ritesh Batra's vision in an Irrfan Khan film.

But I suppose the Gemini in me comes out – I'm trying very hard to make people see that I *am* capable of much more than they think. The two films I presented around that time – *Baahubali*[†] and *Lunchbox* – are poles apart. *Lunchbox* is that one big moment I will always be proud of, because in my entire career trajectory, I don't think I've had that kind of an acclaimed film. And I made it my own quite easily, even though I don't deserve any credit for the beauty of *Lunchbox*. So major chance *pe* dance I've done around *Lunchbox* and *Baahubali*, where I had nothing to do with the films creatively, but I got a lot of credit.

SG: Did Irrfan tell you this in person?

KJ: Yeah, yeah. We were at an airport, about to board, and he said, '*Yaar*, you really commercialized everything in the film,' and I said, 'Whatever gets the people in, Irrfan.' So he said, 'Yeah that's true.'

SG: So even though *The Lunchbox* wasn't 'your film', it was

---

* A 1991 Lawrence D'Souza film
† A 2015 S. S. Rajamouli film

your film in a manner of speaking and you got the two kinds of Bollywoods together. It was two kinds of Hindi cinema coming together and a synergy was created. That was 2012. I am wondering whether, after that, you wanted to actually make a film with him. Was that a thought in your head?

KJ: There was a film that I was very keen to go to him with. But by then we had already heard of his illness and I knew he was in London. I knew through Homi Adajania, who is a dear friend of his, that he was already unwell. So I just kept it aside. And then subsequently things just went downhill …

SG: If I may ask, what kind of film was it?

KJ: It was actually an emotional film about a husband and wife and a child. Not like a *Hindi Medium*, but it was really quite a beautiful, emotional story that I had been developing for a while. It's developed and written but I don't know whom to go to. That's why I said I don't know if there's a replacement for Irrfan Khan. It's a combination that needed his presence, his performance but also his emotional depth. Which, I think, is rare. Rather, it's impossible to find.

SG: And one last thing. When you think of Irrfan Khan, what's the one thing that comes to your mind?

KJ: The one word that comes to mind is charisma. And I would say that cinema charisma is a different kind of charisma. Everyone will say genius, best actor, legendary performer, best – all that and more. But to me, I found him charismatic. Right before he fell ill, I remember meeting him on a plane. I was getting off at London and he was going to a film festival. I looked at him and I said, '*Sir, aapne bahut weight lose kiya hai.*' [You have lost a lot of weight.] He said, '*Haan, sab log woh* *bol rahe hain.'* [Everyone's been saying that.] I said, 'Is it for a role?' He said, 'I don't know.' Much later I realized that maybe the weight loss was to do with his illness. We were sitting very close to each other on the flight to London. I remember he was reading something. He had his glasses on and the sunlight was kind of seeping into his face. I was sitting opposite him and I saw a cinematic visual in front of me: Irrfan Khan, the early rays of sunlight on his face, him reading with his glasses on. I just looked at that face and thought that there was power and charisma in it. That's the Irrfan Khan I remember.

SG: One thing that has been troubling me and I've posed this to the other people I've spoken to: do you think the fact that he came from a certain community was a barrier between him and getting certain kinds of roles? Bollywood is the most liberal, the most talent-happy place. But in the India that we live in today, do you think that an actor of his calibre would have become a superstar? We've had twenty-five years of the Khans, Mr Amitabh Bachchan – they are still huge stars. Do you think Irrfan would ever have become that kind of a big star?

KJ: Well, I don't think it has anything to do with his last name. He was an artist and that will always remain his strength.

SG: He wanted to be known as just Irrfan.

KJ: Well, I don't know, that was his personal decision – I have no idea why. That was maybe some numerology thing, like the double r that he added, or maybe someone advised him – I don't know.

To answer your question: would he be a superstar? I don't know what we know of superstardom anymore. I think the concept of superstardom has changed drastically and it has nothing to do with the times we live in; it's to do with the fact that the content is changing and it is no longer elevating one individual but elevating the entire content itself. But he would have been a strong pillar. Would he have had the stardom that we know Shah Rukh Khan has? I don't know and I'm not sure, because that stardom I don't know if anyone from the young generation can have, you know? Even the young actors that are in the star zone – are they going to be mega stars? I'm not sure. Because I think the times are different; we are not putting stars on pedestals anymore; we are putting films on pedestals, content on a pedestal. A film or a show that you love is no longer a star vehicle; it's a writer's vehicle, it's a directorial vehicle, and I think that's what Irrfan would have scored in.

SG: Would it be a lasting regret that you actually didn't work in a film with him?

KJ: It will always be a regret. There are two regrets I have in my life. One is that I never got to direct Sridevi and the other is that I never got to direct Irrfan Khan. They're completely opposite artists in the landscape of Indian cinema, but those are the two regrets I will always have.

'Irrfan is irreplaceable'

ANURAG KASHYAP

How did Irrfan miss doing an **Anurag Kashyap** film? Intense, rooted hinterland stories – the kind Kashyap made his mark in – practically begged the presence of an actor who could fully inhabit that terrain. Kashyap speaks of getting to know Irrfan in his early TV days, how his brother Abhinav Kashyap knew Irrfan much better, and how he finally got onto an 'Irrfan project' as co-producer of *The Lunchbox*.

SHUBHRA GUPTA: It's hard to believe that you and Irrfan did not actually work together.

ANURAG KASHYAP: Yeah, we had a lot of opportunities to work together ...

SG: Tell me a little about those opportunities. When did you first meet Irrfan?

AK: *Bahut pehle* – a long time ago. Irrfan is one rare actor from the National School of Drama who knew extremely early on that he wants to do cinema. He did not pursue theatre at all; he just left and came to Bombay. At that time, everybody used to wonder why he left. And the struggle was so long. My first interaction with

Irrfan was very early on, thanks to a series called *Darr* which my brother Abhinav [Kashyap] directed. It was on Star TV, with Kay Kay [Menon] and Irrfan. That's when we met for the first time.

That was also a phase when *Satya* released, and Manoj Bajpayee had just broken out. He was working on getting Irrfan to play the villain in *Ghaath**, I think, directed by Akash Deep. He was instrumental in getting Irrfan a mainstream 'negative' role. And then I got busy shooting *Paanch* [Kashyap's first film which is still unreleased]. Aditya Srivastava was in the running for *The Warrior*, but he got busy with *Paanch*, and Irrfan ended up doing *Warrior*. Irrfan's closest friend was Tigmanshu [Dhulia], and my brother and Tigmanshu were very close. Irrfan and my brother also became very close. Actually, *Dabangg* was originally written for Irrfan.

SG: Seriously?

AK: *Haan*. My brother wrote *Dabangg* for Irrfan and Randeep Hooda. And it went to Arbaaz Khan to produce. And he ended up taking it to Salman [Khan], who said, 'I want to act in *Dabangg*.' That was also a time when, amongst all of us filmmakers, there was constantly a juggle between Manoj Bajpayee, Kay Kay and Irrfan. I really wanted to work with Irrfan, but somehow it didn't happen.

In *Black Friday*†, it was supposed to be Irrfan instead of Aditya Srivastava, and Irrfan, somehow, did not want to play Badshah Khan. Same reason Naseeruddin Shah did not want to play Tiger Memon in *Black Friday*. This was a very sensitive time and, being Muslim, they did not want to play these perpetrators.

---

* A 2000 Akashdeep Sabir film

† A 2004 Anurag Kashyap film

Irrfan wanted to play Rakesh Maria [the police commissioner of Bombay at that time]. But casting-wise, Kay Kay Menon had a strong resemblance to Rakesh Maria. So I was like, 'You know, it will be very strange if I get you [Irrfan] to play Rakesh Maria.'

We talked about *Gulaal* [2009]. We were also very invested in doing a musical biopic of Pash [the iconic Punjabi poet]. Irrfan was learning to sing. We talked about that; it came out in the papers as well. But somehow or the other, things never worked out. I could not find the funds to make the film and, later on, he was doing so much work outside India that it didn't happen. *The Lunchbox* worked out – on which I was a producer. Even *Gangs of Wasseypur* was taken to Irrfan first by UTV.

SG: You mean Manoj Bajpayee's role of Sardar Khan?

AK: No, we were thinking of the elder brother's role – Danish Khan [eventually played by Vineet Kumar Singh]. I remember even before the script was written, there was a meeting with Irrfan at Prithvi [Theatre]. We started discussing and he got so invested in it. We did not know how the film would shape up at that time. But the role did not shape up [as planned], and we thought it very unfair to get Irrfan to play it. There were a lot of opportunities – we crisscrossed – but it just didn't happen.

SG: It's so strange because anytime I think of your work, I feel that Irrfan should have been there because, as you said, you crisscrossed from so early on.

AK: Yes, from the BITV* days. *Hum Bambai Nahin Jayenge*, the serial we did for BITV, became a stepping stone for all of us. I was writing it. Shekhar Kapur was in charge of BITV; Tigmanshu

---

* Business India Televsion – a now-defunct channel

was doing *Hum Bambai Nahin Jayenge* for Shekhar. From that world first emerged Tigmanshu, and Tigmanshu pulled out Irrfan. *Bandit Queen* was entirely cast in Delhi and Irrfan was already in Mumbai. Somehow, Irrfan not being in *Bandit Queen* is something we wondered about. Because there was a lot of resistance to Irrfan in the beginning. Barring Tigmanshu, I don't think anybody was investing in him or pushing him.

SG: Why?

AK: See, Irrfan was not a social butterfly. He was not part of any clique; he was just friends with some people. And he was quiet and aloof. He was not somebody who would go and ask for a role. He would happily go and meet people, but even then he wouldn't be able to ask. In his early days, he was all the more shy.

SG: Shy? Do you think he wasn't convinced about his own talent? I'm just wondering about this man, who spent ten years of his life looking for cinema and was sick of doing TV. Tigmanshu said, 'If he didn't get *The Warrior* when he did, he would have left acting.'

AK: *Woh I think thak gaya tha.* [He was very exhausted.] But he was also very quiet. I was also a very quiet person at that time, but only because everybody was senior to me. I did not know whether it was my place to speak. But in my circle, I would talk a lot. His quiet was inherent. See, everybody wanted to somehow be a hero. I didn't think Irrfan had that; Irrfan wanted to act. Irrfan could do that but he wanted to do much more. Even a Manoj Bajpayee wanted to be a hero. Irrfan didn't.

Then one after another came *Ghaath* and *Maqbool*. Around that time, Tigmanshu got the courage to make *Haasil*. He was not getting funding before that.

SG: Was it at this time that Bollywood suddenly realized that here was this guy hiding in plain sight?

AK: Bollywood did not realize it, I think, till *Hindi Medium*. It was always the independent, outsider filmmakers, or a Vishal Bhardwaj, or a Tigmanshu Dhulia. Even after *Paan Singh Tomar*, Bollywood did not embrace Irrfan.

They would still go to him for negative roles. Like when I was doing *Bombay Velvet* [2015], everyone was pushing me to give the role of Khambatta [the antagonist's role, eventually played by Karan Johar] to Irrfan. I said, 'I don't want to.' When I work with him for the first time, I have to do something much stronger.

Bollywood thinks on conventional lines. Villain? *Irrfan ko le lo, chalega. Achha actor hai, villain bann sakta hai.* Bollywood did not look at him as a protagonist. It was always an Asif Kapadia or a Ritesh Batra, from the outside. They saw the actor in Irrfan.

See, Irrfan did not tie into India's obsession with fair skin, chocolate looks, Punjabi-ness and all those things. Nor did Nawaz [Nawazuddin Siddiqui] represent that. Bollywood only started embracing Irrfan when his films started succeeding. Post *Paan Singh Tomar*, what was Irrfan doing? He was doing *The Lunchbox*. He was playing a person older than himself. Or he was doing *Life of Pi*, which was a smaller role; the film was not about him.

That's Bollywood for you. In all the mainstream things they have done with say, Nawazuddin, they have tried to make him funny. Rajkummar Rao gets a certain price only if he does comedy roles. If he does a serious role, they immediately brand it as an arthouse movie.

SG: Even now?

AK: Look at Rajkummar. Why is he only doing funny roles? Because that is the only time he gets paid. He can't do another

*Omerta**; the budget of the film would probably be what they pay him to act in a funny role. So what happens in comic roles is: they think Irrfan and Nawaz and Rajkummar Rao are odd-looking people. Odd-looking people, who don't look like heroes, are okay in comic roles, or negative roles. But they can't be heroes. There is a very fixed notion of things.

SG: But I thought that things have changed a little bit in the last five years?

AK: I'm saying, Rajkummar and Ayushmann [Khurrana] are still represented as the middle-class, small-town Indian in most roles by mainstream Bollywood. They'll be cast differently only by filmmakers who don't represent mainstream Bollywood. Mainstream Bollywood will typecast you, because that's the only way they know how to sell something. If Irrfan would have been around, they would have kept casting him in funny roles, where he would display his comic timing. Because he's a great actor and his comic timing was great. And he could do it with a straight face.

He could do anything. For me, Irrfan is the only actor – including everyone from Manoj Bajpayee to Nawazuddin to Naseeruddin Shah – who made me believe the character he played every time. There have been times when I did not believe what Manoj Bajpayee was playing or what Nawaz was doing, especially when they did those mainstream stories. Naseer also – sometimes he was over the top. But Irrfan I have always believed no matter what character he's played. He's a great actor.

SG: Did you spend time with each other?

AK: I like my seclusion a lot. Manoj Bajpayee says, 'If I meet Anurag three days in a row, I'll start hating him.' Which is true.

---

* A 2017 Hansal Mehta film

I never go to the office, I never leave my room; I straightaway go to the set. I've been all the way to Irrfan's house in Madh Island. Which I can't say for a lot of people. But I have spoken more to Sutapa than to Irrfan. It was around the time Sutapa was working with [Sanjay Leela] Bhansali. I think she wrote the dialogues for *Khamoshi* [*The Musical*], Bhansali's first film. That's when I used to interact a lot with her.

The longest conversation Irrfan and I have had is around these three things: *Black Friday*, *Gangs of Wasseypur* and Pash. And he would always say, '*Hum log kyun saath mein kaam nahi karte hain?*' [Why do we not work together?] In my head, Irrfan was so much larger. I just did not know how to go to him with what role – which would also come across as respectable.

SG: So what you're saying is that the two Bollywoods still do not collide. Mainstream Bollywood will still only typecast you, rather than create roles with a difference.

AK: *Nahi*, they don't collide. What happens is, they co-opt people. Like Rajkummar Rao got co-opted, now Pankaj Tripathi has got co-opted. When, say, a *Stree** happens, Rajkummar Rao gets co-opted. Ayushmann Khuranna is not represented by agents and he takes his own calls, so he is a separate case.

SG: Everyone I have spoken to for the book has said that if Irrfan had been alive, this would have been his time.

AK: Yeah. I think today is the right time. He started off this change. Today, Manoj Bajpayee, Pankaj Tripathi, Rajkummar Rao, Ayushmann Khurrana – these are our stars. They're making things happen. Cinema somehow – even mainstream cinema –

---

* A 2018 Amar Kaushik film

feels like and looks like it is India. There was a ten-year, fifteen-year period where our films did not even look like they were about India.

SG: So things have changed a little, haven't they?
AK: Sure, a little.

SG: And casting directors these days are meant to be more cinema-literate than the people before.
AK: They are cinema-literate, but in mainstream movies, it's the producers and the directors who give the brief.

SG: So Irrfan never appeared on the radar of all these people?
AK: He was always on the radar, but they didn't know what to do with him. They know now what to do with a Pankaj Tripathi because they have made him an endearing elderly man. After a while, seeing someone succeeding in six–seven roles – leading to success at the box office – they start casting him in the kind of role that he has already succeeded in. Mainstream Bollywood cinema is all about likeability. And there is more likeability with endearing fathers and quirky gangsters.

SG: So you're saying that it was only with *Hindi Medium* that Bollywood woke up to Irrfan?
AK: Bollywood only wakes up to the box office. Bollywood does not wake up to anything else.

SG: Is that why Irrfan went Westwards? Or did the West come looking for Irrfan?
AK: The West gave him respect.

SG: How did they know he existed?

AK: They always have casting people scouting; they send people out here. They keep a lookout, and they always reach out when they think you would be a good fit. Irrfan's big breakout performance was actually *The Warrior*. It was seen the world over; it travelled a lot in the festival circuit. One other role that championed him was in Mira Nair's *The Namesake*.

Imagine Spielberg seeing Irrfan as the guy who owns Jurassic Park – a millionaire. Because their idea of a millionaire – or billionaire – is not the Indian idea of a millionaire. The Indian idea of a billionaire is very Punjabi, *gora chitta*.

SG: But none of his Hollywood films were especially fantastic.

AK: They are not great films. But they gave him enough money for him to be able to do a *Qissa*. For many of the films that he did back home, not enough money was paid to him. For *Lunchbox* we could not pay more than fifty lakhs. The whole cost of the film was so low. I don't remember the exact figure but there was more of a backend than there was upfront money.

SG: So what I'm hearing is that this fantastic actor who was available and free to do everything that he wanted to do, wasn't able to, for various reasons.

AK: It's like this. The budget that I will make *Mukkabaaz** with, Netflix would pay me as fees just to do something preliminary. So what Hollywood did for Irrfan is what Netflix does for me.

SG: What are your favourite Irrfan performances – if I had to ask for your top two or three?

---

* A 2017 Anurag Kashyap film

AK: Irrfan's performance was amazing in *Bhoron Ne Khilaya Phool* [a *Star Bestsellers* episode]. I loved him in *Haasil* and *Maqbool*. *Qissa* and *Paan Singh Tomar* as well.

SG: And in all of these, what was the one thing that said to you this is an Irrfan role – only he can pull it off?

AK: You know, Irrfan had a rare understanding of his craft. If you take a complex character and give it to an actor who would take out each complexity individually and articulate it, it becomes overacting. He would take it all and imbibe it in a way that it all became normal. He simplified it.

I'm saying that we are all complex people, but we don't act out our individual complexities. Irrfan understood that. Irrfan knew how to keep it within. He was also not insecure because he understood that cinema is about evocation. He is one of those rare actors who did not say, '*Meri kitni lines hain?*' [How many lines do I have?] He knew as long as he was evoking something within the audience, it would be great for the film, and great for the filmmaker.

Lots of times, filmmakers are just handling actors' egos, trying to balance lines between them. Ninety per cent of the actors think the power of your role comes from how many lines you have. Irrfan understood cinema was about evoking, which is very rare. It's very hard to sell a silent character to an actor. It's hard to tell an actor that silence will matter in this; you don't need to talk.

SG: Any particular incident with the two of you together that makes you smile?

AK: A long time back, around the time of *Maqbool*, we were drinking together. *Maqbool* was made after *Satya*. And Vishal said, 'In the opening scene, I want to kill the writer of *Satya* and redefine the gangster genre.' So we shot an opening scene where Irrfan kills me.* It was so much fun. We took out that scene later on. And later, outside Vishal's studio in Oshiwara, we got drunk and were sitting in the car with Irrfan – I don't remember whose car. Irrfan, drunk, would become a poet – it was amazing, that conversation about films, writing, people.

SG: Do you feel his absence?

AK: There's a big lacuna that can't be filled. But in a sense he has set things in motion that is good for a lot of people, in a much larger way than, say, for example, Saeed Jaffrey or Roshan Seth did. They are Anglicized, English-speaking theatre people, not rooted in small-town India. Irrfan's is not an easy place to fill. It's not like, *Irrfan nahi hai toh, chalo, Nawaz hai; woh nahi toh yeh hai*. Irrfan is irreplaceable.

---

* Anurag Kashyap co-wrote the screenplay of *Satya*.

'Irrfan's death is a permanent damage'

DIBAKAR BANERJEE

Most of **Dibakar Banerjee**'s films (*Khosla ka Ghosla!*, *Oye Lucky! Lucky Oye!*, *Love, Sex Aur Dhokha*) are situated at the intersection of current events, political undercurrents and individual aspirations. The director who brought welcome freshness into Bollywood and the actor who switched things up would have made a winning combination. But Banerjee only worked with Irrfan in a few advertisements; they did speak about possible roles, but nothing materialized.

SHUBHRA GUPTA: I'm going to start with my preamble: why didn't you work with Irrfan Khan?

DIBAKAR BANERJEE: I really wanted to. In 2013, we were actively talking about *Detective Byomkesh Bakshy!*, where I wanted him to be the villain. I remember the exact exchange. I said, '*Ram–Raavan ki ladaayi hai; aap Ravaan ho.*' [It's a battle between Ram and Raavan; you are Raavan.] So Irrfan called me up and said, '*Mujhe Ram banna hai, bahut bann liya Ravaan.*' [I want to be Ram; I've played Raavan enough.]

None of my films are sure shots; they start as risks every time. For the producer, for the financer. There's a very polite discussion around the table. Even if they genuinely like the film, it's written on the wall that it's a risk. And how to mitigate the risk? That's the first premise on which my films are financed and greenlit. So I was always looking for risk mitigators. Of course, without damaging the film too much.

When I was speaking to Irrfan, I was looking for the surety that if Irrfan is the villain, nobody will be able to ignore the hero. He was already a star then. Irrfan in a YRF [Yash Raj Films] film, as a villain – it looked to me like the perfect risk mitigation.

I knew that I had no chance of having Irrfan as a detective. Unfortunately, the story I had written at that time was of a twenty-four/twenty-five-year-old detective who's doing his first case, who's just been through a break-up, and doesn't even want to be a detective. He's a completely confused guy who's blundering into something and, through what happens to him, he manages to get somewhere in the end. It's a coming-of-age story. I genuinely couldn't have done that with Irrfan. He understood, and said, '*Dibakar, jab Ram ki kahani hogi, mujhe batana.*' [When you have a story about Ram, let me know.]

Then I started working on a lovely story in which Irrfan was the main character. Irrfan had notionally said, '*Yaar, yeh toh achhi lag rahi hai; karte hain.*' [I like this one; let's do it.] I was working on the *Sandeep Aur Pinky Faraar* [2021] edit and I thought, let's start this. I called Irrfan's manager and said, '*Woh baat hui thi, chaar–paanch mahine pehle*; let's start talking.' [We had spoken four–five months ago.]

She said, 'Dibakar, which planet do you live on?' So I said, '*Boss, mera planet toh alag hai, yeh main maanta hoon* – I do live on another planet. What's happened?' My heart started beating faster. She said that he has a very debilitating illness – it wasn't looking good. That was about two years before he went

– probably 2017 end. So that's how it happened. I was building up to working with him.

SG: You said that when you reached out to him, he was already a star. Was he?

DB: *Bilkul.* Just like Amjad Khan was a star. For me, Irrfan was a complete star. I mean, by that time, we were watching his Indian and international projects. We knew who he was and, in fact, we were all rooting for Irrfan – *usko aur bhi aage jaana hai* [he will achieve much more].

SG: 'We'?

DB: Me, Vishal [Bhardwaj], Anurag [Kashyap] and some other directors who came up around the same time. Vishal presented Irrfan to the world in a way that was a complete cinematic experience in *Maqbool*. I didn't know Vishal at that time. I walked up to him and said, 'I'm a struggling filmmaker; my first film is stuck. *Aaj aapki film ne mera haunsla badha diya.*' [Today your film has given me courage.]

In one way or the other, we were also trying to fight to get into the system, like Irrfan. And we were getting in. And after that, it was three things: dates, the script, whether you got along or not. You might ask somebody as big as Irrfan, '*Boss, meri chhoti si film mein kaam karoge?*' [Will you act in my low-budget film?] Irrfan's manager might as well tell me, 'Look, Irrfan's doing *Spider-Man* [*The Amazing Spider-Man*], *yaar.* Why will he do your film?'

SG: Irrfan's manager may have said so. But would Irrfan himself have said this?

DB: I was just giving you an example. Let's say one is speaking to Priyanka [Chopra Jonas]. It's the same case: Priyanka started in

Bollywood but now she's abroad. And I'm a Bollywood director who's saying, 'Arre, ek Bollywood comedy hai – aap karoge?' [Will you do a Bollywood comedy?] And Priyanka's business entity tells me, 'Arre yaar, she's busy, and your film is an indie.' And Irrfan or Priyanka or Nawaz [Nawazuddin Siddiqui] or whoever has gone beyond your reach. That also happens.

SG: Do you remember your first meeting with him?
DB: In the nineties, Irrfan had come to Bombay and he was waiting for a break. In 1997, I was making a film for World Wildlife Fund [WWF] and I'd come to Bombay looking for the actors. I was a young twenty-six-year-old ad filmmaker [from Delhi], as alien to the Bombay world as possible. Westernized, grown up on MTV, Channel V, VH1. After '89, I hadn't watched any Bollywood film. I still haven't watched the classic nineties movies that a whole generation has grown up on; that cultural staple is not in my system.

My casting director said, 'There is a very good actor – Irrfan Khan. Usko bula lo.' [Call him.] I wanted to do a screen test. Irrfan would have been thirty/thirty-two. I called him and said, 'Irrfan, I want to test you.' He said, 'Kya yaar, test kya karoge tum; bhej toh diya script.' [Why do you want to test me; you've already sent the script.] I said, 'Nahi, I want to do it.' Irrfan came to my friend's flat in Bandra, where I was staying, and he did the parts, but I could see that he's killing himself.

SG: So this part that he tested for was for that WWF ad film?
DB: For three ad films with one guy speaking about the need to save tigers.

SG: Did he do it finally?
DB: Irrfan said, 'Tum video mat lo, yaar. Main tumhe dikha

deta hoon kaise karoonga.' [Don't make a video. I will just show you how I will play the part.] But without the video, the client wouldn't approve.

At that time, I was told he's a very talented but struggling actor. We all knew about Irrfan, just like the subculture always knew about Nawaz, after *Black Friday*. Those who were looking for alternatives; those who had a healthy scepticism about Bollywood and its tropes; who had paid our dues and come in from outside, weathered the assault of Bollywood and still somehow managed to survive – for us, that awareness was always there.

SG: It was Vishal Bhardwaj who gave him *Maqbool*, finally.

DB: Vishal is different. By virtue of starting earlier and finding that perfect story and finding that perfect Macbeth and Lady Macbeth, Vishal was poised at the right time. So Vishal is in a different category. But Anurag and I? Slightly later, slightly younger – only slightly – and trying our own methods of coming through.

SG: Neither of you actually worked with Irrfan. That is the funny thing.

DB: By the time we were getting ready to hit bigger apples and becoming a little surer of our casting abilities and our ability to convince the financers that we can make commercial films with Irrfan, he became very busy with his international career and other stuff. But I did work on those commercials with him. We used to have great fun.

SG: What else do you remember from that first meeting?

DB: The moment Irrfan walked in the room, I thought *ki iske saath toh kuchh aur kar sakte hain.* [I can do something else with him.] When I did *Khosla Ka Ghosla!*, I was considered only a one-film director. It's only after *Oye Lucky! [Lucky Oye!]* and the subsequent films that people started taking me seriously. By the time Irrfan took notice of me as a director, it must have been 2012–13. That's when I met him and spoke about the film I wanted to do with him. He was very enthusiastic, and we had pretty much verbally agreed that we were going to work together on this story. And it would have been amazing. *But hua nahi …hua nahi.*

SG: Why do you think it took so long for Irrfan to get a break in Bollywood?

DB: Something happened, which is not connected to Irrfan, but connected to all of us. The momentum that built up 2003 onwards came to a head with *Haasil, Maqbool, Paanch, Black Friday, Khosla, Oye Lucky!, Dev D, LSD [Love Sex Aur Dhokha]*. By 2010 – this is my belief – Bollywood had figured out a counter strategy to fighting this invading force. And that was the '100-crore club'. If you go back to your cinema history, 2008–09 is when you first started hearing about the 100-crore thing.

SG: With Aamir Khan's *Ghajini**, yes.

DB: And by the time the privatization of the media had begun, the star system was learning tricks to collude with the media in new ways. And the media being the arm of corporate and political interests, was also figuring out new ways. That collision between the media and the entertainment industry and the star system happened in a way that made the 100-crore war a very potent counter-thrust to the so-called indie wave.

---

* A 2008 A. R. Murugadoss film

By 2013–14, entrenched Bollywood had managed to dent the indie wave a lot. Only a few of us survived. Those who were, I would say, hard to kill. More cockroach-ish, somehow adept at survival. I think that particular counter-thrust slowed down the rising curve of actors like Irrfan and Nawaz to a large extent.

And yet, it is to the credit of their talent that they still managed to survive. But if the 100-crore club hadn't arrived, we could have had success much faster with these actors.

But India had firmly committed itself to late-stage capital growth. And this is beyond cinema. What it does is affect other things. If India had a controlled, leftist economy in 2008–2009, a lot of other things wouldn't have happened, we wouldn't have the money to make so many films! Maybe then actors like Irrfan and Nawaz would have hit their peak; they wouldn't have had to struggle for so long.

This is not to take away from the struggle that Naseeruddin Shah, Om Puri and all those actors and directors have had to go through, because we don't know the real story of the seventies and eighties. What we know is that there was a prolific output of films, which helped people like Naseer do *Manthan** and *Junoon*†, while at the same time experimenting with *Jalwa*‡ and *Hero Hiralal*§, which were independent films bowing to Bollywood conventions *and* doing something different. Imagine *Dabangg* with Irrfan. That would have been a perfect 2013 and '14. *Jalwa* was a hit, right? And imagine Irrfan working on his body like Naseer did. Remember how Naseer had muscled up for *Jalwa*? He was looking like Salman [Khan]. Irrfan muscled up like that and doing *Dabangg* would have been a very nice cultural addition.

---

* A 1976 Shyam Benegal film
† A 1978 Shyam Benegal film
‡ A 1987 Pankaj Parashar film
§ A 1988 Ketan Mehta film

What is irreparable is that he died. You know, I worked with Naseer [in a film forthcoming from Netflix] for the first time and realized that we are bloody lucky that Naseer is alive. We are lucky that Tabu is alive. That Raghubir Yadav, Neena Gupta are alive. They are making Indian cinema survive by being there – you know what I'm saying?

Irrfan's death is a permanent damage. We can say Indian cinema has truly lost ground. There are already lots of things pulling it down, but Irrfan's going is as if somebody just hamstrung it from behind.

SG: Let us go back to your meetings with him. You did a few other ads, right?

DB: There were two or three films: one had Saina Nehwal, one had Irrfan, another had both. Typical ad films. The films were not the thing; we would just sit and chat and laugh.

Our jokes were mostly around the tropey Bollywood dialogues. We used to laugh about the perennially whiny, teary Indian hero. *'Main kya bataoon tumhe,'* he would say, *'Lalita, iss dil mein kitne nasoor hain, jo main chhipata hoon.'* [What should I tell you, Lalita, I hide the many wounds of this heart.] And we would laugh because it was connected to a class of Indian hero so afraid of a sexual encounter that he either whines or stalks. You're behaving like an absolute predator, and the heroine is supposed to find it attractive.

SG: Irrfan was so sexy, but you wonder why he didn't get to do more romantic roles.

DB: Of course he was sexy. And I was planning a film with him about infidelity. He would have been perfect. See, I have no attachment to the trope of man-woman attraction, which forms the spine of Bollywood. It's not really that important to me. Gender is. Sexual desire isn't that important to me because it's normal. That song sequence in *Maqbool*, between Irrfan and Tabu – those are the kind of sequences which will make me see a love story in that Bollywood environment.

Otherwise, man-woman love is passé. In *7 Khoon Maaf*, Irrfan's role is so deeply layered and dark. That slightly effeminate, slightly softer Irrfan gave it a lot of watchability. I watch Bollywood for films like *Satya* or *Maqbool,* or broad camp, broad comedy.

Irrfan is actually one of the few romantic heroes I could have watched. He had that thing. Imagine *Arth** with Irrfan, in Kulbhushan's role. Because Kulbhushan Kharbanda is very good-looking, but he's not romantic! You can't think of romance too much when you look at Kulbhushan, even when he's young. You're fascinated by him when he's Shakaal.† Irrfan was deeply romantic, which comes out in *Piku* in an absolutely effortless way. Therefore, for me, the eye goes to Irrfan. It's like the [Jeff] Goldblum rule; the eye goes to Goldblum. Whenever Irrfan was in the frame, I would only watch him.

SG: Some feel that he changed the face of the Bollywood hero. Did he?

DB: I don't think Irrfan was ever given that kind of power. Even after delivering a 100-crore film, Irrfan was not cast in *Dabangg*. That means he doesn't have power, even after he delivers. That means the system is skewed; where you give a person an entry ticket after he delivers something ten times, twenty times beyond the mark where you have pegged him, and then you give him mere smoking rights. You have to deliver a 100-crore hit to

---

* A 1982 Mahesh Bhatt film
† The campy villain played by Kulbhushan Kharbanda in a 1980 Ramesh Sippy film

enter the room. This doesn't happen to star kids, or the elite, or the ones with Bollywood family connections, *na*? They can give flop after flop, but they are still in the room. But even after a 100-crore film, Irrfan will only get room rights. You hear that he is too 'dark', too 'old' – that's when the absolute asymmetry and the power skew of the system reveals itself.

SG: So are you saying that even now, post pandemic, post OTT, this skew that has hobbled Bollywood will continue to remain where it is?

DB: It'll magnify. Because the platforms are basically entrenched in and allied with capital. And capital allies itself with political power, because political power dispenses the licence to own capital. It will do everything in its might to get eyeballs, while figuring out ways and means of allying with the political *and* business dispensation of the time. The only difference is that in the new world, the power of capital is so great that it'll take a few risks, because their greed is to have everything. In that greed to have everything, people like us will slip in.

But our films will not be marketed, our vision will not be celebrated; we will not be signposted. We will be left in the jungle and if, somehow through the quirks in the algorithm and by dint of our product, we manage to get some kind of a viewership which convinces a deeply flawed, machine-learned algorithm that these films are commercially viable, then we'll survive. Our films will not be headlined. They will be put into the feeder stream and we'll be left to the vagaries of the ecosystem to be discovered, or to be ignored.

SG: If he had been alive today, this would have been Irrfan's time. Would his films have been given the kind of push that you're talking about?

DB: Depends on the film. If he had done a deeply transgressive, political film with me, then it wouldn't have been. If it had been the story about infidelity, then it would have, and the platform would have played up the part which deals with sex.

SG: So you're saying that even someone like Irrfan, who would have managed to find his pinnacle post *Hindi Medium*, would have to struggle, depending upon the kind of film he did.

DB: He would have had to cherry-pick. *Irrfan ki picture hai toh ek level toh milega.* But Irrfan is at that level for twenty years; what's so great about that? He knew; that way he was a known man, he was a star.

SG: Did his being Muslim ever come in the way?

DB: It would, today. Everybody who is a Muslim is struggling with that. It would have worked against him. In some silly, petty and extremely squalid way. That's where we've come. Self-goal *ke taraf jaa rahe hain.*

SG: When you close your eyes and think of him, what's the first thing that comes to your mind?

DB: His smile. Every time I used to meet Irrfan, we used to smile and that smile used to say, '*Dekho, tumhari bhi lagi hai, meri bhi lagi hai. Main samajh sakta hoon tumhare saath kya ho raha hai, tum samajh sakte ho mere saath kya ho raha hai. Abhi batao karna kya hai.*' [We are both screwed. We can empathize with each other. Now tell me what we should do.]

'An actor with great interiority'

CAMERON BAILEY

Cameron Bailey, one of the chief architects of the Toronto International Film Festival (TIFF), is among the few global programmers who have consistently and knowledgeably tracked Indian cinema. Currently CEO of TIFF, where several of Irrfan's films premiered (*The Lunchbox* and *Talvar*, among others), Bailey speaks of the widespread recognition and admiration that the actor enjoyed in the West.

——

SHUBHRA GUPTA: You've been heading TIFF and you've been following Indian cinema for so long, so here is a question leading from that. In the West, before Irrfan, there was Naseeruddin Shah and Om Puri? They made appearances in and had started to get recognized as good actors and were in demand, especially Om Puri. But they were also boxed in as, for the most part, stereotypical brown characters – cab drivers and so on. I think Irrfan came and shifted something. I wanted to talk to you about that shift. Do you think that there was a difference between his presence in Hollywood and the actors who had gone before him?

CAMERON BAILEY: Irrfan was a man who spoke with great humility and he would have seen himself standing on the shoulders of his predecessors and building on what they have done. But I think he really had a singular career in cinema; I don't know another actor who's had a career that's quite like his.

It's hard to explain why that is, but I do know that he had a singular presence on-screen and off-screen as well. He carried himself with the grace and the wisdom of a prince and yet, he was also very humble. We know that he came from fairly humble beginnings; he wasn't part of a renowned film family. And the combination of his regal bearing and his humility allowed him to really connect with audiences on screen. He never seemed to be above his audience, he never acted out or spoke down to people in person or on screen, and that allowed him to connect with audiences in India and all over the world.

At the same time, his bearing, the way he performed, the precision and form of his acting technique were so impressive that you couldn't help but admire him; you looked up to him but you connected with him at the same time. I think there are few actors who do that across cultures and continents. He was able to do it in both very serious independent drama, in the biggest Hollywood blockbusters and everything in between. I don't know that we'll see another actor like him again.

SG: Mira Nair's *The Namesake* got him a lot of visibility in the West but it had started with *The Warrior*, Asif Kapadia's film. At what point were you aware of Irrfan?

CB: Oh, that's a good question … It might have been *The Warrior*. For me, I think he came into focus in layers. I would have seen him in films before I took note of him specifically as a screen presence. So *The Warrior* is certainly one, *The Namesake* later on. And then there was a period in the early–mid 2000s when he was doing films like *A Mighty Heart* for Michael Winterbottom,

The Darjeeling Limited for Wes Anderson; he seemed to be everywhere, even if they were sometimes smaller roles. Then, of course, there was *Slumdog Millionaire*, that's when *everybody* saw him. But there were many other films before where you would note his presence; in some films he was just so striking and such a foundation of the film's appeal that you couldn't help but pay attention.

SG: He did the big tent-poles and the small independent ones, but I can't help wondering if Hollywood really knew what to make of him.

CB: Look at *Life of Pi*, which is a Hollywood film certainly, but Ang Lee is a very global director. I think that allowed him to cast Irrfan, or to use his presence on screen, in maybe a slightly less traditional Hollywood way. If you look at *Jurassic World*, where he plays the CEO of some big, scary company, what you see is Hollywood using his compelling presence. He *can* play someone who seems like the master of the world; he has that kind of carriage to him. And yet, at the same time, he's an actor with great interiority; that's one of the things I most responded to in him. I saw that the most in *Lunchbox* but also in many other films, where he seems to be thinking and feeling things that he's portraying not just through external behaviour, but you really get a sense of the depth of a human character. There's some of that in *Life of Pi*, although his screen time isn't a lot in the film, but the scenes are so powerful that you can feel the pain in that character, through his performance. So I think Hollywood actually did alright by him, all things considered. He's an actor who can portray interiority, who has great dramatic heft and presence. In some cases, Hollywood will say, 'We used that.'

In the series *In Treatment*, I thought his performance was really magnificent and speaks to what I was saying before in terms of how he's able to convey a rich interior life on screen.

SG: So let me get to TIFF. Was *The Lunchbox* the first film of his that you programmed?

CB: No, we had *Slumdog Millionaire*. What was that, 2008? I don't actually remember spending time with him as much then because there was so much was focus on Danny [Boyle] and Freida [Pinto] and Dev [Patel]. But I think that was certainly a moment; that film certainly took over our festival and everything about it was being celebrated. But there were many other films as well. *Lunchbox* was another kind of phenomenon, because that had come fresh from Cannes, having won an award there. At that point, many people knew Irrfan, that the film did so well, and I spent a little more time with him. Then we actually did an on-stage conversation at the Abu Dhabi Film Festival shortly after, which was lovely as well.

SG: Are there any Indian films that you remember him in the most?

CB: Sure. We showed *Qissa* at the festival as well, and I ended up speaking with him a fair bit about that. I'm always glad to see him take on a leading role, so that was one I quite liked. Then there were other ones. *Paan Singh Tomar* I remember seeing and being impressed by his performance. But I think those two in particular I consider very strong, apart from *The Warrior*, which, because Asif is a British filmmaker, doesn't entirely qualify as an Indian film.

SG: That's a very striking performance. I saw it again after so many years and was completely blown away all over again.

CB: When you mention that, we have to talk about his eyes. His eyes were so compelling; I hope you're writing about that as well …

SG: And one last thing I've asked everybody with whom I've spoken for this book. What is the one thing that comes to your mind when you think of Irrfan?

CB: I think of him as a wise man; he could just *be* on screen. He wouldn't have to do anything; he just had that presence where you looked into those eyes and you felt his soul, and it felt like he had lived and experienced and attained wisdom somehow. He was wise in many ways and he could convey that without saying a word.

'I still feel that Irrfan is alive'

SUNIL DOSHI

Sunil Doshi, independent filmmaker and long-time observer of the Indian film industry, brings his knowing of Irrfan to the fore in his sharp assessment of the industry, the rules it plays by, how Irrfan navigated the tricky landscape and how his presence changed certain truisms in the industry. Doshi has been the backbone of many significant TV ventures (*Satyameva Jayate*, *Koffee with Karan*, *Kaun Banega Crorepati*) and spearheaded a number of films as creative producer (*Bheja Fry*, *Mixed Doubles* and *Bioscopewala*).

———

SHUBHRA GUPTA: As a long-time observer, participant and somebody who has moved things along, I want you to place Irrfan in context for me. In the manner that he came in and stood for something which was very different at that time; somebody who was a complete actor, who wanted to act in Hindi movies, which are so formula-driven. He had to wait for a long time to get that one break.

SUNIL DOSHI: It's very interesting how Irrfan is one of those personalities in the Indian film industry who are always the alternative, the other. In our industry, Rajinikanth to Dilip

Kumar to Rajendra Kumar to Rajesh Khanna to Amitabh Bachchan to Dev Anand, they were all a kind of a common language. They were larger than life, mythological. People extended godlike status and started building temples to them. Come Irrfan, qualified, with proper training as an actor. He was the other one, an actor for the thinking class. Just as Netflix and Amazon and Hotstar today provide premium content to premium audiences, Irrfan had long ago defined the premium content for Indian audiences.

As I always say, being uneducated and illiterate is a billion-dollar business in this country, and Irrfan changed the status quo. Irrfan came in and started to grow. In a manner of speaking, he was the best of the alternatives, because he was genuinely a great actor. And the second thing: there was something about his face which was melancholic – a sense of deprivation. The kind of a character that you saw in *Salaam Bombay!* – I have nothing but I'll dream of the stars. This is a man who really broke all those conventions and traditions. And he had an amazing ability to transform into the character he would play. Not many actors – including the prominent names in the business – would be able to do that. I think the West was much more receptive, and noticed this. All these actors serve four hundred million people in this country, okay? These actors are the people whom you treat like a god – it is an escapism. And I'm not condemning that cinema. But the premium audiences all around the world, whom are educated, who are aware of the syntax and grammar of cinema – film acting, method acting, non-method acting – saw that spark for the first time in Irrfan.

Irrfan had done a lot of great roles. In spite of that, he was not accepted, until the West started acknowledging him. It was an Anurag Kashyap phenomenon. Kashyap made many films in India, but the moment he went to Cannes, his acceptance shot up.

Irrfan had wonderful eyes – so expressive and emotive. I think that was the great pull factor.

The third factor was that Irrfan came from one of us and people could touch him, they could see him, they could feel him. All the others were inaccessible. The last time we travelled together, we were sitting with Ang Lee and Anurag Kashyap at Cannes after a screening. And he was like, '*Yaar, Sunil, mujhe yeh karwa na?* I want a good experience of Cannes.' So there was a child-like thing. He could be amongst twenty-five people but you would not notice him as a kind of star. You'd know that there was a pull factor in him, but he was always the 'other'. And he excelled at being the 'other'.

SG: Before Irrfan, there was Naseeruddin Shah and Om Puri, right?

SD: Not even Naseer saab as much as Om Puri. Because Om fitted into the formula of the 'other'. He was not the most good-looking guy, but by the sheer power of his acting talent, he was recognized in the West.

Om led the way. Irrfan benefited from that, with all the talent that he had. I mean, there were lots of others. But nobody else capitalized on the way that was paved by Om Puri, and by Naseer to some extent. Also, you must understand, in recent times, technology has aided personalization and localization. The seamless distribution of films – Tamil films to Hindi audiences, Hindi films to Tamil, Telugu and Malayalam audiences – has happened recently. Today, I have no problem; I can watch films in any Indian language. Irrfan came at a time when Hindi was the predominant language in the film industry. Though the Tamil–

Telugu film industry was bigger, we never paid attention. There were perhaps many Irrfans that had happened in south India but they never got due attention or prominence. People from the West also came looking to Bombay, not the south.

Now people are talking about Fahadh Faasil; we only knew Mammootty and Mohanlal at that point of time. Bharath Gopi never became as great as Irrfan, though he was an Irrfan equivalent in Malayalam films. So what I'm saying is: due to this ghettoization, this narrow-mindedness as a society, as a consumer, as an audience, we never went to the south. And Irrfan benefited from all of that. He was not lucky; he had to work hard. Obviously, after getting that little break, Irrfan became Irrfan. Because he was a metaphor for versatility. You could ask him to do anything. When we were shooting *Ek Shaam Ki Mulakaat* [a 1999 *Star Bestsellers* episode], Mazhar Kamran [director of photography on this episode] was looking more like an actor than Irrfan Khan, you know? It was amazing. He was one of us, and the moment the camera went onto him, he turned into somebody else. In fact, there are a lot of people who have not seen one of Irrfan's best works: *Ek Shaam Ki Mulakaat*.

SG: Why did it take so long after *Star Bestsellers* for Irrfan to be noticed? There was such a ferment, so much talent, but it took each of these directors many years to actually find a foothold in Hindi cinema, before they could do their first movie. Anurag's *Paanch* got stuck, Tigmanshu [Dhulia] only made *Haasil* many years later. Tigmanshu and Irrfan being such good friends, of course, Irrfan got to work in Tigmanshu's first film and that's when he got noticed in India. *The Warrior* had already come before that, and he was noticed globally. People who know him say that if *The Warrior* hadn't come out at the time that it did,

Irrfan would have stopped acting. He was so upset with the whole system; he was not getting the recognition; he was not getting the movies. Why did it take Bollywood so long to understand that here was this guy who could do everything? Why was he stuck in TV for so long?

SD: This has multiple answers, Shubhra. I think the very economy of the Hindi film industry was centred around a film releasing in theatres. It involved a higher stake. In a country where we are making more than 1,500–1,600 films, there is always traffic of an unprecedented nature to get into the theatres. There were lots of gatekeepers in the way: the distributors, the exhibitors, the producers. They did not understand the power of talent; it was all a money-making, conveyor-belt mechanism of churning out film after film. Mindless, senseless, whatever was popular.

Second reason: the literacy of cinema was nearly absent. It was thanks to the internet that travelling became cheaper, with the arrival of Airbnb. Technology played a much bigger role than literacy in our country.

Third: in a country where only sixty students are graduating every year from cinema courses in a country of 1.3 billion people, I think cinema is a profession for a few people.

It has industry status. We follow an American way where only whoever is the richest, whoever can put forward more equity, can participate in the cinema business. For many of us independent filmmakers, we just got some recognition in the last eight to ten years. Before that, there was nothing. And Irrfan represented that 'other'; he represented the independence of a filmmaker. Irrfan represented alternative filmmaking. I am not saying art film versus commercial film, but independent filmmaking.

It took all this time because of illiteracy, because of the way our culture is and how we closely associated religion, mythology with our cinema-making. I mean, thanks to all these platforms and the templates and references that have come now that we have started to make horror and dark noir and other kinds of films. Otherwise, it was good versus evil all the time. It was another interpretation of Ramayana and Mahabharata.

When the economic renaissance happened post Manmohan Singh and the world became much more accessible to the middle class, things started to become affordable, accessible. Multiplexes started coming up and further segregated the premium audience from other Indians. So I personally feel that Irrfan was not a mass actor; he was an actor for intellectuals, for the people who consume premium content. The people who own the American Express card – that was Irrfan's constituency. It was not the constituency of Paytm users, if you know what I mean.

SG: By 2006–07, Irrfan was trying to move away from this narrow casting of being premium content for the kind of intellectual people who wanted to watch 'real cinema' as opposed to mass-driven vehicles. He wanted to explore a wider world, right? He did *Hisss** with Mallika Sherawat, he did all kinds of terrible films in which he was the best thing. Even then, he was an ensemble actor. When did that shift happen for him? Or did it happen at all? Even after *Hindi Medium*, was he still going to be the actor that only one kind of class would go for?

SD: By the time 2006–2007 came, Irrfan also became more ambitious. It was the Smriti Mishra [an actor known for *Sardari Begum*† and *Is Raat Ki Subah Nahin*] syndrome – you came from a small town in Banaras and then you were noticed for *Sardari Begum* and, suddenly, you wanted to equate yourself with Madhuri Dixit because somebody said you are a great Kathak dancer. I

---

* A 2010 Jennifer Lynch film
† A 1996 Shyam Benegal film

remember in 2010–14, Irrfan and I had multiple conversations as to whether he should get an agent who would ask for a lot of money on his behalf. If Irrfan asked for a crore, people would say, 'Yeh paagal ho gaya hai.' [He's gone mad.]

At the same time, in other parts of the world, the agents were doing a fantastic job for him. He was getting due recognition, and there it was not about earning money. He wanted to work with Ang Lee, with the greatest filmmakers. He knew that if he did that, he would get money here. So he became fiercely ambitious; he started to dream a lot. He diluted not his values or principles, but many other things for achieving that ambition. He wanted to have a big car and a big house. So he said yes to a lot of people, and that worked for those directors because he would bring in a differentiator. He would not cost as much as Ajay Devgn or Akshay Kumar. He would play the inspector, and it would be nice to give something to the intellectual audience. So it was not for any compelling desire that they wanted Irrfan to do their film. I think he was a part of a smart programming mix.

Hindi Medium was one such example. By that time the ecosystem had completely changed. People were more accepting of that kind of cinema. Suddenly you realized that besides the three Khans and the Bachchans and the Roshans, there were others also. People were watching *Money Heist** while watching *The Family Man*†. Irrfan corresponded to that school of filmmaking which came from abroad. Irrfan became a currency for people to transact on. Also, with Irrfan, you had an economic proportion; you could not do a 200-crore film; you could at best do a fifteen–twenty-crore film. Every talent has a

---

* A 2017–2022 Netflix web series
† An ongoing Amazon Prime Video web series

tag, unfortunately, in this part of the world. So I think it was an index of popularity, a differentiating factor, cost factor, etc. I think it was also the Aishwarya Rai Bachchan syndrome. She had done all the greatest, successful commercial films but she was still dying to work with a Rituparno Ghosh to get a national award. In a very similar manner, a lot of us cast Irrfan Khan so that we have his face, which was familiar to the international community, and we would have access to that. So I think there were multiple reasons, besides just the talent, to cast Irrfan Khan.

SG: When did you first meet with him? Do you remember?
SD: I think it was in 2001–02. Tigmanshu was writing from my home for *Star Bestsellers*. It was pivotal for harnessing new talent. That was an amazing thing Shailja [Kejriwal] did – hats off to her. It gave so much talent to this business.

I met Irrfan thanks to Tishu and we hit it off extremely well. I have been a confidant of Irrfan, with regards to lots of his personal issues – domestic and otherwise – what he wanted to do, what kind of fun he wanted to have. He wanted to go out with all the interesting men and women around the world. Because I travel quite a bit, he has accompanied me to a number of places.

SG: Was he a very serious kind of character, or was that just a facade? Was he a fun-loving guy?
SD: He was an absolute fun-loving guy. He [exuded] joie de vivre. When he was around, women went crazy. He didn't do anything. He would stand tall, have a smoke and a drink – he was very fond of a good life. Like every one of us, you know? I have had the privilege of being associated with a lot of A-list talents in the Hindi film industry. For different reasons, people were attracted

to those stars. But the reasons for being attracted to Irrfan were so completely esoteric and different. It was a very different type of attraction. Not that Shah Rukh Khan didn't do that, you know – putting out his arms, like that act he kept on repeating. Irrfan invented, in every movie, a new idiom and new context of attraction. He kept on increasing his constituency. Unlike the stars who only serve their constituency, in a manner of speaking. That is why their stardom was limited, as compared to his.

SG: I asked Karan Johar why he did not cast Irrfan in his movies. Was it because he did not have the looks, he was not a chocolate boy, he was not a *hatta-katta* Punjabi fair guy that Karan wanted in his movies? And he said, 'I never had a script worthy of Irrfan.'
SD: I think that is a very nice response, very respectful to Irrfan, but that's not all of it. I think it's about, say, the kind of coffee place that you would go to. Karan was habituated to a certain kind of a coffee house, within which he found everything. And so, talent was kind of self-sufficient within the bubble of that coffee house. Why would he look outside?

SG: Sutapa Sikdar told me that during his illness, even towards the end, he was getting some really great scripts. He would have benefited from the *Hindi Medium* success, because that was his first solo success, and he would have been a star of the kind that he wasn't. Where would he have gone from here, if he hadn't been ill?
SD: That is a very difficult question to answer. It would be logical, if a particular film has surpassed commercial expectations, for you to get five other projects thereafter. And knowing Irrfan's talent, he would have excelled in all of them. But in a manner

of speaking, Irrfan also had limitations as to what he could and could not do.

SG: Now this is the first time I'm hearing this word 'limitations'. Because he literally could play anything.

SD: I mean to say that he could not play a conventional lover boy, in the way Shah Rukh Khan played in *DDLJ* [*Dilwale Dulhaniya Le Jayenge*]. It is not that he did not have the talent to do it, but people would not buy that. See, in your own country, you require a familiarity. As I told you, Shah Rukh Khan had that *paisa vasool* quality; even if people believe the film is crap, they will come back. The problem for Shah Rukh began when he started to do roles which were against the expectation of the audience that he has served. With Irrfan, it never happened. Please understand: he was so wise and intelligent that he excelled within the limitations. You tell me one great film where he is singing in the garden and pursuing a woman. Could you imagine him doing that? [But if you were to see that in a garden, a couple is singing, and behind the trees observing them, about to do something sinister – you could see Irrfan Khan fitting that role. But you could not see him playing a man running behind a woman. He was not a conventional hero. We are seeking this in Irrfan Khan because, for three decades, we have seen only that and we want somebody else to do the same. But he is not that. That's what I meant by limitations.

SG: What is the one thing that comes to your mind when you think of Irrfan?

SD: I don't know what is that one thing, but I am still not able … I still feel that Irrfan is alive. I don't think he is dead, in my mind.

I refuse to accept that. It is impossible for me to imagine that he is not there.

What I can say is that Irrfan wanted to become very famous – in the last few years. He wanted to become so famous that he would take on the top-notch talents of the world. It was not arrogance ... I think a little bit of that came in as well, to be honest. Just because he is dead, or he was my friend, I will not hide the truth. But his talent quotient was so high that he earned that arrogance through his talent. A lot of people earn arrogance through the money they make. Irrfan earned arrogance through sheer talent.

'A sufi spirit that cannot be contained'

SANTOSH DESAI

Santosh Desai, well-regarded social commentator, has written extensively on trends emanating from Hindi cinema. Irrfan's journey in Bollywood was unique, and Desai is perfectly poised to parse that trajectory, looking at the times the country, and cinema, has passed through, from the 1970s to the present day.

SHUBHRA GUPTA: What do you make of the phenomenon that was Irrfan?

SANTOSH DESAI: The kind of outpouring of emotion after his passing, of feelings from across a whole wide spectrum of people – I remember being a little surprised by that because, while I get the fact that there is something that he represents that cuts across, if you look at his heralded work, a lot of it is actually the kind of work that goes out to limited audiences.

I mean, he has of course acted in more mainstream or commercially successful films also, but his work that one keeps going back to does not have that same kind of widespread, mass appeal. And yet, there was something about him that connected beyond the narrow audience that would have seen those particular films, right? To me, that was really intriguing because, say, Rishi Kapoor's passing, which is broadly in a similar time frame, was different. Of course when any popular actor passes, there's a certain sense of connection and nostalgia. But there was still a difference: the intensity of feeling that one came across, that sense of a personal loss that Irrfan seemed to represent, was in spite of the fact that Rishi Kapoor had been around forever and there's a whole generation that has grown up with his films and he has gone through a transition that would mirror a transition that a generation has itself gone through. In spite of that, it was remarkable the genuineness of the emotion and the extent to which it kind of welled up – it was something I hadn't seen previously in the same way.

For an actor who is not a classical lead actor without blockbusters to his name and a bit of a chameleon, it's not as if there's a particular image or a particular kind of role. So if you look at it, you find that he actually doesn't fit into virtually any of those constructs. And normally someone like that who floats in between categories and labels and characterizations is someone you would not expect to get that kind of popular resonance. So it just seemed very interesting, both with regards to Irrfan and perhaps even our relationship with cinema and how it has evolved. That someone like him can come to mean so much to us, you know? I think in some ways, it probably speaks to both.

I remember I had a piece about Rishi Kapoor but I didn't write about Irrfan simply because I found that everyone had the same things that I would have liked to say. Normally, in a column, you try and find a slant of some kind, which you feel is your slice on things. It was just this idea that Irrfan had a certain honesty, a lack of pretentiousness. And that honesty really stood apart, I think, both in the context of Hindi films as well as the times. There was something so real and refreshing and unrehearsed and truthful about Irrfan. And it felt like everybody got it. You might characterize it differently, but I just found a remarkable convergence in how people were speaking about him. This was quite interesting because of course there are those normal, standard characterizations, you know – you agree on Rishi Kapoor being the romantic hero. But I think this was something deeper than that. At one level people talk about the fact that he played the common man in a variety of ways. But what is interesting is the uncommonness of the common man that Irrfan actually represents. If you go back to the Amol Palekar kind of representation of the common man, you converge on a broad archetype of the common man: a little lost, overwhelmed by the system, who tries to find a way and uses all kinds of subterfuge or devices in order to make his life meaningful and worthwhile. Whereas if you look at Irrfan's common man, each of them is actually a very finely etched portrait of commonness. So even if the role that he's playing is itself not of a common man, so to speak, there is a commonness, a humanness that he brings even to those roles. Which is why you can relate to him. Even if he is playing a character which is far removed from you, you recognize something human and universal in him. And the fact that in Hindi cinema you had space for that kind of a nuanced representation, and that it resonated with audiences, is a measure of the distance we have travelled. Irrfan actually represents that more than anything else. I can't think of anybody else who has that kind of range and specificity of nuance.

SG: I was very intrigued by what you said about the evolution of our relationship with cinema. Everybody has their own take on why cinema, and particularly Hindi movies, speaks to us. I would like you to expand on this, and how you see Irrfan fitting into it.

SD: In an earlier time, cinema was mythological. It spoke to us at the level of the psyche. If you look at most of the storytelling, it is retellings and reinforcements of archetypes. Broadly, storytelling in India is therefore the virtuous woman, the straying woman, who is good-hearted but has been led astray by circumstances; the righteous man who is the hero, who represents all the values which are mired in a system of values that he seemingly upholds. These are retellings of almost mythological themes.

I think a lot of people have written that it's almost a womb-like existence in an auditorium. And you go back to themes that were womb-like. For instance, there was a time when the lost-and-found film was so much in vogue. I remember we used to go to the theatre ten minutes after the film started, after the classic transition shots from the young to the adult. You could have film after film after film playing to the same trope in such a mindless way and there was still an audience for it. There were about twenty to twenty-five films in that period that were all versions of a lost-and-found formula.

Classic cinema in India has tended to be full of these archetypal notions which served to reinforce traditional values. The role that it was playing in society was maintaining a homeostatic kind of balance. And so the role of popular culture was very much to keep a sense of order in terms of values, and to limit the dislocation that is caused by external change. Therefore, it keeps reinforcing, barring the films that would break that – but the spine of cinema was engaged with this order-making, continuity, through retelling.

In fact, newness was the problem. So you had old stories told in the same way: this one will die, this one is going to get raped, this one is going to get sacrificed. It's not as if there was anything left to the imagination when it came to how a film would resolve itself. From the very outset, you know how things are going to go and the pleasure was in the mode of telling and not in the story itself. Not in the outcome of the story but in the experiencing of it. I don't mean it in a judgmental sense, but it left the audience infantilized. You are watching these stories that are psychologically reassuring, where they tell and retell; it's how mythology stories are told to you, over and over. Through repetition, you kind of feel reassured, comforted.

So the one big shift I see is the storytelling moving from almost a psychodrama and a psychological mode to where you are separating from the archetype, and that is delicious. And it happens in a whole lot of small ways. It doesn't necessarily happen in only the breakout films which are unconventional. So not *Fire** – I'm not talking about those. I'm talking about the characters – the whiskey-drinking mother-in-law or grandmother. Where you start taking the idea of the mother, which is an archetype, and then break it open in some ways. Similarly with shifting the notion of the virtuous heroine, moving from the reinforcement of the familiar to the teasingly unfamiliar. Then you start enjoying the unfamiliar, it starts becoming delicious. Of course you have many manifestations that go much further, which are full-blown, more experimental.

But that's the one central transition that I think Irrfan, in particular, represents – moving away from the classic archetypes of an earlier time. And that is why he is perhaps the single most skilled practitioner of that. He in some ways epitomizes that. Almost everything he did would be difficult to fit into classical [definitions]. Even if the role was archetypal, his representation

---

* A 1996 Deepa Mehta film

of it was never that. There was always something about it that made it an individual speaking, not a template speaking to you.

SG: Because he never did anything that was expected. I mean, after a point, you went to watch an Irrfan movie. It was not that *iss mein Irrfan bhi hai;* it's that *iss mein Irrfan hi hai.* He shifts something, doesn't he?

SD: Exactly. Both the fact that he was doing unfamiliar things as well as doing familiar things in an unfamiliar way. And always making it his own. I think that's what people really recognized. That change in the relationship we have with cinema here, where we are now looking for cinema to surprise us and the pleasure therefore is in the storytelling. When you take the time particularly between the mid-sixties and the early to mid-nineties, maybe even beyond, from the Amitabh Bachchan/multi-starrer time to the Jackie Shroff and Anil Kapoor period and the hideousness of the T-series video cassette culture of the eighties and nineties, you see the repetitiveness of those characterizations. The Kader Khans, the Shakti Kapoors … You have some freshness when Govinda happens, but by and large, the storytelling is nothing but such familiar tropes. What we see today, over the last fifteen–twenty years certainly, is a distinct shift.

SG: So do you think Irrfan just happened at the right time, right place? How do you see him breaking out of that long television stranglehold, where he did *Star Bestsellers,* which saw the advent of new filmmakers such as Tigmanshu Dhulia, Anurag Kashyap, Imtiaz Ali, and coming into the movies, which is where his heart lay?

SD: I don't think Irrfan is necessarily the cause of the shift in our relationship with Hindi cinema. Irrfan is there, but these new directors, who are new kinds of storytellers, have new eyes. And you see so many of them come up at broadly the same time. This is the part where the archetypical storytelling shifts to more inventive forms of storytelling – it's also part of a deeper underlying shift which has to do with social shifts. As you move into a society where choice-making becomes important, the notion of individuality starts becoming important. There are many factors that feed into the shift, technology being a big one. The mobile phone individualizes all of us, right? It gives every individual a personal relationship with the world. So I think there are larger forces that are shifting which are not just reflected in cinema but also reflected in many other walks of life.

You have a whole bunch of new people who are now speaking to and representing an audience that is looking for more diversity, for choice-making, for something that they can call their own, who are asking: What is my kind of film? What is my kind of story? It is the emergence of an audience like that, which is fragmented, that needs storytellers for it to start becoming real. New storytellers, from Anurag Kashyap, Anurag Basu, Tigmanshu Dhulia, all of them are looking for performers who can do justice to their form of storytelling and their vision of cinema. I think that's where someone like Irrfan and the accidental convergence of film directors in television helped enable this move. It's part of a more organic process, and he did happen to be in the right place at the right time, in that sense. Had he been around a little earlier, there wouldn't have been people to harness that kind of ability. So to that extent, it was important that he was where he was, when he was. Although it is not only a function of that, but the fact that he was what was needed for that form of storytelling, and he was recognized – because he was around.

SG: Quite right. Which are some of your absolute favourite Irrfan roles?

SD: There's *Maqbool*, *The Namesake*, *Haasil*. There is *Haider*. I actually quite liked him in *Piku*. I liked him in *Hindi Medium*, *English* ... what?

SG: *Hindi Medium* and *Angrezi Medium*.

SD: I haven't seen the second one; I've only seen the first. Even that's not a great film, but I just found the freshness that he brought to it amazing. I would struggle to name Irrfan roles that I didn't enjoy. There's something about him that is absolutely arresting, that just draws you in, and that is his power. What Irrfan also managed to do is lift the mainstream audience's standards and understanding of what constitutes acting. In the period I was going to films almost all the time, Sanjeev Kumar was considered *the* actor. But a lot of his acting was very studied mannerisms. If you look at the kind of refinement of the craft that Irrfan represented, it also elevates how audiences understand the craft itself. Otherwise, the understanding often has been that craft is very performative; people who *perform* acting are the ones who get branded as actors.

My sense as a lay audience member is that you find a lot of hammed-up roles that both Naseeruddin Shah and Om Puri have played in popular cinema. Irrfan manages to rise above the script in a way that I don't think they necessarily did.

SG: What did you think of his making this transition from an Indian actor to someone who was internationally starting to get known? And my other question is about faith, his Muslim-ness or the absence of it.

SD: The international thing is quite intriguing because, at one level, you could say that there was a sort of openness; he defied labels. He clearly had a very finely honed craft but he also represented the Western notion of Indianness in a sense. The fluidity and the ease with which he flows into any representation, there is something that comes to mind.

That being said, I wonder if that is not applicable to Om Puri as well. In a certain sense, I think Naseer saab tried too hard when it came to international roles. Whereas Om Puri has done a fair amount of interesting work internationally. Om Puri and Irrfan, in a sense, have a somewhat similar ability to mould themselves, whether it was for directors, forms of storytelling, the narrative. Versatility is a terrible word because it doesn't express the fullness of that. I think it's the fluidity. You know, he's an open text, he's not a closed box of aptitudes. Therefore, there is the sense that anything is possible, any character. With Om and all of them, there is a certain shape that takes place around them, which indicates that he is suitable for this, will make sense in that. Now that can be a dangerous thing because it becomes formless. But because Irrfan is so compelling as a presence on screen, you recognize his power, which does not have boundaries attached. I think that is what allowed him to make the transition into the international sphere that much more easily. It strikes me that in some ways, it's also a nature of the evolution of the kind of roles people from this part of the world have started getting. It's also the fact that you have directors like Ang Lee, Mira Nair, people with a sensibility which goes beyond the classic moulds in which an Indian character or a subcontinental character was conceived. And you look at the Indian context now, where the nuance and the specifics of a character have started becoming more important. If you look at how South Asian characters are being imagined, you see a much bigger range of roles that they are being asked to play. Where, in the role, you are not just an Indian. The fault line is not India versus the West. The representation of South Asians in Hollywood films would be as archetypal as in Hindi cinema for so many decades. The only fault lines that existed were intergenerational – between a new generation that has grown up in the West and an older generation that carries the displacement of migration; you leave a culture and you come to another. In the more serious films, two or three broad tropes existed. They continue; it's not as if they have changed completely, but I think there is more room within that for nuance and storytelling which highlights individual stories and not stories of collectives. This is true for communities as well as people. Just like in India, when you need a particular character to be brought alive, I think Irrfan becomes a more natural choice. I just wonder whether the same thing is at work even when it comes to Western directors.

SG: When you think of a Salman Khan or a Shah Rukh Khan, their identity is more limned by their faith, even though they may not be performative Muslims. And they played the Raj/Rahul/Prem kind of roles in their most popular films. Irrfan wasn't really seen as a 'Muslim' actor; I think he was just seen as a fantastic actor. He dropped the Khan from his name. Why do you think he did that?

SD: There is a certain essential humanism about him both in terms of the roles he plays and as a person. I use it in a loose way, not a specific way, but there is about him a certain Sufi spirit or a spirit that cannot be contained within these identity labels. It's almost as if he floats away from these categories. It's not as if he's a counterpoint to these; it's just the fact that he detaches himself and he's a free spirit, above and beyond. In a sense, it is a dropping of the weight, which is almost an imposed anchor. A surname, in an Indian context, particularly one that signifies religion, is something that weighs you down; it's what defines you. What's interesting is that the older Khans have made their mark playing the Prems and Rahuls of the world, but they are unmistakably, very crudely speaking, Khans. It's a very peculiar kind of a co-existence of a Hindu on-screen identity, with a very clear Khan identity off screen.

So the dropping of the surname may have been to avoid having that attribution, that here is one more Khan in the industry. But, more significantly, it is simply a reflection of the fact that those identity weights drag you down and willy-nilly frame you. So you are looked at through that filter. You say, 'Look at me without that filter. Look at me as an actor, as a human being.' I remember some of the interviews where Irrfan talks about this – going beyond the notion of doctrinal, organized religion which, I personally think, was the motivation to truly represent an everyman and not be boxed into these human contrivances of religious and caste categories. It's not about disowning faith in any way, as much as it is about disowning the baggage that comes with faith being on display.

ACKNOWLEDGEMENTS

For a film critic used to filling crisp column inches, the thought of writing a book – SO MANY WORDS! – is intimidating, even if said critic has done one and got it out of the way, so to speak.

This is my second, and it all started with Mimi Choudhury reaching out to me with her idea of a book on Irrfan. It was May 2020, just a month after Irrfan's passing away from an incurable cancer. I was not really sure at first: an Irrfan biography was already out, and there was talk of several other books. Did we need another?

Yes, the world did indeed need a critical appreciation of one of our greatest actors from a long-time film critic's perspective. It was Mimi's conviction and clarity which persuaded me, and got Pan Macmillan India on board. She has been an invaluable sounding board and staunch editorial companion through the journey of the book, from the draft stage to the complete volume.

My editor–publisher at Pan Macmillan India, Teesta Guha Sarkar, diving deep into voluminous edits and spending many hours across many months poring over multiple drafts, and knocking the material into shape, has been the pillar that this kind of sprawling book requires. At this point, I must wave a grateful paw at Arsalan, Teesta's gorgeous black-and-white cat, who trained a watchful eye on us as we toiled, and kept us going.

Acknowledgements

My thanks to Shreya Gupta, who read the manuscript so closely and thoroughly, helped with the Hindi translations, and was a great support during the final phases. Also, to Amartaya Gupta, who helped with annotations and translations and provided many finishing touches.

A big shoutout to Shreyoshee Bandyopadhyay, intern at Pan Macmillan India during 2021–22, now pursuing a master's at Oxford, who transcribed the conversations so diligently and beautifully, adding very useful notes in the transcripts. And another one to Chitrang, who unravelled the mysteries of transcription apps, and other Mac things.

A special vote of thanks to my friend, film-festival head and author Aseem Chhabra, whose biography of Irrfan was published at the beginning of 2020. As ever, Aseem was generous with his contact list, and chats with him about his experiences while working on his book were both instructive and fun.

Many thanks go out to more people than I count, but let me start with my constant companion Madhusudan, who has spent years listening to me go on about the movies, and seen me through them all. It isn't easy for a non-film lover to live with someone who loves and lives them. This book is dedicated to him. Thanks also to my dearest friends Lekha and Nalin, amongst the busiest and best people I know, always ready with their precious time and a glass of red, both deeply useful things in the life of a stressed author.

As also to bright spark and film enthusiast Kanishk Devgan who helped pull out articles for my research. And to Md Wahid for helping me find other resources.

Thank you to my yoga teacher Jaya P., who made it possible for me to hit the desperately needed focus button whenever

Acknowledgements

I most needed to. She has been an incredibly calming and energizing presence in my life for the past few years.

My heartfelt thanks to Sutapa Sikdar, who said yes when I told her about the book.

Thanks also to all the film people – directors, producers, actors – present in the book, for agreeing so generously to share their memories and perspectives.

And, of course, to Irrfan, who made cinema better.

FILMOGRAPHY

Salaam Bombay! (1988)

Kamla Ki Maut (1989)

Drishti (1990)

Ek Doctor Ki Maut (1990)

Pita (1991)

Mujhse Dosti Karoge (1992)

Karamati Coat (1993)

The Cloud Door (1994)

Vaade Iraade (1994)

Purush (1994)

Adhura (1995)

Private Detective: Two Plus
Two Plus One (1997)

Such a Long Journey (1998)

Bada Din (1998)

The Goal (1999)

Ghaath (2000)

Kasoor (2001)

The Warrior (2001)

Kali Salwar (2002)

Gunaah (2002)

Pratha (2002)

Haathi Ka Anda (2002)

Bokshu – The Myth (2002)

Dhund (2003)

Haasil (2003)

Supari (2003)

Footpath (2003)

The Bypass (2003)

Maqbool (2004)

Charas (2004)

Aan: Men at Work (2004)

Shadows of Time (2004)

Road to Ladakh (2004)

Rog (2005)

Chehraa (2005)

Chocolate (2005)

7½ Phere: More Than a
Wedding (2005)

The Film (2005)

Dubai Return (2005)

Yun Hota Toh Kya Hota (2006)

The Killer (2006)

The Namesake (2006)

Deadline: Sirf 24 Ghante (2006)
Sainikudu (2006)
Mr. 100% (2006)
Partition (2007)
Life in a… Metro (2007)
A Mighty Heart (2007)
The Darjeeling Limited (2007)
Apna Asmaan (2007)
Aaja Nachle (2007)
Tulsi (2008)
Sunday (2008)
One Two Three (2008)
Krazzy 4 (2008)
Mumbai Meri Jaan (2008)
Chamku (2008)
Migration (2008)
Slumdog Millionaire (2008)
New York, I Love You (2008)
Dil Kabaddi (2008)
Billu (2009)
New York (2009)
Acid Factory (2009)
Right Yaaa Wrong (2010)
Knock Out (2010)
Hisss (2010)
Yeh Saali Zindagi (2011)
7 Khoon Maaf (2011)
Thank You (2011)
Paan Singh Tomar (2012)

The Amazing Spider-Man (2012)
Life of Pi (2012)
Saheb Biwi Aur Gangster Returns (2013)
The Lunchbox (2013)
D-Day (2013)
Qissa: The Tale of a Lonely Ghost (2013)
Gunday (2014)
The Xposé (2014)
Haider (2014)
Piku (2015)
Jurassic World (2015)
Jazbaa (2015)
Talvar (2015)
Bajirao Mastani (2015)
The Jungle Book (2016)
Madaari (2016)
Inferno (2016)
Hindi Medium (2017)
Raabta (2017)
Doob: No Bed of Roses (2017)
The Song of Scorpions (2017)
Qarib Qarib Singlle (2017)
Puzzle (2018)
Blackmail (2018)
Karwaan (2018)
Angrezi Medium (2020)
Murder at Teesri Manzil 302 (2021)